Wherever the Sound Takes You

Also by David Rowell
The Train of Small Mercies

Earlier, briefer versions of "In Switzerland Nothing Is Easy," "Complicated Rhythms,"
   "Going for the One," and "Into the Darkness" were originally published in the
   Washington Post Magazine. An earlier version of "In Switzerland Nothing Is Easy"
   was also previously published in *Best American Travel Writing 2016* under the title
   "Swiss Dream."

Lyrics from "Do You Feel Like We Do" reprinted with permission from Peter Frampton.

Lyrics from "Swiss Lady" reprinted with permission from Peter Reber.

Lyrics from "Lesser Animal" and "Murder Blossom" reprinted with permission from
   J. R. Hayes and Relapse Records.

Lyrics from "Hokie Karaoke: Are You Just Another Wannabe" reprinted with
   permission from John VanArsdall.

Lyrics from "I Wanna Know," "Bug," "Rise Up and Fight This Shit," "Nothing but Time
   for the Blues," "Sell My Soul," "Been a Long Time," "Sad," "Long Time," "Chasm,"
   "50 Bones," and "Free (Waitin' for the Rain)" reprinted with permission from Bob
   Funck.

Lyrics to "Free St." and "Commercial St." reprinted by permission from Alex Milan.

Lyrics to "The Toothbrush" reprinted with permission from Erin Fitzpatrick.

WHEREVER
THE SOUND TAKES YOU

Heroics and Heartbreak in Music Making

David Rowell

The University of Chicago Press

Chicago and London

The University of Chicago Press, Chicago 60637
The University of Chicago Press, Ltd., London
© 2019 by The University of Chicago
Published 2019
Printed in the United States of America

28 27 26 25 24 23 22 21 20 19   1 2 3 4 5

ISBN-13: 978-0-226-47755-8 (cloth)
ISBN-13: 978-0-226-60893-8 (e-book)
DOI: https://doi.org/10.7208/chicago/9780226608938.001.0001

Library of Congress Cataloging-in-Publication Data

Names: Rowell, David, 1958– author.
Title: Wherever the sound takes you : heroics and heartbreak in music making /
    David Rowell.
Description: Chicago ; London : The University of Chicago Press, 2019. | Includes
    bibliographical references.
Identifiers: LCCN 2018029033 | ISBN 9780226477558 (cloth : alk. paper) | ISBN
    9780226608938 (ebook)
Subjects: LCSH: Musicians—Anecdotes. | Rock musicians—Anecdotes. | Musical
    instruments—Anecdotes.
Classification: LCC ML385 .R82 2019 | DDC 781.1/7—dc23
LC record available at https://lccn.loc.gov/2018029033

♾ This paper meets the requirements of ANSI/NISO Z39.48-1992 (Permanence
of Paper).

For Lynn Medford,

who let me follow the beat

SET LIST

The Necessary Equipment

When I was young, I was under the direct influence of two people who were keenly interested in shaping my musical landscape: Bob Funck, who was two years older and lived two doors down, and my brother, John, almost six years older and one bedroom door down. My parents enjoyed music, but their record collection was a modest stack of albums by Perry Como, Doris Day, and Jim Nabors and included *The Ballad of the Green Berets* and the Partridge Family Christmas album. (My dad also liked bagpipe music.) Those records were played only occasionally on the curio, and mostly my parents were content to hear the music at church every Sunday — the organ, the choir, and the occasional guest trumpeter.

John was the music fanatic in the family. His great passion had formed, as far as anyone could tell, completely organically and was as instinctive as his first steps or first words. John loved show tunes. In his bedroom he sat listening, transfixed, to the original cast recordings of *Man from La Mancha*, *The Sound of Music*, and *South Pacific*. Most days it was as if Rodgers and Hammerstein were renting the room the next door. It's not that I disliked the music—those classic Broadway anthems are highly tuneful and blithe—but for John it was urgent that I develop the same deep reverence he had. He was constantly dragging me into his room and making me listen with him. Or he would trick me into coming in by saying he wanted to show me something, and once I stepped in he'd close the door and drop the needle, and the overture from *South Pacific* would come streaming from his speakers.

There were no albums by rock bands in the house, though John did have a swinging record by Herb Alpert and the Tijuana Brass Band, *The Beat of the Brass*, whose cover showed Alpert and his group dressed in tuxedos and looking perplexed to find themselves standing in a field of yellow flowers.

While I endured another listening of "I'm Gonna Wash That Man Right Outa My Hair," my friend Bob was starting to discover the progressive side of rock, thanks to his oldest sister, Roberta, the first hippie I ever knew. Bob had access to Roberta's ample collection of albums and eight-tracks, including Pink Floyd, Yes, and Emerson, Lake and Palmer. (She had painted the cover of Rush's *Fly by Night*—one of the few rock album covers to feature an intimidating owl—and hung it on the wall outside her room, which featured a bead curtain for a door.) Bob and I sat in his dim room and listened for hours. There was so much great music to absorb, and for me, the albums' liner notes conveyed information far more interesting than what I was learning in school. We discovered, for example, that Robert Plant was the only member of Led Zeppelin who didn't have a credit on "Moby Dick" and that on Yes's triple live album *Yessongs*, drummer Bill Bruford played on only three of the tracks whereas newcomer Alan White was on all the others. For me, why Richard Nixon was kicked out of office was of minor consequence, but what could have possibly happened to make Bill Bruford leave Yes?

Looking back at that time, that essential education I was getting at his house, Bob told me recently, "I felt like I was giving you something important, like I had something to offer, a purpose."

When I entered seventh grade, my school created its first concert band. By that point my love for rock music was in full bloom, but I had never given any thought to actually playing music myself. There was a ukulele in our house that stayed untouched, and a bugle John had picked out with his accumulation of S&H Green Stamps that only I sometimes tried. (The sound I was able to produce was as musical as if I'd blown into a chest of drawers.) We had an upright piano, and John took lessons, but to the consternation of my mother I somehow managed to avoid them. Still, I was intrigued enough to show up at the band sign-up table that first week of school. Maybe it was Herb Alpert I was thinking of when I said I wanted to try trumpet. But the band director, a peppy man with a moustache straight out of CBS's *Cannon*, told me that because I had braces, I wouldn't be able to perform a proper embouchure to play it. I took a few seconds to think about that, then asked, "How about the drums?" It would be one of the most significant choices I ever made.

I was issued a large plastic suitcase that held a chrome Premier concert snare as well as a small xylophone. I dragged it home and began to bang on my new instruments.

It turned out that I had a natural aptitude for drumming. I loved how the drumstick felt as it bounced against the snare head—that little jolt of friction against my palm—and drum rolls came relatively easily. For me, learning to read music was like learning geometry: I displayed no genius for it, but I understood the shapes, the calculation of spaces, and the particular sizes well enough to do the work required. At the end of the year I won the school's first Excellence in Band award, which stunned me—and my bandmates. This rare bit of success was far from my areas of expertise, Atari games and *Star Wars* sound effects, and it made me take music all the more seriously.

When I moved on to high school—E.E. Smith, in Fayetteville,

North Carolina—the only band was a marching band called the Magnificent Marching Machine. It was known to "get down" and I was not, but still, that first day of practice, it was at least clear to the other drummers that I could play. My mother taught at Smith's rival school, where John had been student body president his senior year. After he graduated the district lines were redrawn, and I had to go across town to a school to which I had no real connection. This development was more crushing to my mother than to me, and as she pulled into the parking lot to pick me up from that first day of practice, she saw me with the rest of the band in formation and moving in a way she'd never seen before. This caused her to burst into tears. She was still in shock that I couldn't attend the school where she'd taught for nearly eighteen years, and whose marching band stepped with the precision of the Queen's Guard, and in her emotional state she pleaded with me to drop out. Even then I realized that this was an unfair request, but it troubled me to see my mother so upset, and by the time we'd gotten home I'd begrudgingly relented. For the next couple of years I would occasionally pick up my drumsticks to keep my drum-roll skills in reasonable shape, but otherwise my days of playing music with any aspiration seemed behind me.

In 1983, on a Friday night during eleventh grade, I was driving a classmate named David Morketter to our school football game. We were just starting to get to know each other, and David mentioned that he played guitar. I said I played the drums. Neither statement was quite true. But by the end of the night we decided it was only natural that we put together a band for the school talent show.

We soon began rehearsing in his garage. I had a rubber practice pad that came with my snare, and by putting it on the drum head and hitting it in the middle, I could produce a lower sound than if I hit it on the edge; in that way I approximated the effect of a bass-snare combination. On guitar, David was the equivalent of a beginning speller. He could play the simple riffs of the Who's "I Can't Explain," the Rolling Stones' "Let's Spend the Night Together," and the Kingsmen's version of "Louie Louie," but that was about it. Yet after a few nights of this, we decided it was time to fill out the rest of the band.

As we announced our intentions, our friends mostly said, "You guys play?" or "That's awesome!" but no one claimed to sing. Or maybe they sensed it was a good idea to lie. After a few days we were getting desperate. Then Mark, who was a senior, told us he sang a little. Mark was a nice guy, always ready to laugh. He was a bit nerdy, with black hair parted in the middle. We liked him. We didn't know if he really could sing, but in David's garage a couple of nights later, Mark was deliberate and largely unselfconscious. He knew the words to the few songs we could play, and he gave the impression of singing, though there was no microphone. He sang into his balled fist, and we could hear almost nothing.

Mark pointed at my drum several times through each song, as if to cue me, but I was willing to forgive that—it was, I figured, an attempt at showmanship. He bounced his head over David's guitar lines too eagerly. He seemed almost impressed by what we were doing, and that should have endeared him to us, but instead it worried us. Still, we had him come over for another rehearsal. As we played he pointed more this time, showed some inclination to gyrate—not dramatically, but in quick flashes. After we went through "I Can't Explain" and "Let's Spend the Night Together" about ten times each, we wrapped up, and Mark said good-night and got in his car.

"Well," I began.

"He's not really . . ." David added.

I nodded. We felt bad, and maybe it just came down to the effect of Mark singing rock songs in an Izod shirt. But we knew we didn't have our singer yet.

Finally one guy we didn't like very much, Jimmy, stepped forward. We figured pretty immediately that Jimmy couldn't sing, but he was tall and surprisingly cocky, considering he was also a goofball. He was not unpopular with the girls. And he was willing. Talentwise, we seemed to have our match.

David wasn't skilled enough to produce any kind of guitar solo, and we would need some other element to break up the repetitive nature of just the riff alone, whatever we played. There was a kid named Danny on our bus whom we had never really talked to before, but he always carried his alto saxophone case with him. All we knew about him was that he played in the marching band and got off at David's bus stop. He had a perpetually faint smile over his faint moustache, and wore eyeglasses of the kind commonly seen on hardware-store employees. David and I made our pitch. Now we had exactly one person in the band who knew what he was doing.

Once the four of us convened in David's garage, we gravitated toward "Louie Louie" because the riff was so rudimentary, though David, on his Hondo Sunburst, didn't know what chords he was playing and just kept his fingers pressed down on two strings. We liked the song's swagger. Too, we were comforted by the fact that the Kingsmen's singer couldn't really sing, either. In fact, he sounded unhinged. Never mind that musically what stands out most is that a rollicking organ, not a guitar, powered the main melody.

But what were the words? Unbeknown to us, we weren't the first ones to struggle over what the singer was saying. For more than two years the FBI had conducted an investigation because it was believed that the lyrics were, quite possibly, lewd and graphic. Over several nights David and I put our ears to his boom box and listened over and over to a cassette that featured the song. We transcribed what we could and made up the rest. (Ultimately, the FBI also gave up trying to decipher the lyrics, thus ending the investigation.)

With just days before the talent show, I still had not played an actual drum kit, so I called my friend Mike Fowler, who had been a fellow drummer in concert band. Mike had been playing a kit for several years, and he graciously let me borrow it for a night. I put it together in David's garage and tried to transfer the beat I'd been keeping on my snare to a bass drum, cymbals, hi-hat, and three toms—plus the snare. In that first hour it felt like my limbs were guided by a remote control—a remote control that a bunch of people kept wrenching out of each other's hands. It was also exhilarating. Later that night in bed, I pumped my arms over my head and tapped my left foot to the beat of "Louie Louie," practicing the 4/4 rhythm that I would need to maintain for exactly two and a half minutes onstage.

The day before our big debut, my father paid a visit to one of the many pawnshops in town because this one had a full drum set. He knew the owner and struck a deal to borrow the set for twenty-four hours. In David's garage we kept practicing. There was, by the strictest of definitions, progress. Jimmy had found a respectable amount of bravado, and David and Danny were playing the song's main riff more or less in unison now. I was, of course, still trying to learn how to play the drums.

"That doesn't sound good," Jimmy said of a fill I was working on.

I knew he was right, but I told him, "You don't know."

"No, seriously," he said.

Once more, from the top.

The next day, we were one of more than a dozen performers — mostly dance groups, lip-syncing acts, and a couple of singers tackling R&B torch songs. We huddled on the side of the stage, nervous but excited as we waited. I was dressed in a red dinner jacket and bowtie I'd rented from a tuxedo shop, copying Ray Davies's look on the record sleeve of the Kinks' *Give the People What They Want*. Jimmy wore beach shorts, a tie, and wraparound sunglasses. David, taking his cue from both Van Halen and the YMCA, where he refereed flag football games, had put slashes of white tape on black warm-up pants and paired them with a ref's shirt. For some reason, David and I had encouraged Danny to wear a cape, perhaps because he was the most unlikely person in the world to wear a cape and we liked the boldness of that. Also, Rick Wakeman, keyboardist for Yes — my favorite band by then — also wore a cape. But Danny met us only halfway. He'd fashioned a cape out of his gym towel and hung it from the back collar of his plaid shirt, which was tucked into black shorts. When we eyed this, as students were filing in for the show, David and I conferred with each other.

Maybe just forget the cape, we told him.

The school receptionist, Mrs. Allen, served as emcee, and we were in the middle of the lineup. We'd named ourselves the Com-

mons 4 because there were four of us, and there was a commons area
where Jimmy, David, and I hung out during break and after lunch.
(Danny went there, too, but he tended to sit on the half-wall next to
his sax case.) When the time came to announce us, Mrs. Allen mis-
read her program notes and told the crowd we were playing "Lovie
Lovie."

Once onstage, David plugged in his guitar, and Jimmy moved to
the mic. The thing Jimmy was most excited about was break dancing during Danny's brief sax solo, which was to be a rough approxi-
mation of the Kingsmen's guitar solo. The problem was that Danny
forgot to turn on his microphone, which we realized too late. No one
heard a note he played. As this became clear to David, he improvised
his own attempt at a solo, carrying it out on one string and giving it
all the consonance of a bug zapper.

I couldn't tell if I was playing on the beat or if I had multiplied it
by a factor of four, but I felt a joyous thrill as my foot worked the bass
pedal and I attacked the snare and hi-hat; I was the fireman in the
ship's engine room who just happened to be dressed like the dining
room maître d'.

We were in a talent show and had no talent, except for Danny.
But the whole point of this adventure had been the exploration, to
see not so much what we could produce together, since David and I
had already confronted that, but what we would take away from this
first experience of playing live rock music. Though I'd surely recognized the truth of this before, now I could experience the power of
it firsthand: the drummer is the one who sees everything. He lets
the other musicians carry the melody and, through their solos, tell
their particular stories. That was a pretty apt musical fit for someone
like me — more listener than talker, more observer than participant,
whose habit was always to sit near the back in class, to stand on the
edge of the crowd at a party and take in the dynamics. The drummer
wasn't the jock or the brain or the class clown. The drummer was the
one who knew the answer but was content not to raise his hand. In
any case, what was unfolding in front of me was chaotic and even

theatrical, and I was doing my best to direct it all from behind the kit while absorbing every nuance.

Though we'd rehearsed our ending plenty, we finished the song like a multicar pileup. Yet as we walked off stage, David and I raised our arms in triumph because that's what it felt like to us — a triumph in something we couldn't quite name.

We did not, needless to say, win the talent show. We didn't achieve musical bliss with our incipient performance, but I, for one, had glimpsed the possibility of it. And it was the possibility of that kind of fulfillment that got so fully inside my system. It had been easy to make bad music together, but what would it require to make good music? If you could master your instrument, would the music automatically be good? When you were that young, were you already confronting the limitations of your own equipment?

David and I became best friends through that experience. We still talk about it today — the ways we tried to inch forward each night we practiced, the grandiose vision we had for our performance versus what we delivered. The thrill of discovery, the acceptance of compromises. That band played one song publicly one time, and that was it. But for me it was the beginning of a lifelong journey of wanting to understand how and why we make the music we do. And trying to grasp what music can give us — and also what it can't.

The stories that follow, which ultimately make up the bigger story about music I'm trying to tell, represent a broad range of abilities, ambitions, and genres. As I shadowed various musicians, from industry legends who've toured stadiums to a guy who plays in a storage facility, I was exploring a particular set of interests: What was their connection to their chosen instrument? What did they feel when they played? What had they put themselves through — and were still putting themselves through — for their music? Through it all I studied the ways musicians utilized their equipment — figurative and literal — and focused on the hard-earned truths in the licks they played. I asked lots of questions, but mostly I was there to listen and see where the music took them, on stage and off. I went to their homes, attended their rehearsals, and watched their performances—at festivals and in concert halls, clubs, bars, restaurants, studios, a radio station, open mics, in living rooms, a senior center, a log cabin, hospital rooms, a church, and on street corners—where the audience responses spanned from long, raging ovations to utter and unbearable silence.

In music the distance between sorrow and joy can be surprisingly narrow, and sometimes I glimpsed this even within the performer's same set. In the years I spent reporting this book, I traveled as far as Switzerland and just a few miles from my house, always searching for the telling moment as the performer or band took the stage, anything that further illuminated the ongoing narrative of a craft carried out by hands but sprung from the soul.

CHAPTER 1

"In Switzerland Nothing Is Easy"

I had been walking around for an hour trying to find a street musician—more precisely, a street musician playing a particular instrument—when I heard the buzzy strain of a clarinet. That wasn't what I was looking for, but maybe it was a start.

Here in the crowded foot traffic of Bern's Old Town, it wasn't clear where the sound was coming from. I took a few steps in a couple of directions until I heard the muffled darts of a Middle Eastern drum accompanying the clarinet. I walked past Stauffacher, a bookstore that featured in its window not one but two books on the pop group Abba, and past Magic X, an erotic megastore. At the end of the narrow alley were the clarinetist and a much taller man playing a small darbuka with a stick as thin as a baton.

I leaned against a wall, waiting for the song to end. I pulled out my laminated picture of the hang—an elusive percussion instrument, which I had come all the way to Switzerland to find. Under the picture I'd typed, "Have you seen this musical instrument?" Every time I thought the musicians were winding down a song, they segued into another. After twenty minutes, they'd gone from smiling at me (*Hey, this guy really likes us!*) to looking annoyed (*This guy is creepy, right?*). Finally I stopped them midtune. The pair looked at my picture, then at me. They wore the stony expressions of bouncers.

"Dutch," the drummer said. They didn't speak English.

In my desperation I mimed playing the hang, as if that might clarify the situation, though it must have looked as if I was warding off bees. They shook their heads again and glanced at each other. I sighed and started to leave, but not before the drummer grunted and pointed with his toe toward the basket in front of them. I fished out two francs.

As I walked away, they started up "Over the Rainbow," a song that always freezes me in my tracks. The skies were blue, with the clouds far behind me—that much was true—but my troubles weren't exactly melting like lemon drops. I had a sinking feeling that my troubles were just beginning.

In Switzerland I was on the latest stop of a crusade that started the night I first put together Mike's drum set in David's garage. After college I ended up in Boston, where I had a tiny studio apartment, and the wall that divided me and my neighbor, Maria, was more of a partition wall—we could hear when the other hiccupped. So it was hardly realistic for me to bring my drum set, which my parents bought for me after the talent show for my seventeenth birthday, up from home. But the separation was tough, and I missed my kit.

Around that time, world music was becoming popular, and in the music stores in and around Boston, new kinds of percussion instruments were showing up alongside the standard fare of tambourines, maracas, and cowbells. At Jack's Drum Shop I came across a tongue drum. It was a rectangular wooden box and had only had five notes, but I was drawn to its crisp timbre, and it would be quiet enough that I could play it softly in my apartment. It came with two mallets, and just having sticks in my hands felt restorative.

I was instantly hooked. And so began a lifetime of collecting percussion pieces.

I bought a kalimba next, or African thumb piano, which had little keys that produced shimmering tones. I found a balafon from Mali, a rain stick from Chile, an udu drum, more tongue drums, more kalimbas, and an angklung from Bali. I ordered a dumbek from Pakistan, a tamborim from Brazil, Bao Gongs from China, and Noah Bells from India. I have a talking drum, a djembe, all kinds of African shakers, clay bongos from Morocco, an American Indian drum, a berimbau, a dulcimer, a guiro shaped like a frog, and a shekere. There are singing bowls from Tibet, an Ipu from Hawaii, a glockenspiel from Sweden, tank drums (tongue drums made of metal), an ocean drum, a thunder drum, a steel pan, wooden spoons, and a waterphone. Birthdays, Christmases, Father's Days—they have all become occasions to add to the collection. Some instruments I am better at than others, but the ability to produce so many sublime sounds all around me has made daily life more enjoyable. The sounds from these instruments—every one of them—stirs something inside me.

When YouTube came along, I was forever seeking out drumming videos. One night I came across a blond man in Rasta dreadlocks playing what looked like a giant wok, with a cover that had indentions on the side and a bubble on top. There was an echo of the steel drum in the sound, but it was richer, more resonant. His hands moved over the instrument like flowing water, the melody like a message from outer space. The sight of a piece of metal being played like a hand drum left me spellbound. Excluding the vibraphone or xylophone, metal percussion pieces are often meant to sound a dramatic, sustained note—think of crashing cymbals or gongs or the solemn blare of orchestral bells. The full notes of Armageddon. The fluidity of notes on this strange-looking instrument—in one moment as bright as chimes, in another as muffled as bells in a sack—was beguiling and bedeviling. I wanted to know everything I could about this wonderment.

It was called "the hang" (pronounced *the hong*), or "hand" in the Bernese German dialect, as I would learn, and created by Felix Rohner and his partner, Sabina Schärer. Felix had previously been a maker of steel pans when he and his colleagues discovered a new kind of sheet metal, which led to the hang's creation. The only way you could get one was to write a letter—not an email—making the case as to why you were worthy of owning the instrument. Most applications were denied. The lucky recipient, however, had to fly to Bern to pick up the hang in person—and pay about three thousand dollars, though not right away; there was a waiting list of a year or longer. Thousands of people all over the world wanted one, none of them more than I did.

With two sons to send to college, I was no more likely to buy a hang—even if I was one of the chosen few—than I was to start driving a German tank. Instead, my want was modest: I would seek a single encounter. My idea was to visit Felix in Switzerland and write about the hang as a travel piece for the *Washington Post*, where I worked as an editor. The story would delve into the creation of the hang—what Felix's hopes had been for it, for example—and I could learn how the instrument had worked its way through the musical landscape of Switzerland. In doing that, I could introduce the instrument of my dreams to a wider world.

I discovered that Felix had cowritten papers for the International Symposium on Musical Acoustics, and sometimes the name Uwe Hansen appeared as coauthor. He was a professor emeritus at Indiana State University, where he had been a member of the physics faculty for thirty years. (Hansen didn't play around. Back in 1966, his PhD dissertation in physics was titled "Dielectric Anomalies in the Cyclotron Absorption Spectrum of Lead Telluride.") I called him to see if he could put me in touch with Felix. "Felix is kind of an interesting, interesting, interesting guy," he told me. "He's sort of a part musician, part scientist, and part theological philosopher." He thought Felix would be interested in my idea, so he sent me Felix's email address.

"I've been playing drums and world percussion instruments my whole life, and I've never heard an instrument so mesmerizing as yours," my message to Felix began. "Basically, I feel like it's the most beautiful thing I've ever heard." I went on to sketch out my story proposal and closed by saying, "I would travel all the way to Bern for the chance to play a Hang even for five minutes." How could Felix resist?

In his response, he thanked me for my interest, but the very thing I thought would move him most — my willingness to travel so far for so brief an encounter — was what alarmed him. He quoted back that sentence to me, and then wrote, "This sounds like a project of a pilgrimage. We are not a place like that." He went on, "It seems you were touched by the virus of the Hang. This virus is rather strong, and people travel around the world to get touched again." But, he informed me, "the Hang chapter is closed, and we turned the page." His company, PANArt, had modified the hang, and now it was called the gubal. Still, there was a shard of hope toward the end: "Please clarify what is your deeper interest about." The email was signed by Felix and Sabina.

In my follow-up, in case I had come off as a stalker, I changed tactics a bit and made clear that I'd also be writing about other music in Switzerland. He responded that their goal was to stay humble — "We do our daily work like monks" — and that in working on the gubal, "we are in the refinement of a new art form."

I tried one last angle. If he would not meet with me, would he put me in touch with other hang players? But by then Felix had, essentially, hung up on me.

Still, Switzerland had more hang players than any other country, judging by the videos I'd seen. I could track them down before I left. And I did, some of them. First I found Daniel Waples, the blond guy I'd seen in that first clip, though it turned out he didn't live in Switzerland. But there was still so much I wanted to ask him. "I am about to go into a 10 day meditation retreat where I will have no access to the internet," he emailed me, "but I assure you, I will connect with you as soon as I get out again." That meditation must have been hard to come out of, since five months passed before he got back to me — and long after I'd returned from Switzerland.

One hang player, who did live in Switzerland and understood that Felix wouldn't speak to me, wrote, "I do not want to tell second hand stories about people who do not want to take part in the story." Two others didn't respond. Another hang player let me know he would be away on tour the very week I'd be in Switzerland, but we could talk by phone, and he gave me his number. "Hear from you in June," he wrote. And he did. I just never heard back.

I didn't know anything about Switzerland, but it was hard not to think that I had stumbled onto some bizarre percussion conspiracy. If I went through the city streets asking about the hang, would I end up on the wrong end of a Swiss Army knife? I was too determined to give up. I'd go and find the hang myself, somehow. And if I struck out completely, well, there were other Swiss musicians I could interview for my story: the country was crawling with yodelers.

After the clarinetist and drummer in the alley, I met Michael Dmitrischin, who was playing his accordion a few blocks away. He looked at my hang picture and told me he had seen one before, but he had mixed feelings about the instrument and what it could do. You can't play classical on it, he said.

Suddenly street performers were everywhere. There were two young men — boys, really — singing an a cappella version of Simon and Garfunkel's "The Sounds of Silence" in a thick German accent. "Hello dockness my old fhwend . . ." Around the corner was an acoustic guitarist teaming up with the player of an erhu, or Chinese violin, which filled the air with a mournful groan. The guitarist had seen a hang in the area just recently, he said. I had every reason to believe I was getting warmer, but maybe it was too much to think I could spot one on my first day. Not far away, though, was someone who could fill me in a bit more on the hang's beginnings.

I went to meet Thomas Burkhalter, a musicologist who ran a world music website called Norient. Thomas had reinvented himself as a journalist after ending his days playing alto sax in jazz groups in and around Bern. In 2001 he interviewed Felix Rohner for a story about the hang that he was writing in the local newspaper. "He was very open," Thomas recalled, "but then, he wanted to sell the hang, you know."

In 2002, Thomas started Norient to showcase experimental music. As Thomas and I talked about the website, his colleague Theresa Beyer joined our conversation. An editor at Norient, Theresa was studying for her PhD in Swiss folk music and knew three people with hangs. "Everybody who has one is really proud," she said. She had been to a party where the host had a hang and brought it out to show people, but then the host suddenly turned nervous as the hang was handed around and said, "'Be careful, be careful!' So it's a sacred thing."

We talked about how the hang fit in with the current music scene in Switzerland. Thomas said the traditional music of Switzerland — largely made up of yodeling, accordions, and alphorns — had grown in popularity because of the recent rise of the conservative movement. "In Switzerland we have a big struggle between the left and the right," he said. "You have the conservative side, and that is against Europe, against foreigners, against everything, basically. And then you have the more left side, where we are the part that wants to show another feature of Switzerland that is modern and open to the world." Theresa added that the country's traditional instruments had been co-opted by the right wing of the country, as if to say, Why would we ever need anything else? "So there's the motivation to show, for these musicians, that they are not part of the right wing," Thomas said.

It was creeping into evening, and as we said good-bye they wished me luck on my hunt, though by then most of the street musicians had packed it in for the day.

On day two I was headed east to the Emmental, a countryside of rolling hills, chalet-style farmhouses, and cows and sheep that dotted the plush landscape like snowflakes. The area is most famous for its cheese production, which plays a major role in the Swiss economy, but there's another production that goes on here to create some of the country's most recognizable music. I wasn't likely to find the hang on this excursion, but makers of other instruments had agreed to talk to me, and I was hoping that, as fellow creators, they might offer a useful perspective on Felix's off-kilter sales philosophy. Plus, in getting an education in the instruments that had, for better or worse, helped shape part of the country's musical image for the rest of the world, I'd have a deeper appreciation of the hang's place in the pantheon.

Our first stop was what my driver and interpreter, Christian Billau, called the Rolls-Royce of accordion makers: Hansruedi Reist's workshop. Hansruedi made a Schwyzerörgeli, a distinctive accordion with buttons on both sides (no keys) that was also notable for its slender size and elegant craftsmanship. When we walked into the two-story factory, the air was so thick with the scent of lumber it was like walking into wood itself. Normally the place would have been teeming with employees, but many Swiss were on holiday, and there was just Hansruedi, one of his sons, and one other employee. Hansruedi told me the story of the business's origins, and Christian translated.

Back in 1966, Hansruedi's father, Rudolf, a mechanic by training, found himself out of work. To put food on the table, Rudolf decided to sell everything he owned—even his beloved accordion. His only idea to earn money was to build an accordion to sell. But how to make it stand out from all the others in the marketplace? Rudolf's stroke of genius was to modify the treble key arms, which control the air coming in and out, by making them out of metal instead of wood. The difference was significant. In humid conditions, the wooden parts made the sound inconsistent. Metal solved that.

He sold that first instrument to a good friend who was a truck driver. "When he was making a break at the truck stop somewhere, he [brought out] his instrument and played in the restaurant," Hansruedi said. People were curious about the instrument, and he would tell them that his buddy Rudolf made it. That word of mouth, Hansruedi said, is how the business "keeps rolling" today. Hansruedi took over the business from his father in 1994, and now Hansruedi's two sons worked under him. Rudolf, at eighty-eight, still liked to come in each day.

As we toured the shop, where saw blades were arranged on the wall like family portraits, Hansruedi said the waiting list for a Schwyzerörgeli was at least a year. Roughly 140 instruments are produced annually, at prices ranging from three thousand to thirteen thousand dollars each.

Hansruedi had grown up around the accordion, and he was an accomplished player himself, but I wondered if at the end of a day's work, the accordion was the last thing he wanted to pick up. He chuckled at the very idea. "The goal," he said, "was less work, more playing."

Before we left, I fished out my picture of the hang and asked if he had ever seen it. He studied it, then shook his head no.

Back in the car, Christian said we were now about to meet the Rolls-Royce of alphorn makers. (Was this just a Swiss way of seeing things? Was there also a Rolls-Royce of fondue pots?) The alphorn's sound is common in traditional Swiss music, but you might know it more for the way it looks: typically about ten feet long, its silhouette conjures an indoor plumbing pipe. The alphorn has no valves, so it's played like a bugle, with no keys or buttons. All the variations of sound are produced by manipulating the shape of the mouth and the force of breath; notes push down through the instrument like downhill skiers.

Bachmann's Alphornmacherei sat in an emerald-green valley. Inside, Walter Bachmann greeted us in the dimly lit workshop while his father, also named Hansruedi, sanded an instrument on the far end. In front of Walter was a near-complete alphorn, as smooth as a new boat. And just as with Hansruedi Reist, Walter had a story to tell about how the company began.

His grandfather Ernst Schuepbach was thirteen when he wanted to play the alphorn, but his family was too poor to buy one, so he set out to make his own and completed it in 1925. He, too, sold his creation to a friend — for two francs. When he made his next sale, it went for fifty. Originally, Walter explained, "the idea of this alphorn was this communication instrument because you can hear it [from] ten kilometers." The instrument would let you "communicate with different tones — about the weather, different things. Warnings."

"The melody explained the mood," he continued. People played it, "and the people on the opposite hill could imagine what the needs were."

Unlike the accordion, though, the alphorn was a poor farmer's instrument and didn't have an easy time finding acceptance among the more well-to-do members of society, Walter said. Farmers came into the city during winter to play for spare coins, and the ungainliness of the horn didn't improve its reception. During World War II, Walter told me, the main method of transportation was the bicycle, and carrying the instrument could be tricky. Fortunately, the alphorn was usually made up of two pieces that could be taken apart rather than being fashioned from a single length of wood. That didn't make the instrument any lighter, but it may have cut down on cyclists clotheslining one another.

In 1977, the alphorn got an unlikely boost when Pepe Lienhard, a Swiss bandleader with a resplendent moustache, appeared on TV to perform the hit "Swiss Lady." The song not only featured the alphorn, it was about the alphorn!

> But when we're playin' our music, it's like a dream coming true
> My little Swiss Lady — she's a little bit crazy
> But when we're playing our music, I'd like to be an alphorn too

Suddenly, an alphorn boom began, and even furniture makers with no musical background decided to get in on the newfound popularity. They produced alphorns by machine rather than by hand. This "made the quality go down, and the price went down," Walter said. He estimated that there were now thirty professional alphorn makers in the country, but only three others, like Bachmann, made them all by hand. Their waiting list — two years — was even longer than Hansruedi Reist's. (If Switzerland is ever in need of an official motto, they might try "The Waiting Capital of the World!")

Walter trolled through a collection of mouthpieces, then fitted one onto the grand horn and motioned for me to give it a try. The prospect filled me with trepidation as I recalled my efforts on the old bugle at home. I put my lips to the horn and had the distinct feeling that I was about to summon a dragon. I pulled back, inhaled deeply, and blew into the horn, making a long, anemic note that, had someone been listening over the hills, might have been translated like this: "Hi, Didier. Your cows are long and my luck here is grass seed."

As we were leaving, I took out my hang picture. Walter hadn't seen one in person, but he'd heard bits and pieces of the hang's lore. He spoke to Christian, and Christian relayed the by now familiar report that to acquire a hang, a letter of application had to be submitted to Felix Rohner. Christian laughed in amazement. "I didn't know that," he said. "That's weird."

"He's quite extreme," Walter said.

Next, Christian, who was the head of an Emmental tourist office, drove us another twelve miles to meet Switzerland's foremost expert on the zither, if not the world's. (I was sorry, though, to learn that his name wasn't also Hansruedi.) While the alphorn and the accordion were doing brisk business, fate hadn't proved so kind to the zither, which might date back as far as the 1500s. Generally the zither is a flat, wooden structure with multiple strings that are plucked or strummed while the instrument is either held in the lap or laid on a table. I knew just a little about the zither, and I was amazed to learn it had its own museum here. When we stepped inside, I took out my picture of the hang right away to show Lorenz Mühlemann. Lorenz, who spoke English in a quiet, unfluctuating manner, said he had heard it on the streets of Bern. "Sometimes it's there, and sometimes it's not."

I told him about my quest and trotted out my premise that the hang was one of Switzerland's great musical contributions. His face tightened, as if he'd just suffered a hypodermic needle injection.

"There are also other great things in Switzerland concerning music," Lorenz said. "For example, the zither." And so began his tour.

Lorenz's museum is made up of two rooms that showcase an astonishing range of zithers from earlier centuries, some decorated with fresco-like art on the main body, or sound box, with the number of strings ranging from 4 to 122. Lorenz picked up an instrument from 1830. Around this time, he said, "We can say that the zither is a popular instrument in the Alps, especially Switzerland. It was an essential part of early Swiss music," but its historical significance was not well known today. "That's why I started the museum." When I asked him why the zither wasn't better known now, he showed the needle face again. "Well, just because," he said.

Running the museum was just one aspect of Lorenz's labor of love. He gave concerts, wrote books, taught students, repaired instruments, and researched and collected old zither sheet music. He spoke on the radio and TV about the zither. He had also made more than a dozen recordings himself. And when he played a zither, its euphony cascaded through the room. Lorenz played impeccably, intensely, and it was easy to think of him as a man simply born about one hundred years too late. In another time, he could have been the Eric Clapton of the zither.

I asked him if it had been easy to get visitors to the museum. "In Switzerland nothing is easy," Lorenz said, and released a tight smile.

Considering the zither's long life, its struggle for attention had been relatively recent. "Before World War II," he explained, "it was absolutely cool to play this for the young people, and after World War II, it was absolutely uncool." As bebop took off, the trumpet and saxophone became more popular; then, as rock and roll emerged, the electric guitar made the zither feel like . . . the zither. Plus, there had been no hit song by a 1970s band singing about the desire to be a zither.

Lorenz picked up a zither from the twentieth century, coaxing a rather sad melody from it, but playing it seemed to fill him up again. When he was done, the echo of notes drifted through the room like mist. He sat very still. "Nobody plays it anymore," he said. "It's absolutely forgotten."

In Bern I was staying at the Hotel Innere Enge, also known as the Jazz Hotel. I had taken it as a positive sign that I was booked into the Ahmad Jamal room because Jamal, who was a major influence on Miles Davis, is my favorite pianist. On the walls were Ahmad Jamal album covers, sheet music for his songs, reviews, and also a letter of commendation from President Bill Clinton: "Through your talent, dedication, and love of jazz, you have given us an invaluable legacy," he wrote. "Hillary joins me in extending best wishes for every future success."

Downstairs, Marians Jazzroom, which the hotel boasted as being one of the top jazz clubs in the world, was closed that evening, but peering through the window I could see a hologram of Dizzy Gillespie. On the way to the second floor was a wide-eyed bust of Louis Armstrong, and on the third floor a set of vibes Lionel Hampton used while touring Europe. But one of the chief advantages of staying at the enchanting Innere Enge was its proximity to PANArt.

Even though Felix had been clear he didn't want to meet with me, I decided that a single drop-in couldn't hurt. I bargained with myself that I would go just this once, and whatever happened, that would be it. But by the time I got there, after all the stops in the Emmental, the lights were off. I pushed my nose to the glass and peered in. What I could see, about four feet away, was a shelf of sixteen gubals. The new design resembled Saturn. For several minutes I stood there and studied this wine rack of extraordinary music.

It was raining, which seemed appropriate enough. The instruments were right there, yet I felt as if I were still four thousand miles away. If I had had an alphorn, the message I would have sent would have been shorter this time: *Feeeelliiiixxx!*

On my third day, I walked over to a store called Musik Müller to talk to Tom Günzburger, the head of the drums and percussion section.

Tom had had his own experience with Felix Rohner. In the beginning, Felix had let him sell the hang in the store. "And then suddenly [Felix] says, 'Stop,'" Tom recalled. Apparently Felix had decided to sell the hang himself rather than through other merchants, Tom said, and "that was it."

Over time, Musik Müller began to sell the hang knockoffs that slipped into the marketplace. (PANArt was late and, ultimately, unsuccessful in trying to patent its own design.) One knockoff was the German-made caisa that Musik Müller displayed in the front window, which Felix happened to notice as he walked by. "He came in," Tom said, "and was very angry and said, 'With this instrument, you destroy your shop.'"

"What the hell?" Tom said now at the memory of that encounter. Sometime after, there was a repeat performance when the store started carrying another knockoff, produced in France, called the Spacedrum. "This is not a good copy," Tom said Felix told him. "They all make shit."

There was, of course, a waiting list for the Spacedrum, too. For me, trying the Spacedrum was like encountering a Marilyn Monroe impersonator. A little intoxicating at first, sure, but to feel anything more was to give myself permission to feel dishonest. And I hadn't come all this way for a substitute.

After my stop at Musik Müller I retrieved my map of Bern and went looking for a spot where Theresa from Norient told me she'd seen a hang player not long ago. It happened to be in front of the Einstein House, where Albert Einstein lived from 1903 to 1905, when he was developing his special theory of relativity. Inside, I took in the parlor room where the great thinker might have scribbled notes on the space-time continuum.

There wasn't a hang player around, but while I toured the house a dulcimer player had set up. He was playing something familiar, but it took me a minute to place it: "Smoke on the Water," by Deep Purple. On the dulcimer, the simple, Neanderthalish guitar riff sounded as though Deep Purple had been turned into a phalanx of fairies.

I walked across the street to the Bern Conservatory, where

Markus Plattner, the assistant director and an accomplished guitarist, had agreed to meet me. Markus's office was airy and orderly, and his keyboard and acoustic guitar were within easy reach of his desk. Tall windows opened to a pleasant breeze. Years ago, he told me, he and the director were invited to Felix's house to see the hang. "We went there because we were generally interested in maybe having the hang at the school," he said. "I remember, I felt a bit strange. We never got to talk to [Felix]. He didn't actually talk. [Sabina] took care of the conversation."

The conservatory did get a hang, but after a while, Markus said, Felix demanded to have it back without explanation. At that point, the plinking sounds of round two of "Smoke on the Water" cascaded in. Markus stopped to listen and said, "What we're hearing out there, the dulcimer, that's very popular right now." He said there was a new folk scene in Switzerland, with influences from jazz, pop, and rock but also a modern sensibility. That got him on the subject, as it had for Thomas at Norient, about the identity of the country. Conservatives, he believed, were saying, "'We don't need all that modern stuff. We have our folk music, our yodeling, our Schwyzerörgeli.'" But, he pointed out, "for artistic musicians, that doesn't cover it all, does it?"

Markus was one of those artistic musicians. After hearing the Beatles in the 1960s, he knew playing music was what he wanted to do and got his first guitar, though over time it became full of wormholes. He discovered blues and jazz and eventually became a prominent jazz guitarist in Switzerland. Now Markus was one semester shy of retiring. Afterward, he planned to sail on — quite literally — by going to live on a boat. "Something new is coming," he said wistfully.

Before we parted, I asked him if he'd play something for me on the guitar. He cradled it in his arms as if it were a toddler and began "The Nearness of You." It was soulful and strained with a little melancholy, I thought. Or maybe that was just the mood I had fallen into. It was late afternoon, and I had only one full day left to find the hang.

I seemed to be the only journalist who had struck out with Felix. Jessica Dacey had interviewed Felix and Sabina for a Swiss website two months earlier. When we met that evening in a wine bar she said she was still surprised she had even gotten the interview. In her story, she referred to the hang as "a kind of Holy Grail for tens of thousands of people around the world." And she quoted Felix on the extraordinary impact it had on people: "Twenty thousand letters and everyone is talking about the same thing. They tell us the story of when they first encountered this sound." When I asked her why she thought he wouldn't speak to me, she had a guess. "They want to keep it a small production. They're not interested in making money. For them it's all about the artifice. In fact, they don't even call it an instrument—they call it a sound sculpture."

Jessica knew plenty about music: her husband was a British recording artist who went by the name Merz. (In one of his videos, set in the woods, he plays with a drum ensemble that keeps the beat by hitting trees and rustling leaves—perhaps to invoke nontraditional forces. Or maybe the budget was really low.) She suggested that the musical experimentation in the country, and also the jazz influence and the very openness in Swiss culture, were a perfect combination for the unique qualities of the hang. "It's one of those things that kind of transcends culture," she said.

The night sky was turning pink and violet, and Jessica needed to head off. The streets were quiet, and on the way back to my hotel it occurred to me that my being booked in the Ahmad Jamal room had been all wrong. I was in search of a percussion instrument; I should have asked for the Louie Bellson room. Bellson pioneered the use of two bass drums at once, and Duke Ellington called him "the world's greatest musician." The Louie Bellson room had drumsticks on the wall, a mounted snare drum!

I felt more behind the beat than ever.

A musician named Andreas Gerber, who lived in Liestal, a fifty-minute train ride north of Bern, was one of the hang players I'd contacted before leaving on my trip, and he had expressed an openness to meeting. The way my luck was going, I figured I'd reach Liestal only to spend hours waiting in vain. On my last day in Switzerland, though, Andreas pulled up on his bicycle exactly when we said we'd meet. Andreas, who had the wiry build of someone who has been too busy to eat his whole life, took me up to the loft of a building that also housed a movie theater. He opened the door to a cavernous room, which looked like Santa's workshop if Santa Claus were a Nigerian percussion master. There were steel drums and a whole wall of African bells. There were shakers and gongs and pouches of decorative mallets posted on wooden beams, berimbaus and a balafon. There were string instruments, a piano, and more hand drums than I could count. And in front of all of that, Andreas had set out two hangs—not unlike the way a date might set the table for a romantic dinner—next to each other on stands.

Here is what followed: we played the same hang together, and we played the hangs separately, improvising melodies. Andreas jumped over to the piano as I played, and he picked up the guitar, grabbed shakers, played the melodica, and lorded over the rantang. Sometimes he sang as we played—in English, in German, in no language at all.

For me, playing the hang was like a first kiss, or maybe it was like driving an exotic sports car for the first time: delightful, yet not exactly what I had imagined. I didn't always know where to put my hands. I went too fast. I felt unworthy. (Wait, did I just describe my first kiss again?)

Because you play the hang with your hands, there's a warmth that comes through that's the opposite of what you usually get from the icy feel of other metal instruments. You can better control the range of sound, and what might come across as a light shuffle on a djembe or conga still carries a melodic murmur on the hang.

Andreas had a story for each of his five hangs (here was the one his wife sang most beautifully with; here was the one he loaned to a friend whose friend was dying and wanted to play it while he still could . . .), and he had me play each one. When I asked him how music had come to take such a hold on his life, he told me that his father was a preacher and that he was raised in a fundamentalist Christian environment. Church music pervaded the house. But then his two older brothers introduced him to the music of the Rolling Stones. "That was a turning point," he said. "It gave me electrifying feeling for my body."

As a teenager, he'd started off playing piano and electric violin in rock bands, but being in bands proved not to be his thing. "I'm not in show business," he said. "I'm in flow business." He studied music in Brazil, Korea, Africa, Bali, and California. Those experiences led him to the study of TaKeTiNa, which emphasizes the healthy effects rhythm has on the mind, body, and soul, the belief that the body is an instrument. He had been teaching TaKeTiNa and the art of improvisation for decades. But even for a world traveler and musician, the discovery of the hang cast a particular spell. "It's the most beautiful sound I ever heard," he said. That was one thing we had in common.

After acquiring his first hang, he kept going back to Felix for more. No two hangs are exactly the same, and Andreas kept falling in love with another and expanding the family like a musical polygamist. He wanted to use them in groups, with choirs, whatever musical context interested him. But, he said, Felix became disapproving of this approach, and their relationship became more tense.

Andreas recalled how Felix began insisting that the hang was not merely a drum or percussion instrument. Rather, Felix said, "the hang brings you back to yourself. The role of this instrument in the world is to bring people back to their self, their center." This "is a beautiful thing," Andreas told me. "I respect this vision, but here's my 'but': I find it not okay to say that people who do something else with it mistreat it, are doing wrong. That, for me, goes too far."

That shed some light on why the other hang players wouldn't speak to me—they didn't want to risk a falling-out with Felix. I wondered what the implication for Andreas might be since our meeting was clearly going to be in my story. He understood that Felix might end their relationship. This would be particularly difficult, he explained, since Felix and Sabina were the only people he knew who could tune a hang. But, he said, "I'm a free man."

In our final hour together, we kept hopping on different instruments—Andreas on the hang, the piano, various drums. I moved over to one of the steel drums, and for nearly fifteen minutes we built to something like a musical farewell; the groove grew slower and slower, and though I, for one, didn't want it to end, we both knew when those last notes had sounded.

By the time I stepped outside again, I was amazed to realize that, as much as I had loved playing the hang, I no longer harbored the fantasy of owning one. I had something better now: the memories of meeting all these good people over these four days and hearing their stories—and also their wonderful playing. And memories wouldn't need tuning. Maybe Felix was right: maybe I had had the virus. But now I seemed to be cured.

At the station, as the train rounded the bend to take me back to Bern, I reached out to shake Andreas's hand, but he pulled me into an embrace. We broke into laughter—we were two people who took such immense pleasure in the beating of a drum, and we were always searching out a vast range of musical instruments and the stories they told. The endless roads you travel to find harmony.

CHAPTER 2

Do You Feel Like We Do?

On the stage of Baltimore's Lyric theater, I was holding a piece of equipment that had proven to be much easier to find than the hang. Its grip on me was different but no less significant, and I was still trying to understand it forty years later. Unlike the hang, this device had found a mass audience, with millions touched by it.

In my hands was Peter Frampton's Talk Box. It produced an iconic sound that combined the guitar and the voice, which Frampton had famously used on his epic "Do You Feel Like We Do" from *Frampton Comes Alive!*—once the greatest-selling live album of all time.

All around me men in black were scurrying to get the stage ready for the concert that evening—just Frampton, with no opening act. It happened to be the fortieth anniversary of *Frampton Comes Alive!*

"You can feel how heavy it is," said Aidan Mullen, Frampton's guitar tech. And it was, especially considering that it was no wider than a board book. The Talk Box was worn and square, with one button in the middle.

Was it complicated inside? I asked.

"No! It's a speaker—that's all it is," Aidan said. A hose connected to the box, and the other end was wrapped next to the microphone and blew air into Frampton's mouth. The Talk Box was like another larynx—the guitar did the riffing, Frampton mouthed the words, and the sound that produced went into the microphone. "It's not rocket science," Aidan added, "but it's interesting."

With his short hair, glasses that constantly came on and off his face, and hands that perpetually tightened, twisted, and tinkered, Aidan projected more the vibe of a handyman than a member of a rock crew. He had been with Frampton for only a couple of years, but in some ways he'd been working toward the job his whole life. "I went to see a show at Oakland Stadium," he said as he was getting Frampton's massive guitar rig up and running. "It was July Fourth, 1977, and it was Peter Frampton, Lynyrd Skynyrd, Santana, and the Outlaws. And I was fifteen years old. I was right down on the barricade. Peter Frampton was my favorite guitar player at the time, Garry Rossington from Lynyrd Skynyrd was my second favorite guitar player, and the correlation there is that both of those bands had *huge* live records that year." Lynyrd Skynyrd's was *One More from the Road*. "For me, *Frampton Comes Alive!* was a game changer in so many ways because back then it wasn't about MTV, it wasn't about videos, it wasn't about downloads. You went to a record store and you bought a record. You opened it up and you listened to it and you looked at the pictures. That was it for us as music fans, and certainly as a guitar player.

"'Show Me the Way' was the first song I heard off that record, and that had the Talk Box on it, too, right? And that was kind of one of those things—I was probably in the car with friends and heard it on the radio. I'm like, *Whoa! What's that?* I learned that album cover-to-cover as a guitar player back in my teens. I know every note and every nuance of that record."

So it was particularly meaningful for Aidan that Frampton was currently on a joint tour with Lynyrd Skynyrd—tonight's show was one of the few dates Frampton was playing on his own. But the joint tour was complicated, too—maybe more so for Aidan than anyone else in the crew. "On the Lynyrd Skynyrd tour we have ten minutes to have [the equipment] completely off the stage," Aidan said with a note of wonder. Frampton's immense rig looked like it had been lifted straight out of NASA. "A lot of people look at it and go, 'Why? What's the point when you can get a little box that can make any sounds?' But he's a purist. There's a setup for every song, and then within each song there are six separate parts that are available at the push of a button. He's always been a gear guy. He's always had an awesome set. He's famous for it. It's all part of the package, right down to the Talk Box." I counted fourteen guitars in a nearby rack.

Aidan said that before the tour started, he brought much of Frampton's equipment to his house and spent two weeks just staring at it, trying to wrap his mind around how it could be streamlined and easier to work with.

One of the things that surprised me was that this tour wasn't much playing up the fortieth anniversary of *Frampton Comes Alive!* I had imagined that would be a marketing dream, but there was barely anything in the promotion. I mentioned this to Aidan, who said it hadn't been his place to weigh in on that, but he had encouraged the idea in his own sly way; he reached into his pocket and gave me a handful of guitar picks he'd had made that showed the album cover in miniature—Peter with his shirt unbuttoned, hair flowing, his guitar raised, his eyes cast skyward, his mouth slightly agape, his face set in what could be a moment of musical bliss, or, with the two round lights on either side of his head, a close encounter.

Another crew member overheard our conversation and reminded us that Frampton did a big thirty-fifth anniversary tour, which produced another live album—and DVD—called *Frampton Comes Alive! 35 Tour*. "Just five years apart, it might have been a little odd to do another," he explained.

"Thirty-five is a weird year to celebrate," Aidan said.

He scanned the stage, which looked like a snake pit with all its loose cables. "Has anybody laid eyes on the black stool today?" No one had. Then he spotted it behind the drums. During shows, the stool held Peter's tea, picks, and throat lozenges. Aidan said that sometimes, when they were tearing down the stage after a show, a crew member might find a half-eaten throat lozenge on the stool; Frampton would put it there so that he could put the tube from the Talk Box in his mouth. Aidan pondered the alternative. "The amount of sheer sound pressure coming out of that hose, it would probably blow [the lozenge] down his throat," he said, then acted out a choking Peter Frampton trying to get through "Do You Feel Like We Do."

Frampton Comes Alive! was released in 1976, when I was nine years old. My musical education at Bob's house hadn't yet started in earnest, but I did acquire my first 45 that year: KC and the Sunshine Band's "(Shake, Shake, Shake) Shake Your Booty." I became more aware of Peter Frampton by the time I was in middle school. In Fayetteville, you could hear the softer hits of the day on the AM station WFLB—Boz Skaggs's "Lowdown" or Orleans's "Still the One," say—but I eventually discovered the FM station WQDR, out of Raleigh, and the three hit songs from *Frampton Comes Alive!*—"Show Me the Way," "Baby I Love Your Way," and "Do You Feel Like We Do"—came on as regularly as traffic updates on the Beltline. "Show Me the Way" featured the Talk Box more minimally, but "Do You Feel Like We Do" indulged in it at length, in stages. (By the time I was sixteen, I could drive from one end of town to the other before the nearly fifteen-minute song was over.)

Throughout the decade I heard the main six-note riff constantly pouring out of the cars that passed my friends and me on our bikes or when someone's older brother or sister drove us to Putt-Putt or the YMCA. I hadn't yet been to a rock concert, but hearing "Do You Feel Like We Do," which was recorded at San Francisco's Winterland Ballroom, made the idea of it seem as visceral and death-defying as the chariot race scene in *Ben Hur*. The crowd cheered uproariously at the slightest development—the fans' screams were so loud they became another instrument. But the part that enthralled my friends and me the most was when, halfway through the song, the crowd responded to an action we could only imagine. We didn't know what a Talk Box was, but we knew Frampton was using something to create those mechanized sounds. Did he step into some kind of iron lung wheeled on stage and set upright? Was *that* what the crowed was cheering? Or was it a breathing apparatus being lowered onto him, like Darth Vader's mask or a deep-sea diver's helmet? Then those first Talk Box notes would burble out. First, it was about forty-five seconds of gibberish, then, more clearly, the words "Do you feel like we do?" This was a time of UFO mania, and Frampton sounded to us like an alien from a distant but friendly planet. Next we could make out, "That's all right, that's all right with me." My friends and I would turn to each other like pleased code breakers and repeat back what he'd said. Then he continued: "Do you feel like we do?" Did we? We wore braces and Whacky Pack and motocross T-shirts and coasted on our bicycles with banana seats while obsessing over the times on *The Price Is Right* when Barker's Beauties appeared in bikinis. How could we feel even remotely like Peter Frampton and his band? Not that it wasn't nice of him to ask.

Then Frampton seemed to say something a bit stranger. All of us were convinced he then told the crowd, in Talk Box speak, "I want to fuck you." And the crowd roared even harder!

We snickered—we were of the age when the best response to anything sexual was to snicker. Snickering let you not fully understand the thing in question without letting on. A small scraping from the back of your throat and kind of a hissing sound—that was all you needed to cope with anything. But that moment in the song also made us sort through some complicated issues. Did he want to fuck the entire crowd? We reasoned that even though he hadn't specified, clearly he meant he only wanted to fuck all the *women* in the crowd. So why did all the guys—and we could tell by the deep-voiced responses that the audience was easily 75 percent dudes—respond so eagerly? Was that simply the generous nature of 1970s hippies? (Only in my forties did it occur to me that he was saying, "I want to thank you," which was disappointing.) For the next two minutes, Frampton produced cosmic-sounding stage banter before releasing an orgasmic groan and blasting into the last, torrid guitar solo.

There was only one other song on the radio that played as long as "Do You Feel Like We Do." Iron Butterfly's "In-a-Gadda-Da-Vida" is two and a half minutes longer; with its terrifying guitar line, eerie organ, and growling vocals, it sounded like rock for the undead but didn't get nearly the same airplay. And while none of us had heard the studio version of "Do You Feel Like We Do," we were sure that there was no way it could have sounded like this. There was too much in the live version that radiated spontaneity and verve. It captured everything we imagined live rock was about.

By the time I was in my twenties, "Do You Feel Like We Do" and the other two tracks from the album had become staples for classic rock channels on the radio, a kind of old folks' home for all the bands from my childhood that I loved. There were other songs that featured the Talk Box—Joe Walsh's "Rocky Mountain Way" and Aerosmith's "Sweet Emotion," for example, and "Tell Me Something Good" by Rufus featuring Chaka Khan. Stevie Wonder, Steely Dan, and, much later, Bon Jovi used it. In 2005 the band Weezer used a Talk Box on its song "Beverly Hills," but Weezer had always seemed to me a band of smart-asses, and I couldn't help but think this was their idea of musical parody. They had released five albums of ironic pop-punk, and everything about this song, despite its catchiness, was disingenuous. The main chorus declares, "Beverly Hills—that's where I want to be!" Weezer was mocking the very idea of a Beverly Hills lifestyle. The video for the song, which features Hugh Hefner, was filmed at the Playboy Mansion, just to reinforce the charade. The singer, Rivers Cuomo, in his hipster glasses, sings amid a crowd of busty, comely young women. To me, their use of the Talk Box was the original middle finger to excess and indulgence.

The Talk Box! Ha ha! Oh, man. Those old farts.

Hearing that song then made me consider a question I'd never thought of: Was the Talk Box ultimately one of rock's coolest sounds, as I'd always believed, or, just possibly, was it really the whoopee cushion of rock? Was it even truly musical?

In searching out Peter Frampton's Talk Box now, I wanted to understand why whole generations had such deep affection for such an odd effect. And I wanted to know what it meant to Frampton forty years later. Could he have possibly glimpsed how a single piece of equipment would affect his life and career so fully? The other part of that was more personal. I was going back to my childhood and trying to learn how much I had evolved as a listener. How much, I wondered uneasily, was my love for my favorite music rooted in the memories wrapped around it versus the music itself?

In 1966, Peter Frampton joined the Herd at age sixteen, after the band had gone through some lineup changes. The Herd, which formed in London, scored a few hits, but despite Frampton's ambitions as a serious musician, he couldn't steer the band away from its pop trappings or the relentless attention on his boyish good looks. After two years, it was time for a reset.

In 1969 he joined Steve Marriot to form Humble Pie, and the heavier sound and downplaying of image and looks were a tonic for Frampton. The band recorded four studio albums and a well-regarded live album, *Performance: Rockin' the Fillmore*, but the music was becoming increasingly raw and heavier under Marriot's leadership, and creative tensions about the band's direction took their toll; Frampton bowed out in 1971. He was a songwriter and a singer, but playing the guitar was the most important role for him, and this time he was glad to be on his own.

"When I left Humble Pie, and it was, like, '71, I was doing a lot of sessions," Frampton told me. He was speaking from his home in Nashville after the fortieth anniversary tour. "I met a lot of incredible musicians — and Beatles." He laughed, still awed by the memory. "Which was a very heady experience for me. At the age of twenty-one I was in the studio with two Beatles." This was a recording session for George Harrison's first solo outing, *All Things Must Pass*. "It was like my mind was blown. I was just enjoying the heck out of it, obviously.

"So we're doing *All Things Must Pass*, and on acoustic was myself and George—I was on George's left, and to the right of George was three [members] of Badfinger: Joey Molland, and the two writers [Pete Ham and Tom Evans]. So there were five acoustics because it was Phil Spector and one is not enough, or two, or three. And then Gary Wright would be on piano or organ. Billy Preston. Ringo was there, too, and also Jim Gordon, who was the drummer for Derek and the Dominos." Another drummer, Alan White, who would be in Yes from 1972 on, played on the album, too. "So incredible, incredible band."

In a down moment in the session, Harrison introduced Frampton to pedal steel guitarist Pete Drake, who had flown in from Nashville. Drake was a fixture on the country music scene, an ace session man who had played on Bob Dylan's three recent albums, *John Wesley Harding*, *Nashville Skyline*, and *Self Portrait*, which had been Dylan's foray into country. "And we were doing a Bob Dylan song— 'If Not for You' was one of the songs," Frampton recalled. Frampton told me he'd always assumed Dylan had recommended Drake to Harrison for the session.

"I was getting calls from all over the world," Drake told Douglass Green of *Guitar Player* magazine in 1973. "One day my secretary buzzed me and said, 'George Harrison wants you on the phone.' And I said, 'Well, where's he from?' She said, 'London.' And I said, 'Well, what company's he with?' She said, 'The Beatles.' The name, you know, just didn't ring any bells.'" Still, Drake flew off to London for a week for Harrison's *All Things Must Pass* sessions, which would be significant for Drake but even more so for Frampton.

"So there I am—I'm set up right opposite of Pete," Frampton continued. "He sets up his pedal steel and blows all us away. It was phenomenal. So we're having a break, and all of a sudden he says, 'Check this out' to me—I mean, we hit it off straight away, you know. He got this little box out, put it on the top of his pedal steel. And plugs something in here, plugs something in there, and put the pedal steel into this and that, and all of sudden he got this plastic tube and put it in his mouth, and the next thing that happens is, the pedal steel is singing to me."

The sound was strangely familiar to Frampton — it reminded him of listening, as a boy, to Radio Luxembourg, which was a station that broadcast illegally at night to England. When the voice announced the station's call sign — 208 was the identifying number — it came through in a distorted, Talk Box style.

"So I always wondered, what *is* that? Well, there it is in front of me, and my jaw dropped. I said, 'Oh my God. That's incredible. Where do I get one?'" Drake told him he made it himself. Frampton was mesmerized. "I had to find one of these," he told himself. But first he would have to find the right song to put it in.

In 1972, Frampton started up his solo career with *Wind of Change*, which Ringo Starr and Billy Preston played on; the album didn't make much of an impact, peaking at number 177 on the *Billboard* album chart. But Frampton was happy to be in charge of his musical destiny for a change, and as a solo act he proved to be a capable, confident lead singer and front man and, of course, a dynamic guitarist. As his band prepared to tour behind the album, there was a single moment, a musical flash, that would alter his life. "What happened was, we were rehearsing the band," which was given the name Frampton's Camel, "and so we went to America for our first tour," Frampton told me. "But this was rehearsal, in London, and we were just jamming. I would always bring my Revox reel-to-reel [tape recorder] and a couple of mics. I've always been pretty much an engineer on the side, so we would record everything we played so that we could see how we sounded, see how it was going, and also catch any jams that might happen throughout the rehearsal. Well, we did this jam, and when we stopped the whole band just turned around and said, 'Wind it back like two or three minutes. There was a lick you did, Peter, that could be the beginning of something.' So we wound it back and played it, and they went, 'There it is, there it is!'"

He hummed the "Do You Feel" riff for me. Even hearing Peter Frampton *hum* it brought chills!

I asked him if he had realized he'd played anything special in that moment. "No, it was just an unconscious, or subconscious — the way to play freely is to not think at all. The time for thinking is when you're practicing and stealing great riffs from other people that you make your own, you know." That made him laugh again. "But this was something that I didn't even remember playing until I listened back, and there it was.

"When the playback came through, I definitely heard it," he said. "And then the four of us just started working on that riff." The initial idea was that the song would be an instrumental. Then, a couple of nights earlier, "I had a couple of glasses of wine too many, and I woke up with a slight hangover. And then I started writing this chorus. It was about, 'Are you feeling all fuzzy like I am?' And so I said, 'Guys, I've got this little chorus idea,' and then we worked the riff. We worked it into the key of this chorus that I had written, and then I came up with a verse. I said, 'Give me a second, I'll write some words that will do for now, and then I can go home and make them better.' Well, I never changed them. And it was there that I wrote them on the spot in that rehearsal room. And I might have written the third verse later, but I definitely wrote a couple of verses right there in the room, and we spent probably a couple of hours just putting it all together."

They played the song live before recording it, and from the beginning crowds responded to it. "When it comes down like three-quarters of the way through and just down to nothing, basically, where on the live record it's the Talk Box, that was just ad-libbed guitar at that point and a few 'Do you feel like I do?' kind of things, which I think probably came in as a communication thing at that point because that's a perfect place, as everybody comes down before the climax there, for communication to the audience. And when I did finally get a Talk Box, it was obvious to me that that would be the place to introduce it.

"Whether you knew the song or not," he said, "it was uplifting to the audience. It was like, 'OK, how do you feel? Do you feel like I do? Ugh, I feel awful.' Or, 'I feel great today.' It was just like this colloquialism that just turned into this major question to the audience. It was just one of those songs that was — we hit the nail on the head with that one. You can't work out what's going to work and what's not going to work. I've never been able to do that, and if I did I'd write a hundred 'Do You Feel Like We Do's.' And sometimes it works and sometimes it doesn't, but from the very word go on the intro there's something very special about that track."

Curiously, for the next album, *Frampton's Camel*, in 1973, the band recorded two versions of "Do You Feel," one significantly slower than the tempo of the live version, and that's the one Frampton went with. Reflecting on that decision now, he was slightly mystified. "It sounds very embryonic to me now," he said. The song, the only one on the album credited to the whole band, wasn't released as a single, and *Frampton's Camel* failed to crack the top 100 on the *Billboard* album chart. With the following release, *Something's Happening*, in 1974, not much was.

Before Frampton recorded his next LP, his girlfriend at the time, Penny McCall, wanted to get him a special Christmas present. "I get a call from her and she said, 'I need a Christmas present [for Peter],'" Bob Heil told me. "'Can you help me?' And I said sure."

Heil is a legendary sound engineer, famous, in part, for developing the Who's quadraphonic sound system. Bob had also worked with Humble Pie and developed their sound system, so he knew Frampton well. "She knew that I was close to the band and I could get him some musical gear. She didn't know if it was going to be a guitar or amplifier or what." But Heil knew right away what that present would be.

In 1973 Joe Walsh, who had left the James Gang, recorded "Rocky Mountain Way," which was the first rock track to feature the Talk Box, although it wasn't called that then. In fact, Walsh used Pete Drake's very same Talking Actuator, recording it in Drake's Nashville studio. (Heil maintained that it was Nashville pedal steel guitarist Bill West and his wife, Dottie, who made the Actuator that Walsh used at Drake's studio.) Walsh didn't attempt actual words in the solo, but his guttural, swampy scatting was oddly seductive and otherworldly and fit right in with the overall deviant-sounding vocal.

When it was time for Walsh to go on tour, he needed something more substantial than Drake's fragile three-inch box, which was made for the studio and not for the rigors of touring. "Joe and I got together because I was doing sound for the James Gang," Heil told me, "and we were helping put the equipment together for his new band called Barnstorm. They were about to go out on tour, and one day in rehearsals Joe said, 'Hey Bob, what are we going to do about that box, that voice thing?' And I said, 'Well, we'll build one.'" And they did.

Once "Rocky Mountain Way" became a hit — reaching number 23 on Billboard's singles chart — and people wanted to know more about that strange, hypnotic sound, Heil figured out how to put the device into mass production. Originally, it had no case, or backing, around it. "That first one, Joe put it in a paper sack," Heil said. "He tied a rubber band around it; it looked like a wine bottle."

So when McCall called Heil, he got what was now the Talk Box ready and sent it to her. Frampton was thrilled. "As soon as I got the thing I locked myself away in a rehearsal room in New York," Frampton told me. He and McCall were living in Westchester, New York, at the time, but each day he would go to New York City, where he was "borrowing" Foreigner's rehearsal room. "Just me and a guitar and a Talk Box," he said. He figured out how to manipulate the sound by the way he shaped his mouth, using his mouth, essentially, as a resonant chamber. "I locked myself away in there for a week and came out learning how to talk with this thing."

When the tour for Something's Happening kicked off, Frampton was anxious to see how the new version of "Do You Feel," which had already become the highlight of his live shows, would go over featuring the Talk Box. "It was quite unbelievable, the reaction," he said. "It was one thing when I started just playing notes the very first time. People started screaming. It was funny — it's a funny sound. And then when I spoke with it and said, you know, 'Hello everybody,' or I think the first thing I said was, 'Do you feel like I do?' I felt the audience move towards the stage, so there was this sort of immense attention focusing that I had not felt before. From that moment on it was something that we did every night, and we'd get the same reaction, on a sliding scale of different audiences, but it would be the same reaction just about everywhere."

After the tour came to an end, Frampton put the Talk Box to use in the studio, injecting it into "Show Me the Way" for the next album, titled simply *Frampton*. Rather than waiting late to introduce it, as he did in "Do You Feel," Frampton brought in the Talk Box before the opening verse, right after two bars of acoustic strumming. It's sparsely used, on the opening and brief second solo, and in the background of the second verse, trailing behind the recorded vocals. It was like a calling card for the real Talk Box demonstration he'd deliver in concert.

Frampton fared much better than *Something's Happening*, peaking at number 32 on the *Billboard* album chart, but it was his fourth album in four years and hardly an encouraging place to be this far into his solo career. "Show Me the Way" was released as a single, but nothing came of it.

Frampton went back out on tour, but this time he kept only his drummer, John Siomos. He brought in Bob Mayo on keyboards, who would also accompany on guitar for some songs, and bassist Stanley Sheldon. Frampton thought it was the best band he had assembled, and the shows were blistering displays of arena-rock musicianship. Where the studio efforts had sometimes been too tight and restrained, like frozen-food versions of a delicious meal, performed live the songs flowed with a new energy; tempos were pushed, and there was new attention to the groove. Some of the shows were recorded, and when Frampton and the band listened to them, it confirmed what they knew. They were remarkably in sync, and everyone's playing was outstanding.

As Frampton and I were talking about the ways the audience comes through on the live version of "Do You Feel," I told him how fascinated I had always been with the audience's sense of anticipation right before the Talk Box solo. "I walk from my left stage mic to the center stage mic, where the Talk Box is," he explained. "You'll notice right before I play the Talk Box there's a huge ovation." I'd noticed!

"Did I drop my pants at that point?" he said, and laughed. "No, no. I didn't do anything, I didn't take my shirt off or anything. It was the anticipation of what was to come because they had seen me in San Francisco play the Talk Box because I was opening the bill; I was in the middle spot; I'd played all around this country so many times, which also contributed to its success." The word of mouth about the shows kept growing. The Talk Box "was something that they knew was coming, and they couldn't wait for it.

"When we got to the point of June '75, when we were doing those shows, those California shows, we were so relaxed with 'Do You Feel' that there was no rush. There was no, 'OK, this is how it's supposed to go.' We have signposts that [signal], 'OK, we're going to change gears here.' And how many gears we change is up to what happens that night. That's why I've been able to play for so many years doing some of the same numbers—for forty years, you know. Because it changes every night. They know they're going to get the same songs, but they're going to be different. It has to be different; otherwise, I couldn't do them every night."

Before *Frampton Comes Alive!* Frampton had toured relentlessly, sharing the stage with the Steve Miller Band, Edgar Winter, the J. Geils Band, Santana, and even Humble Pie; no one questioned whether he put on a terrific show. But that live alchemy wasn't happening in the studio often enough. After that tour he was apprehensive about going back into the studio. But what was the alternative?

Frampton's manager at the time, Dee Anthony, also managed Humble Pie. Just as the Allman Brothers Band, whose first two studio albums generated lackluster sales, did with *At Fillmore East*, Humble Pie had taken their studio efforts as mere jumping-off points and stretched out with extended jams in their live recording *Performance: Rockin' the Fillmore*. And increasingly, live albums had proven to be some of the most important entries in an artist's catalog. There was the Who's *Live at Leeds*, the Rolling Stones' *"Get Yer Ya-Ya's Out!,"* and Kiss's *Alive!* Even *Johnny Cash at Folsom Prison* had reached number 1 on the *Billboard* country album chart. Anthony and Frampton agreed that a live album should be next up.

Jerry Moss, who cofounded A&M Records, was a believer in Frampton's talent, and he was prepared to be bold: not only would he commit to a live recording as the next release, but after hearing the initial tracks, he suggested that it be expanded to a double album. The label even recorded some last shows well after that decision and shortly before the actual release.

Cameron Crowe, then an editor at *Rolling Stone*, contributed the liner notes. "Frampton & Band perform with the earnestness and competence that we've come to expect," he wrote. "*Frampton Comes Alive!* is much more than a souvenir. It is a testimony to Peter Frampton in his natural habitat."

In 1976 Frampton would be named *Billboard*'s Artist of the Year. *Frampton Comes Alive!* would go on to be the biggest-selling live album in music history—it has sold more than 17 million copies—until Bruce Springsteen and the E Street Band's box set, *Live/1975–85*, released in 1986, surpassed it. But perhaps what was most impressive was that the album spawned three top-20 hits out of songs that had never entered the charts in their original studio versions. "Do You Feel Like We Do" was edited down to seven minutes to accommodate the traditional radio format, and it reached number 10 on *Billboard*'s singles chart, but the longer version was the one that would live in music infamy.

It would have been far-fetched to think Frampton could do anything after the live album that could mirror its success. And he didn't. Commercially, the downward slide began with the next album and continued throughout the 1980s. *Frampton Comes Alive!* was simply his *Moby Dick*, his invention of the Chia Pet. In 1978 he would star, along with the Bee Gees, in a debacle of a movie based on the songs on *Sgt. Pepper's Lonely Hearts Club Band*. Its very concept was akin to remaking *The Godfather* with the Banana Splits. (Reviewing it in the *New York Times*, Janet Maslin wrote of Frampton, "he's a musician, not a movie star, and even a plot that merely requires him to look sad, peppy or joyful from time to time is more than he can manage.") He would eventually be dropped by A&M Records. Through the decades, though, he kept growing as a guitar player, kept writing, and kept performing his treasured songs for people who wanted to hear them. The crowds got smaller, sure—he went from playing multiple nights at Madison Square Garden to a single night at the Cape Cod Melody Tent—but his passion never shrank.

Many of his 1970s contemporaries found a way to be a part of the MTV spotlight, however briefly—acts such as Heart, Rod Stewart, Robert Plant, Steve Winwood, J. Geils Band, David Bowie, even George Harrison—but the video era eluded Frampton entirely. His pal David Bowie, though, came calling to ask him to play on his *Never Let Me Down* album, in 1987, and the subsequent Glass Spider Tour. (When I was in college, in Chapel Hill, that tour came to the Dean E. Smith Center, and my friend Doug Blizzard, who lived on my hall and played guitar, and I decided we'd walk over to hear what we could from the outside—we weren't big enough David Bowie fans to pay for tickets. So we pressed our faces to the glass as the show began, the sound coming to us as if underwater. Then, to our astonishment, a door pushed open, and a security guard motioned for us to come inside. We found good seats on the second level, to the right of the stage. We took in the enormous spider that hovered over the stage, then focused on the musicians onstage. When Bowie and the band played "The Jean Genie," Frampton worked the main riff of "Do You Feel Like We Do" into his solo.)

In 2007 Frampton won his first Grammy for *Fingerprints*, in the Best Pop Instrumental Album category. He continued to tour steadily, and just about every show he's played in the forty years since *Frampton Comes Alive!* has closed with "Do You Feel Like We Do."

"I'm so lucky that it's lasted," he said of the song's appeal, but he couldn't say exactly *why* it had. "The amazing thing is, each new generation that comes along gets introduced to it by an uncle, a brother, a father, you know, and it's the same reaction. They weren't there—they weren't there in San Francisco, they weren't there when the album came out—but now it still has the same effect on new listeners."

Must have been a dream I don't believe where I've been
Come on, let's do it again

The Lyric Opera House (or the Modell Performing Arts Center at the Lyric, as it's known now) had its first performance in 1894. Today the stately, two-tiered Baltimore theater, with its red-cushioned seats and pale gold walls, suggests more *Nutcracker* than a rock concert.

On stage Aidan was restringing a guitar for Frampton that once belonged to J. J. Cale, an influential singer-songwriter and guitarist. Over the course of his career, Aidan had performed as a guitarist himself for many years. He played in Eddie Money's live lineup, sometimes handling bass, and later he toured with country singer Collin Raye. As a guitar and bass tech, he had worked for Def Leppard, Darryl Hall of Hall and Oates, Aerosmith, Guns N' Roses, Cheap Trick, and Phil Collins. He was also a guitar tech for Metallica and was on the very bus that, in 1986 in Sweden, flipped on its side — killing original bassist Cliff Burton.

Aidan and the crew were expecting Frampton's arrival any minute, but for now there was a waggish camaraderie among them as they joked around while preparing the equipment. And then Frampton emerged in the wings, sunglasses on, with his tour manager in tow, and immediately a solemnity washed over. Frampton stood next to me, surveying the stage. The tour manager, Donnie Lewis, zeroed in on me since I wasn't supposed to be at the sound check, and he quickly gave me the boot.

Out front of the Lyric there was a Frampton poster mounted under glass — basically an updated version of the *Frampton Comes Alive!* image: guitar in hand, head tilted slightly skyward. Another poster was of the New Age keyboardist Yanni; with his black hair falling on his shoulders, his fitted black T-shirt, and muscular build, the ageless Yanni had the look of a roguish masseur at a Caribbean resort.

In the lobby I took in the slow trickle of avid fans. In a year I would be fifty, but the early crowd made me feel like a teenager. "The old-timers are dying off, so you have to see them while you can," an older man said into his phone, pacing the lobby. When he hung up, he informed his wife, with a palpable sense of envy, that his friend was at the *Field of Dreams* baseball diamond in Iowa. Nostalgia, it seemed, was everywhere.

In front of me a group of friends compared notes on how many times they'd seen Frampton in concert. One woman said she'd seen him perform when he was just eighteen. "Peter was pretty good back then, wasn't he?" said a man with a dubious shade of red hair. His friends obliged with polite chuckles. "It happens to all of us," a man with a braid down his back said of getting older. The group demurely agreed that that was true.

Taped to the front door was a small poster promoting a fall show by Kansas, who were promoting a fortieth anniversary of their own. Kansas would be commemorating their album *Leftoverture*. Only two of the original members were still in the band. And one sported an eye patch.

I ended up talking to a fan named Paul Robinson. Paul had seen Frampton from the very beginning of his career—with the Herd, with Humble Pie, and as a solo artist. "People got sick of him" in the late 1970s due to the overexposure, Paul said. But now he was dismayed that there weren't more people in the lobby.

We got on the subject of another classic rock artist, Steve Miller, who had been inducted into the Rock and Roll Hall of Fame a couple of months earlier. Paul had been the program director of WLIR, a progressive rock radio station in Long Island, when he interviewed Miller in 1973 at the Carlyle Hotel in Manhattan. Miller was touring in support of his album *The Joker* at the time, and when Paul showed up at his hotel room, he was a little shocked to find Miller still in bed—and intending to conduct the interview there. Paul made an observation about the lyrics to "Shu Ba Da Du Ma Ma Ma Ma" that Miller didn't appreciate, and Miller proceeded to jump out of bed, barely clad, and went on a wild rant, as Paul remembered it, about how Miller had left behind his University of Wisconsin–Madison influences long ago and how he intended to leave the Oregon town where he now lived because it was populated by sycophants.

Then the doors to the theater opened, and we all shuffled in.

Four of the first five songs were from *Frampton Comes Alive!* The band was in lockstep with Frampton at every turn, and his solos were the highlight of each piece, his lines soaring and melodic.

Frampton's broad range of early influences had always shown up in his playing. Listening to jazz guitarists as varied as Django Reinhardt and Kenny Burrell had given him a foundation in developing lyrical road maps in his soloing, and bluesmen Albert King and B. B. King had steeped him in the power of simpler, repeated patterns. The string-bending flair of Hank Marvin, of the British instrumental group the Shadows, came through in Frampton's eloquent phrasing as well. There was even some of keyboardist Billy Preston's funk jams that slithered through. Frampton's solos were melodic monologues—expressive and probing, each arriving at a cogent point.

The Talk Box got its first airing by the half-hour mark with "Show Me the Way," which sounded pretty much identical to the version on *Frampton Comes Alive!* A couple of instrumentals followed, which the crowd greeted more tepidly. Next came an acoustic solo set, and Frampton used the shift to tell stories about how those songs came to be.

When the band returned, they played another from *Comes Alive!*—"Go to the Sun," which was Frampton's biggest guitar workout of the night. The notes ascended into a grand orbit, spiraling further from the central melody of the song but never straying too far from the main harmonies. The longer Frampton explored, the more his bandmates worked the groove, like shipmates inspired to row harder. Next he played a mostly instrumental cover of Soundgarden's "Black Hole Sun," though he sang the last chorus through the Talk Box. That effort earned him a standing ovation, and he elevated the fervor with another *Comes Alive!* song, "(I'll Give You) Money," which let him engage in some dueling with his second guitarist, Adam Lester. This was no teacher-student display; after a bluesy tit-for-tat, Lester stayed with Frampton as the solos grew fiery and frenetic. You could see how much Frampton enjoyed being spurred on, and when the song came to an end, he was ready to push even further. It was time for the main event.

Frampton served up the early notes of "Do You Feel Like We Do," which were received with a long-earned mania. From the beginning a notable jab of funk was injected, and now Frampton alternated leads with his keyboardist, Rob Arthur, before the spotlight went fully to Arthur, whose blocky chords fueled an exhilarant, jazzy ramble. Though he had worked out his own solo, it also had echoes of Bob Mayo's famous excursion.

Bob Mayo on the keyboard! Bob Mayo!

That echo was underscored when Frampton announced, "Mr. Rob Arthur on the keyboard."

The arrangement then became stripped down, just as it always does, and the hi-hat became one of the most prominent features as Frampton prepared to step into the void. By this point, my anticipation—and the crowd's—for the solo we'd listened to for much of our lives was reaching the delirious stage; we were like the desert inhabitants in a Mad Max movie, desperate for water. Enjoying the tension in that moment, Frampton began to approach the microphone set up with the Talk Box tube, then moved away from it again, waving his hand in the air to indicate to the crowd, *You know what? No, not tonight. Not feeling the Talk Box for this one.*

The crowd erupted—we knew we were being teased, but we might have ripped him to shreds, too, given the chance. He laughed at his own naughtiness, then sauntered over and took the tube in his mouth. The first sound that came out was "Baltimore," and the relief that swept over the crowd was like the sighting of a rubber raft while floating out at sea. He then proceeded with some lengthy scatting before easing into the back-and-forth of asking the crowd, "Do you feel like we do?" Some of us had waited our whole lives to be asked like this.

That went on for several minutes before Frampton blared that famous *Wwwooooaaahhh!* just as in the *Frampton Comes Alive!* version, then launched into a scorching lead sendoff. When he guided the band into the last-note crunch, we shrieked our ancient lungs out. We stomped our creaking feet and high-fived and wiped our brows. We could have, it occurred to me, stormed outside and started a riot, or at least knocked down some parking signs and newspaper dispensers, though we would have felt it in the morning. Then Frampton and the band took their bows and went backstage.

For his final encore, Frampton brought back the spirit of George Harrison with a reverent working of "While My Guitar Gently Weeps." Pete Drake, for one, would have enjoyed the spectacle.

After my conversation with Frampton, I felt as though I couldn't fully understand the strange life of the Talk Box without learning how Drake had gotten onto his own talking contraption. He'd been enamored of the sounds Jerry Byrd coaxed out of his steel—Byrd played regularly at the Grand Ole Opry—and that set him on the path. Drake's family was in Augusta, Georgia—his father was a Pentecostal preacher—and by eighteen Drake had settled in Atlanta. One day he walked by a pawnshop and caught sight of a Supro, a single-necked steel guitar that could be played while held in the lap. After he saved up enough to buy it, he was gigging in clubs around the city and formed his first band, the Sons of the South.

After a few years the Atlanta scene felt limited, and Drake packed up and moved to Nashville, where he endured shaky times before his fortunes turned around in 1960. He went on to perform on two number 1 hits—"(You Just Don't Love Me) Anymore" and "Before This Day Ends" with singer George Hamilton. Suddenly, "I just couldn't do anything wrong there for a long time," Drake told *Guitar Player*.

During that time, he had neighbors who were deaf and mute, and that had gotten him wondering if there was anything he could create to help them communicate. Then he caught an old movie that featured Alvino Rey playing the steel guitar and making it "talk." "I thought, 'Man, if he can make a guitar talk, surely I can make people talk,'" Drake said. Such a leap might be a little head-scratching, but that belief opened up a new possibility for himself. Which he owed to an earlier musician with visions of making his instrument talk.

"The history goes back to 1939," Bob Heil told me. That was when Rey "took an old throat microphone like they used back in the World War II planes—the planes' cockpits were so noisy in those days a microphone didn't work, so they had these throat microphones, these carbon modules that you strapped onto your throat, and they [amplified] your actual voice box, so to speak. And he took that microphone and plugged it to the output of his guitar amp. So when he would play his wife would sing—it modulated her voice at the frequency of the guitar. It was very crude, but it was an interesting thing."

Rey played the pedal steel in swing orchestras and big bands, showcasing his "talking guitar," or Sonovox, as it became known. His run with it was short, though, and it lay dormant until 1959, when Pete Drake built what he called the Talking Actuator. Of course, what he came up with couldn't help his neighbors, but it did give a new voice to his pedal steel guitar. The Talking Actuator worked mostly in the same ways as Heil's Talk Box would—the speakers were disconnected by the push of a button, and the sound went through the driver in the plastic tube.

Drake first used it in the studio in 1963, on Roger Miller's "Lock, Stock and Teardrops" and Jim Reeves's "I've Enjoyed as Much of This as I Can Stand." Neither song was a notable hit, and after those sessions Drake figured that might be the end of the road for the novelty sound. Then, in 1964, he recorded a song called "Forever" for Smash Records, a division of Mercury. The languid ballad has only a main verse, no chorus, though there is an instrumental bridge, and the words, such as they are, fill out a lover's request: "Hold me," "Kiss me," "Whisper," which Drake articulates sharply through the Actuator. There's a spookiness to Drake's delivery as the singers echo the words back to him. "Forever" sold more than a million copies, and Drake was named Instrumentalist of the Year by the Country Music Association. From then on he was known as the King of the Talking Steel Guitar.

If there was one person who would have insights into both Pete Drake's Talk Box sound as well as Peter Frampton's, I figured it would be Ben Ratliff. A former *New York Times* music critic and author of several books, Ratliff happened to be "a Pete Drake freak," as he put it. Ratliff was thinking about Drake's Smash Records output when we spoke and said it was the emotions his music suggested that were so alluring. "One thing that I think is amazing about the way he uses that [Actuator] is, it's slow, and you hear everything really syllable by syllable," he said. I asked him if he thought the talk effect made Drake's records better, since he put it on so many more records than Frampton did. "Um, I don't want everybody to do it," he said, and we both laughed at the obviousness of his point. "I think that's a vision of hell in which everybody uses the Talk Box."

The Talk Box made Ratliff think of "jazz trombonists who are really skillful using the mute in a wah-wah sense. So much music *is* a kind of talking, or is related to talking. So using that wah-wah mute just intensifies the feeling that you are being talked to." Ratliff could see a connection between some of the great jazz singers and Frampton's Talk Box. "In terms of what he's doing—talking to the audience through his guitar—that's just great showbiz," he said. "That's a supreme act of audience gratification. And it's also not new, you know. Sarah Vaughan used to do it—I think Ella Fitzgerald, too. They would improvise vocally while talking to the audience." He demonstrated by singing an example of the kinds of moments he was remembering. "'You are a beautiful audience, and I'm so glad you came.' Or whatever. And now some people who are influenced by [Vaughan] continue to do it. It's always delightful, you know? But it's a little trick. [Frampton]'s the same thing. He's not saying anything profound. It's like spirit possession."

We talked about "Do You Feel Like We Do" and found that we'd had a similar experience listening to one part of it. Early in the Talk Box solo, "I think he says, 'I want to thank you,'" Ratliff said. "And I feel like maybe me and my friends thought he was saying 'I want to fuck you.'"

In music, as in much of life, we ultimately hear what we want to hear.

The Talk Box had had a tremendous impact on Pete Drake's and Peter Frampton's careers, but was it something you could improve on, like a traditional instrument? When I asked Frampton about that, he surprised me with his bluntness. "It's a cheap gag," he said. "It's just kind of a one-trick pony. It's limited. And I think once you play a note or lick you've kind of showed your hand." He said the length of the Talk Box solo in "Do You Feel" varies from night to night. "Sometimes I tell a story of the Talk Box *through* the Talk Box," he said, and laughed. But "it's not something I can really develop further, I don't think." He said he knew from the beginning that he had to use it sparingly "because a little goes a long way." But with the addition of "Black Hole Sun" in the live set, he was fine with using it for three songs. On *Fingerprints*, he covered the song with the drummer on the original track, Matt Cameron, now the longtime drummer with Pearl Jam. And Pearl Jam lead guitarist Mike McCready also played on it.

"I had no idea or no plans to use the Talk Box," Frampton explained, "and then Matt said, 'Why don't you — even if you don't use it, can you just do a little Talk Box in there, just for us?' So I went out there and did the Talk Box part. It has that effect on *seasoned professionals*." He seemed as flattered by that as he was surprised. The fact that even members of Pearl Jam wanted him to bring it out made me ask him if the Talk Box had ever felt like an albatross. "I've always been very thankful that I used it," he said. "I've never felt, 'I wish I'd never done that,' or '*That's* the star, not me.' I've never felt that at all. The bottom line is, if I've been doing it for two years or forty years, it's still fun to do."

All these years later, Peter Frampton and Lynyrd Skynyrd were playing another outdoor stadium. It wasn't quite the size of Oakland Stadium this time; it was Clipper Magazine Stadium, in Lancaster, Pennsylvania, home of the minor league baseball team the Barnstormers. For late June, the weather was bizarre and worrisome. The venue's security folks stood shivering in their rain gear against torrid winds and rain that smacked like a whip. This was highly concerning to both camps, but Frampton's crew had another problem: the size of the stage.

Production manager John Procaccini, who, prior to joining up with Frampton, had worked for the Doobie Brothers for twenty years, said the stage was smaller than he was prepared for, but Lynyrd Skynyrd's management had signed off on it, so there wasn't much he could do. Most of the Lynyrd Skynyrd equipment had been unloaded before the rain started, and now it sat under tarps. The Frampton gear sat in trucks at the edge of the stadium. But John and Aidan worried how Frampton's rig would even fit on the stage. And would there be any room for Aidan in the wings and for his own setup? And the rack of guitars? Plus, the cover overhead was far from adequate if the rain kept up. After a while it tapered off and the equipment got unloaded, but tensions were still so high that I decided to slip away and sit in the stands.

As I was driving over earlier that day, I talked to my friend Hill Allen, and when I told him that Lynyrd Skynyrd was on today's bill, he warned me, only half-jokingly, "Don't get your ass kicked." I laughed, but then I remembered that Aidan had said yesterday, "Lynyrd Skynyrd has a fairly tough crowd—they've got a thing, right?" A few hours later, though, as the gates opened, the combination of so many long gray beards and walking sticks made it feel like Peter Frampton and Lynyrd Skynyrd were performing in Middle-earth.

The stage was set up over second base, and when Frampton came on he seemed so far away that, in the absence of video screens, I wouldn't have known if it was actually Larry David. This wouldn't be as distracting when Lynyrd Skynyrd took the stage because they were down to one original member—guitarist Garry Rossington. Each member of Lynyrd Skynyrd was excellent in his role, but they were essentially like actors in a musical revue. The band that had produced so many memorable songs had really died in that 1977 plane crash in Mississippi, when singer and lyricist Ronnie Van Zandt, guitarist Steve Gaines, and backup singer Cassie Gaines (Steve's sister) were killed. The other members of the band survived the accident, but guitarist Allen Collins was paralyzed in a drunk-driving accident in 1986 and died in 1990. So that night onstage the spirit of the band was fully present, and for most everyone in the stadium that seemed to be enough. Just not for me. As I walked back to my car, the fading sounds of "That Smell" swirled behind me.

In Baltimore Aidan had said, "I would not want to be Lynyrd Skynyrd following 'Do You Feel Like We Do.' Nor would [Peter] want to be following 'Free Bird,' right?" So I was sorry to miss the finale; Lynyrd Skynyrd had been closing their sets with "Free Bird" every show, every year, every decade just as Frampton had been closing with "Do You Feel." "Free Bird" was clearly the bigger song—more dramatic musically, more poignant lyrically (in concert, Ronnie Van Zandt would say the song was a tribute to Duane Allman). The song defined a whole genre of music—southern rock—and even before concertgoers across the country began to think it was funny to shout "Free Bird" at the moment any band was about to begin its encore, it had already become a glorious kind of cage.

Lynyrd Skynyrd had made it into the Rock and Roll Hall of Fame and were ultimately a more influential act in the annals of rock. On the other hand, they never recorded an album that came close to the sales of *Frampton Comes Alive!* Plus, Frampton appeared on *The Simpsons* and played his Talk Box on a popular Geico commercial.

When Frampton unfurled the opening notes of "Do You Feel Like We Do," the most striking contrast to me between the two acts was that Lynyrd Skynyrd's story was, in the end, a rock and roll tragedy, and their music had endured despite that. But Frampton *himself*, through his immense talent, his determination to outlast the fads that went against him, sheer good luck, and on the strength and phenomenal staying power of a single album and a device you could hold in your hands, was personally and musically equipped to endure. He'd survived disco, punk, 1980s synth bands, drugs and alcohol, the grunge era, three divorces, and a record-buying public that didn't exactly clamor to hear anything new from him. He'd survived a near-fatal car crash and the loss of his precious Les Paul Custom for thirty-one years before it came back to him (he and his crew have since called it the Phenix). He even survived losing his bountiful hair! And he was, on this day, in Lancaster, playing those

CHAPTER 3

Complicated Rhythms

When my wife, Katherine, and I moved into our house nearly twenty years ago, our son was two, and within a few months another was on the way. When I look back on that period, what's impossible to comprehend is that I kept my drum set, unassembled, in the garage for nearly three years. That idea feels as shocking to me now as if I had kept one of our *boys* in the garage. It wasn't irrelevant that the drum set essentially needed its own room, and the thinking was that it wasn't entirely practical for me to play the noisiest of all instruments with a toddler and a baby in the house. It was true, too, that I had plenty of gentler-sounding instruments to keep me occupied. But by the time our youngest son was a couple of years old, there came a day when I went to the garage and, with the urgency of a man digging up someone who'd been buried alive, got my drums out and feverishly put them back together. They've been set up for me to play ever since.

The drum set is considerably bigger than it was on that day. I've added cymbals. I've incorporated the gongs from China, the bells from India, two drum synthesizers and another electronic piece that I channel through an electric bass effects pedal, another tom, and smaller accent pieces. The set is so elaborate that it's like climbing into a helicopter to play it. Sometimes, though, I feel a little conflicted. Many of the most famous drummers in the world—from Elvin Jones to Ringo Starr—played the barest of kits. And every once in a while I'll sit down to my pimped-out set, and I feel like I'm driving a pulsating Humvee with LED neon lights underneath through the quiet streets of Mayberry. I ask myself: is too much equipment possibly getting in the way of my becoming a better drummer?

I was considering this all the more intensely after I got back from Switzerland. Playing with Andreas was both profound and humbling, and when you play with a musician who is so vastly superior, you're left to take measure of all that you still have to learn—and what that will require. But soon enough another musician entered the picture and got me thinking anew about the full meaning of equipment.

When Bill Allen called me at my desk at the *Post*, he said that I should write a story about him, since he had one of the biggest drum sets in the world. It was unusual to get such a brazen request so directly. He explained that he owned a 122-piece drum kit that had been featured in *Modern Drummer* magazine's Kit of the Month column. I'd been reading that magazine since high school. Bill described his setup in detail, including measurements, and mentioned his multiple chime sets, but the math wasn't adding up.

"Wait a minute," I said, "are you including each individual chime?" He was.

"That doesn't count," I said. Still, I was intrigued, and when a friend of his was eventually able to send me a scan of his appearance in *Modern Drummer*—Bill didn't have a computer—I was stunned. I'd never seen anything like it. The main image didn't fully capture the kit's immensity, but in one of the smaller pictures below, I could see three long rows of toms stacked atop each other. They were so high up it was hard to see how he could even reach them and stay on the drummer's stool.

All I knew then was that Bill had an enormous drum set. But that summer I spent visiting him and watching him play, I came to see that the real story was bigger.

At a self-storage facility just inside the Baltimore city limits, Bill lifted the door on space number 41 to show me his life's work. In units all around him were people's living room sets, mattresses, bureaus, and weight-lifting benches, but for Bill, his fifteen-by-twenty-foot unit was more like his office. Five or six days a week he bicycled four miles from Dundalk, Maryland, to play a drum kit that looked as big as a merry-go-round.

It was ninety degrees that day, and Bill, outfitted in green khakis and an olive-striped knit shirt, had the look of someone reporting a condo association's minutes. At sixty years old he had a neatly combed head of red hair and was remarkably slim, and once inside, like a contortionist, he began the tumultuous process of navigating the cramped space onto the drummer's stool — the epicenter of what I counted to be twelve gongs, thirteen cymbals, twenty-four toms, two bass drums, two floor toms, one snare, one hi-hat, six sets of chimes, three triangles, three timpani, and one cowbell. (Bill was a strict minimalist with cowbells.)

"How long do you want me to play for?" he asked once he settled in. "Forty-five minutes?" He wasn't joking. "I'll cut loose."

I sat in the only available spot in the room, which was a matter of a few square inches — and told him to proceed as he liked. Bill lifted two sticks as heavy as plumbers' wrenches and began to create a pulsating rhythm with his bass drums, as snare and cymbals clashed against each other. Soon he ushered in a rain of cymbals and toms, creating an unrelenting storm. It could have been a soundtrack to an army of Vikings being pummeled by a more savage army of Vikings. There was no discernible groove, exactly, not something you could tap your foot to, but the wall-quaking onslaught was riveting. Then he pivoted and brought out explosions from the gongs on the other side of the kit. Was he trying to conjure the Dawn of Man?

The timpani bubbled to the surface, and the mood became orchestral. As he turned back to his stool, he brought back the rolling storm until it had passed and left the area altogether. It was an exceptional show of precision and chops, a master class in how to build an abounding musical narrative.

The room was greenhouse hot, and Allen wiped his moist face. He had intended to go longer. "I was playing in slow motion," he said in dismay. He pulled out a plastic comb and ran it through his hair. Despite the physical rigors of his solos, Bill liked to stay neat.

He explained that he didn't have a steady band, partly because he only wanted to play Christian rock, and Christian rock wasn't exactly the trending music scene in Baltimore. Plus, virtually no stage could handle Bill's set. But these facts didn't deter him from using a stage name: Billy Thunder. Given his relative anonymity, it seemed to me that a stage name was as necessary as another gong, but then, who *wouldn't* want to be called that?

He showed me that issue of *Modern Drummer*, which was so thumbed through and worn it was as fragile as the Dead Sea Scrolls. The pictures of his kit were taken just outside of the storage space — it took him four hours to rebuild the set for the shoot. I chuckled again at the headline "Just Another Garage Drummer," but this was a sore spot for Bill.

"That pissed me off," he said — he thought it was belittling. And the attention he hoped for from the piece never materialized. "I had a few calls, but it was just a bunch of kids," he said. "They asked what kinds of pedals I use and stuff. You know what I mean? I'm looking for somebody who wants to get a serious band together. Right now I got a guitar player and a singer, but I don't know about that singer." They went by Sons of the Prophets, though they hadn't yet had a gig, and the name worried Bill's pastor because, well, they weren't actually sons of prophets. So Bill would change it to Mind Control. (Not to be confused with an earlier band of his, Thought Control.) And then again to Alien Thunder.

After cooling off in the storage site's frigid main office, we stepped back into the sweltering space so that he could start up again. Not many people could spend so many hours in a cinder-block inferno like this. The carpet was threadbare, plastic bags and plastic cups were stashed all around, and the number of cigarette butts in the ashtray outnumbered the drums. Suitcases and boxes stacked up to the ceiling. There were few personal effects on display, except for a picture of his fifth-grade class, at Red House Run Elementary, taped to the wall. (It was, I would learn, one of the few possessions he had left from his childhood.) Still, Bill, who had been a bachelor all his life, enjoyed it here. "I got this place like Home Sweet Home, you know?"

Within the self-storage barracks there wasn't a lot of coming and going, save the security guard, but it wasn't always lonely spending so much time here, he said. "There's a Mexican band right next to me. There's about eight of them when they're playing. They'll probably come in later today. When you hear different things going it just sounds like massive confusion. You just have to put headphones on and deal with it."

Bill had dealt with no shortage of hardships in his life, some of which dictated his daily routine. He had schizophrenia, for one. And his complete devotion to his drum set not only brought him remarkable joy, it gave him a singular purpose: playing solos — solos that only I would get to hear. (Since he didn't own a computer, there was no putting them on YouTube.) As I saw it, the real challenge for Bill was not how he coped with so many hours inside the musty shed every week. It was how he coped with all the hours outside it.

Bill grew up on a large poultry farm in Rosedale, Maryland. His mother played keyboards, and that was his first instrument, too. His middle brother, Fred, also a keyboardist, would later record with Bootsy Collins under the name Frederick "Flintstone" Allen. (He died in 2012.) He noticed Bill's percussive inclination with the keys.

"I had the sledgehammer approach," Bill told me. Fred suggested he might make a better drummer, which proved to be good advice, as

Bill excelled at drums in the school band. Then at fifteen, he experienced the first in a series of dire blows. At a party in his basement, he and his band were taking a break when someone poured something into his drink.

"I drank it all, and then I'm wired to the max," he said. The mixer proved to be a sizeable dose of LSD. Bill was hospitalized for a week. "I was OK after that," he said, "but all of a sudden, later in life, the flashbacks started." He was around twenty and enrolled in Essex Community College. He didn't get to finish.

Doctors gave him a regimen of drugs to keep the flashbacks at bay, and he told me his last one happened eleven years ago. He blamed the LSD for his schizophrenia, but when I talked to his psychotherapist at Key Point Health Services, Jill Grosky, she said there was no way of knowing for sure.

"He doesn't necessarily see schizophrenia as a problem, and that's actually a great thing," said Grosky, who agreed to talk to me after Bill gave his consent, "because it shouldn't be a problem as long as he's maintaining himself in treatment, which he has been [doing] very well." Grosky said that Bill hadn't been hospitalized since around 1982, and that that was "very significant for someone with schizophrenia. You know, that's uncommon." She explained that some people with schizophrenia could function quite capably, but "if they ran into a trigger, it can cause all kinds of problems."

The LSD incident wasn't the only setback of Bill's young life, though. His mother died in 1979, when he was in his mid-twenties. Bill and she were close, and after the LSD incident she took him to regular psychiatrist visits in secret, out of fear that Bill's father wouldn't approve. Not long after, a Pentecostal tent revival was held on the Allens' farm, and Bill wandered in. The church's band members had heard Bill playing his drum set out in the yard — "You could hear it all over the place," he said — and noticed that he drove a bus with a painted cross on the back. They happened to not have a drummer at the time.

Bill was Catholic, but two days after stepping into the tent he was the band's new drummer and had converted to Pentecostal.

"I wanted to get a band going," he said, "and it just happened, you know?"

His father soon remarried, sold the family's lucrative Evering's Poultry Farms, and moved to Pennsylvania without a forwarding address.

"He took off with everything," Bill said. "He disowned us." Neither Bill nor his two brothers ever saw or heard from their father again, though they learned that he lived to be ninety-one.

"I don't even know what he looked like," Bill told me. "He got cremated—that's what I heard."

The complicated rhythms of life.

It was around the time of his father's abandonment that Bill began to develop his vision for expanding his drum kit. He'd lost the big house he'd grown up in, but what if his drum kit got big? He saved up his disability payments and kept acquiring new pieces.

So how big was it, exactly?

I called the editor of *Modern Drummer*'s Kit of the Month column, Michael Parillo, to get his take. "Any time drums are in rows, vertically, we sit up and take notice," he told me. "I would say that [Bill] was fairly well assured to get in the magazine with a setup like that. It's not *the* biggest, but I would certainly agree that it's among the largest ones we've seen come through here."

In his spare time, Bill had filled nine notebooks of drum rudiments—rolls and beats, really—which, to the untrained eye, look like computer code. "Took me two years, two months, and twenty-three days to write it out," he said proudly.

Because he had been on disability for much of his life, he hadn't had a traditional career. He worked at a movie theater—taking tickets, working concessions—for nearly eleven years, and had stints at Taco Bell and National Training Systems, where he handed out fliers and helped recruit potential workers. He had been in a steady stream of bands, but none had ever landed a record deal or played much outside of Maryland.

One day I asked Bill what he got out of all those hours spent on the drum kit each week. He said they were "like a therapy." When he was playing his drums, he said, "I feel like I'm riding through the universe."

Most every week Bill played in the band at Crusaders for Christ Church, in nearby Edgemere. The pastor, Charles Dennison, was also the guitarist. "Drums is his life," Dennison said about Bill. "I could not possibly get out there with my guitar and go out early in the morning and sit in a room by myself, with the amplifier on, and sit there and wham on that guitar all day long, hour after hour. It would drive me nuts."

Bill sometimes lobbied the pastor to let him bring his kit into the sanctuary. "We wouldn't have any room for the church," the bewildered pastor would tell him. The purpose was to worship God, not overwhelm him. The church's kit was standard — three toms, a snare, three cymbals — and Dennison insisted Bill play with brushes. "He would always like to get into something deeper, but he knows he can't do it during church."

I was interested to see Bill play in a band situation, though I knew to lower my expectations, given the setting. One Thursday night service, an hour before the proceedings began, I watched Bill and the rest of the church musicians conduct a highly involved sound check: volume fiddling, strumming, tuning up. "Test, test," Bill said into the microphone. "Praise the Lord. Test."

When the service began, there were four people up front, including Sister Charlene running sound, and four in the congregation. The evening's first song was "When the Spirit of the Lord," in which Bill took a four-measure solo — modest by his standards. The bassist, Brother Marvin, responded with a solo himself. The repertoire was old-time gospel standards: "I Saw the Light," "Amazing Grace," "I'll Fly Away," "I Want Us to Be in Heaven Together." All but one of the parishioners came up and took their turns singing lead vocal. The average age tended high, and one man, who sang a heartfelt rendition of "They're Holding Up the Ladder," asked if he should do another. The band agreed. "They're holding up the ladder that I'm climbing on," he began. But Brother Marvin had to cut him off. "No, we just did that," he pointed out.

Bill often played with his eyes closed in quiet intensity; here and there he snuck in some fancy hi-hat work. Mostly he obliged by providing a shuffling backbeat. During "I'll Fly Away," though, he worked in an intricate fill that brought Brother Marvin to a stop. Brother Marvin turned back toward Bill in surprise, then looked at the pastor. Brother Bill, he and the pastor knew, was filled with the spirit.

After fifty minutes of music, it was time for Dennison to move to the pulpit for the sermon, which was a long meditation on temptation and sin. "Sometimes you hear the devil talking, and you think it's God talking, and then you get into trouble," he warned. At one point, his microphone cut out.

That could be the devil right there, he said.

Sister Charlene quickly jumped into action to see what could be done about the fallen angel.

Bill's ambitions for himself, or his band, were also entirely outsized. He called frequently—on the phone he generally referred to himself as Billy Thunder—wondering if I had contacts who could help him realize his latest idea. Once he wanted to know if I knew how to reach Hillary Clinton. "She's running for president," he said, "and I was thinking I could do a drum solo for her." (Later, when Donald Trump became president, he had the same request.) "Do you have any military contacts?" he asked another day. He was thinking he might get a military helicopter to suspend a stage carrying Alien Thunder and hover over cities as they played. "Do you know anybody at Carnegie Hall?" was another request. This time, he was thinking of a drum-solo concert.

When a friend of his took him to see Yes, the next day he called me and wondered if I could put him in touch with the band. "I want to see if I can get together and jam with them," Bill said. I'd seen Yes live fifteen times. I own all their videos, and I've read four and a half books about them. The first Yes album I ever bought is framed in my bedroom. Yes was entirely personal for me, so this time I went a little off the rails.

"Bill, you're not going to play with Yes!" I said. "They have Alan White!"—their drummer since 1972. "You don't just . . . jam with Yes!"

"Yeah," he said, a bit sheepishly. Which made me chagrinned.

"They've just had Alan White for decades now, you know," I said, in nearly a whisper. But already his mind was racing toward the next thing.

Mike "Spike" Redmond was Bill's current guitarist. He had known Bill for more than forty years and estimated they'd worked on thirty-odd songs together. Spike said he has played clubs up and down the East Coast—and in the 1980s played in bands that opened for the Dead Kennedys and the Circle Jerks. (Bill's band LeftOver, whose sound he described as "Kansas minus the violin," once opened for Loverboy and Johnny Winter.) There was no room for Spike at Bill's storage space, and the lack of a reliable practice facility had meant their progress was perpetually stalled.

At Bill's apartment, which was dim, as smoky as a teachers' lounge in the 1970s, and lined with stacks of musical equipment and crates, Spike was all lament. Living in Dundalk was tough going, he said. "It's like a dark cloud's over this place. You can't get nothing moving."

Spike, his long hair stuffed under a baseball cap, told me he'd spent seventeen years in jail, in various stints, for drug charges, but these days he was a deacon at Merritt Park Baptist Church. Outside of music, he had earned a living as a carpenter and a roofer and was on disability now after falling thirty-six feet and injuring his back. That left him plenty of time to write songs. "They come to me just like they did when I was sixteen," he said. "It's the situation, not having a place to practice, that's holding us up."

One place Bill and Spike could play together—without having the police knock on their door, which happened frequently when they jammed at the apartment—was an open-mic night every Monday at the café Teavolve, in Baltimore. Since neither of them had a car, they were used to biking the eight miles, Spike with his guitar strapped on his back and riding his Mongoose mountain bike, and Bill on his Schwinn ten-speed with a pair of bongos secured in a crate behind his seat. "Like Toto," Spike said.

They'd been playing together at Teavolve for about a year, though Spike had been showing up on his own closer to seven. On a Monday in July, they arrived early, and at 6:30 a notebook was put out for performers to sign up. Sometimes Bill and Spike had time to perform three or four songs, but tonight they were getting squeezed to just two. Spike, in jeans, blazer, and a porkpie hat, led Bill to the back of the café, where they took over several tables with their equipment. They each ordered a cup of coffee and waited. Bill had his wrap-around shades out. "Do I look better with these on or off?" he asked, demonstrating each look. Spike had no stake in the decision, and I wouldn't answer.

The open mic could bring in thirty to fifty people to the airy, comfortable space, though sometimes the crowd was just the performers themselves. At 7:00, the emcee, Sharif Kellogg, announced the first performer. A petite mandolinist named Erin took the stage and sang sweetly. Bill was smitten. "I wouldn't mind taking her out to dinner," he whispered.

Next, Jocelyn Faro brought up her guitar and introduced eleven-year-old Julia. "It's her first time at an open mic, so please give her a little bit of love." As it turned out, Bill was not the only one who had worked out a stage name. Julia went by JC Haven for her music business, her father told me, and she was already starting to record. In a surprisingly soulful voice, Julia delivered the Taylor Swift song "Mean" in a way that galvanized the crowd, and they were clapping with the beat before she was done. After that, she sang "Young and Beautiful," by Lana Del Rey, crooning even more boldly now, though it was disquieting to hear the lyrics "Will you still love me when I'm no longer young and beautiful" from an eleven-year-old girl.

Next up, Tim, in a pale blue shirt and khakis, got ready to read his poem "Sweet as Peaches," telling the audience that this was the date on which Paul McCartney was introduced to John Lennon. "And I personally would not be writing anything if that event hadn't happened," he said. He dedicated his reading to John Lennon.

"Please be my sweet pea. Please be my sweet peach."

By the time he was done with the first poem, no one could quite bring themselves to look up from their table. The momentum got no better when he announced, "I'm writing a musical."

"All right, thank you very much, Tim," Kellogg said after the second poem. "Next up we have Bill and — it's Spike, right? Am I saying that right?"

Bill and Spike proceeded to set up: Spike strummed his guitar for thirty seconds, looking for an acceptable volume from the monitor; Bill, who had decided to go with the sunglasses on, worked his bongos onto his stand and pulled out two mallets the size of meat tenderizers. "Check, check," Spike said into the mic. Suddenly the casual atmosphere had become awkward with this injection of professionalism.

"So we're gonna, I guess, take a minute here," observed Kellogg, "and then we'll get rolling with Bill and —" Blank.

"Spike," said Spike, who kept working his guitar. Finally he and Spike jumped into Spike's composition "I'll Take You There." Bill launched into a booming, highly intricate beat, his bongos detonating through the room. The tempo wobbled like a drunk. Spike strummed harder and looked at Bill, silently pleading with him, but it was impossible to make eye contact with him through the sunglasses, and Bill kept banging away. It sounded as if they were playing from different continents and trying to sync up through a two-second delay on Skype.

"I can't hear the guitar," Spike told Kellogg midsong, ten feet away. Kellogg seemed surprised because everyone else could very clearly hear the guitar.

"Time is running down," Spike sang. He played a nimble solo, but it was barely audible over Bill's clangorous drumming. At one point, the guitar came to an abrupt halt — intentionally, for dramatic effect — and Bill should have stopped, too, but he blazed on. The serenity of the place was quickly on edge. The uneasy crowd couldn't have understood, but Bill playing bongos in a coffee shop was like Mighty Joe Young performing in the Golden Safari nightclub. This was a musician whose *drum solos* had names.

When the song came to an end, Kellogg moved quickly to the microphone. "All right, thanks very much Bill and Spike. Next up is Mr. Tim Harrington." But Spike explained they weren't done and moved into an instrumental called "Stevie's Revenge." When the last chord of the song rang out, the applause was as halting as pegs on a Plinko board.

They cleared the stage, and Tim Harrington stepped up to the mic with his guitar. He announced he had a song about football.

Bill and Spike retired to their booth in back. Both were discombobulated. Seething. Bill announced he was going to find a 7-Eleven for cigarettes. When he returned, before he had fully climbed back into the booth, he said, "Yeah, Spike, I really thought we stunk." Within a couple of minutes, he jumped back up to smoke more cigarettes and pace.

Spike complained to me that Bill had drowned him out. "If I could have, I'd have taken those mallets and flung 'em," he said. "All his life he's been dreaming about being a famous musician. But he does not listen. He's an out-of-control individual." I went outside to see Bill, who was not faring any better. He maintained that the tempo problems were all Spike's. "I'm going to look for a new guitarist," he told me.

After other performers came and went, we got into my car to head back to Dundalk, but Bill was still worked up. "That's the worst we ever sounded," he announced.

But when you've known someone for forty years, friendships develop their own flexible tempos, and both his and Spike's anger soon dissolved. Spike, sitting in the back, suggested Bill switch to brushes as a possible solution. Bill pointed out that the brushes from church belonged to the church, so that wasn't an option. And he couldn't afford a pair of brushes himself. "I've got to eat!" he said.

Spike said he would figure something out. "Yeah, Billy, I don't know if it will be the best of them, but I'm going to scrounge up a set—"

"Scrounge up a set of brushes," Bill agreed.

"I don't know if I can get you the greatest thing ever made."

"I know. I can play anything," Bill said. "I can play pencil sticks."

"I'll get you a good set."

"If you get cheap ones, I'll be playing and pieces will be flying everywhere," Bill said, suddenly alarmed. "You know what I mean? It will just fall apart."

"Them mallets are too loud," Spike said. "It's like marching in the Fourth of July parade. It's just way, way too—"

"We just got to say: it sucked, laugh about it, forget about it," Bill said. "And just move on."

"And come up with different [drum] patterns," Spike said. "That's all it is. Ain't no big deal."

Then, seemingly apropos of nothing, Bill's thoughts were back to his father's abandonment and the family house he sold while Bill was hospitalized—a devastation that came up frequently, and abruptly, in my conversations with him. Maybe the connection was the sting of the night's performance, the echo of letdown. "He fixed me good," said Bill, shaking his head.

As the week went on, Spike decided which songs he wanted them to play at the next Teavolve show and had them working on the arrangements. They just had to get tighter. Besides, they both knew plenty about recovering.

The summer rolled into fall, and throughout I kept thinking about what it meant to Bill to go to the storage facility each day, to glance over at that school picture through the open spaces of his drum set—Bill in the back row, thin, pale, a head of hair the color of a traffic cone—with no inkling of the difficulties to come. Despite what we know about the human brain, the advancements of technology and medical research, no one truly knows what it's like inside anyone else's mind. The brilliant mind, the artistic mind, the troubled mind.

Unknowable. We're all in our own heads, trying to make sense of what life brings each day. That doesn't mean we're ultimately alone, of course, but sometimes we are our truest selves when no one else is there.

Inside storage unit 41, it was difficult to get around. It was often too hot or too cold. Not everything was in a logical place. It was in need of maintenance. During some moments when Bill was there it was as quiet as outer space, but generally what went on inside was an extraordinary cacophony—and wholly original. His drumming lurched forward to a grandiose opus that would go on for thirty minutes or more, then shift to a meditative, pensive mood just as quickly. Placidity. Sometimes it didn't fully settle into a coherent swing, or it was repetitive. Other times it was marvelous bedlam. There was never any audience, no other musicians. Just full-out, manic drum solos, one after the other, all played against the steady metronome of Bill's heart.

CHAPTER 4

The Keys to Happiness

As a child, the greatest pleasure I knew was ordering something "as seen on TV." When magician Marshall Brodien—who, dressed in his three-piece suit, looked more like a bank president—came on to promote his magic set, the idea of manipulating those mesmerizing objects—trick cards! anything that looked like silk!—and impressing my friends seemed miraculous. I urged my mother to order the Veg-O-Matic II not only because it delivered "golden french-fries, hundreds in just minutes," but, to go by the TV announcer's manic tone, it would surely transform our kitchen into the kind of delirious party zone that seemed to exist only for men with sideburns. And then, in 1974, when I was seven years old, I saw a commercial for an album called *40 Funky Hits*.

The cover featured cartoon images of a man on a camel, a soldier licking the boots of a man who might have been General Custer, a bulldog, and a hipster twirling his dice (this would be Lloyd Price's Stagger Lee, who, upset about losing his money, would have his revenge with his .44 Magnum. Funky!). In the ad, the songs, culled from the 1950s and 1960s whose silly-sounding titles rolled down the screen, seemed like the stuff of comics: "Shimmy, Shimmy, Ko-Ko-Bop," "Surfin' Bird," "Kookie, Kookie (Lend Me Your Comb)," "Duke of Earl." The snippets of songs promised a daffy and rollicking time. The top of the album cover read, "As Seen on the Groove Tube!" As a little white boy in North Carolina, I had no real understanding of what it meant to be funky—or a need to be—but I knew enough that I was ready to enter the world this strange record might open up to me.

40 Funky Hits was the first album I ever got for myself; it came with three records, and I listened to each fanatically. Mostly these were novelty records by acts that didn't last long, though there were exceptions. "Tutti Frutti" by Little Richard, "La Bamba" by Richie Valens, and "See You Later, Alligator" by Bill Haley and the Comets were important songs by some of the most essential acts in the early days of rock and roll. The very album seemed to exist for its quirky song titles alone, but that didn't matter to me. (Though, with songs by Little Anthony and the Imperials, Little Caesar and the Romans, Little Richard, and Little Jimmy Dickens, I surmised that rock music and dwarfism went hand in hand.) My love of that album revealed that I already had an impulse toward the 4/4 rock beat, rip-roaring piano solos, and twangy guitar. Still, there was one song, "The Happy Organ," that enthralled me like no other song I'd heard before.

The song developed, as I later came to understand, when Dave "Baby" Cortez found himself in the studio with his band but couldn't sing because he'd lost his voice. Out of boredom the band started jamming, with Cortez pounding out chords on his piano that sounded a lot like "Shortnin' Bread." Hearing that, the studio engineer shouted, "Try the organ!" Cortez wandered over to the corner and turned on the Hammond B-3, and the band went at it again. What came out of that became "The Happy Organ."

The song is a buoyant showcase for Cortez's swirling organ lines, like a skating-rink organist turned maniacal. There's no ignoring the song's repetitive nature, even at just two minutes, but when it was released in 1959, it became the first instrumental to reach number 1 on *Billboard*'s Hot 100.

Cortez would put out a slew of albums during the next thirteen years. And then, after 1972, he would simply disappear. I never heard any of that other music, though. When I had grown past *40 Funky Hits* a couple of years later and put it away for good, that would be the last I'd hear "The Happy Organ" until the internet came along. I never heard it on the radio, didn't come across it anywhere. Still, somewhere deep in the recesses of my brain, the sound of Cortez's Hammond was always whirling around.

The Hammond organ appeared in 1935, and by the time "The Happy Organ" came out, it had developed an intense devotion in listeners and musicians alike. It would go on to be one of the most beloved pieces of musical equipment ever, due, in part, to its ethereal sound and highly flexible nature. (It would also be a crucial element in all the music I would go on to love — from some of my very favorite songs, such as "Green Onions" by Booker T. and the M.G.'s, "Whiter Shade of Pale" by Procol Harum, and, much later, "Don't Dream It's Over" by Crowded House, to some of my most cherished bands, such as Yes, the Allman Brothers Band, Traffic, and Emerson, Lake and Palmer.) Throughout the country, clubs formed around enjoying the pleasures of the Hammond organ. By the time I got to Massachusetts in 2016, the North Suburban Hammond Organ Society was one of the few such clubs left in the country. And, as I would learn, the members weren't just devoted to the Hammond. They were devoted to a long-ago era and the possibilities that the Hammond alone could make true.

It was December, and before the North Suburban Hammond Organ Society could begin its monthly concert, a group of women were finishing their tai chi practice. They were spread out across a large, barn-shaped room at the Veterans' Memorial Senior Center in Woburn, north of Boston. Together they moved in almost imperceptible ways, as if they were underwater.

"OK, everyone, meditation," an instructor called out; she was about the same age as the participants, who appeared to span the seventies and climbed into the eighties. After guiding them through visualization exercises, she concluded by having them grasp their hands together, their thumbs and index fingers touching so they could "bring in a white light that will keep us healthy, happy and safe." Then she had them applaud themselves for the day's effort and said, "We'll see you next week."

Soon after, member Bill Lambert began wheeling one of the two covered Hammond organs out from a corner of the room. The society formed in 1965 and had members who had belonged for decades and some who had just joined in recent years. It got together the first Friday of every month for what it alternately referred to as the concert or the meeting, and today's meeting was different for a couple of reasons. One, it was the Christmas program. But more notably, perhaps, the club's president was going to be late. Since Eric Larson had become president six or seven years ago, this was unheard of, but a close friend of Eric's wife, Elizabeth, had died suddenly, and they would be attending the funeral. The club's vice president, Jim Gregory, wasn't due to make it, so there was a frisson of anxiety in the air.

Bill, who was seventy-one with a full head of gray hair and ruddy cheeks, began warming up the Hammond X-66, a beautiful two-tiered keyboard console built around 1967. He held down a button that activated the tone-wheel generator, essentially the organ's main engine. As he did that, a woman named Barbara, who was eighty-eight and had come with Bill from Maine, got situated near the other organ, a Hammond C-2, built in 1952. "We're both alone, so we keep each other company," she told me.

"OK, so it's working," Bill said, a note of relief in his Boston accent. He played a few chords, and the sound was as full as an orchestra.

"That sounds amazing," I told him. I'd never been this close to a working Hammond.

"Huh? Oh, that's nothing," Bill said. "Wait 'til you hear Eric. I don't even want to play. Wait till you hear when he gets it all set up."

He explained that the sound was just coming out of the Hammond's speaker cabinet, but Eric would hook the organs up to the Leslie speakers — the combination of speaker and amplifier that helped define the Hammond sound. Then "You get that surround — aaahh, it's unbelievable."

Bill tested a few of the organ's preset keys — a clarinet sound, a trumpet. "It has a *beautiful* trumpet sound," he said. "I love it." He played some keys that sounded like flutes, and for several moments he was lost in that. "My A-100 can do that, too. It doesn't sound as good as this because here you have the natural reverberation of a big hall. Things like this belong in a big hall, you know?"

The one younger woman from the meditation class had lingered to watch the organs being set up, and she asked Bill whether there were still people around who could repair a Hammond.

"Eric," Bill said. "If anything goes wrong, he can go into it and fix it. Unless he has to order a part."

The woman said she wouldn't ever want the Hammond to go extinct.

"You wouldn't be old enough to remember Ken Griffin, would you?" Bill asked.

"No," she said.

Bill sighed. He was used to people who hadn't heard of the popular organist who sold millions of albums in the 1950s. "He's the one that turned me on to organs when I was ten years old." He sighed again.

In our phone conversations, Eric had been talking to me about Ken Griffin, but I didn't yet fully appreciate the organist's appeal. So I asked Bill, "What was so great about Ken Griffin?"

"Well, he wasn't among the top-flight artists, but he played beautiful music," Bill said. He then began the first part of a waltz to demonstrate the Ken Griffin style. The harmony he was playing with his left hand, which on keyboards traditionally gets played an octave or more below the melody, was higher than the melody. Griffin didn't create that technique, but his harmony over melody had been a pioneering trait.

Ginny Pratt, who had once been the vice president of the group, was the next member to walk in, but Bill kept playing. "That's an idea of what Ken Griffin sounded like," he said.

With a sense of disbelief, Ginny announced that Eric was going to be late.

"That's what he told me," Bill said.

Ginny, who was seventy-nine and rail thin, her brown hair slightly askew and eyes the color of a tropical sea, listened to Bill a little more, then said, "I can't play this thing, Bill. I hate the thing." She loved the Hammond, but she saw this particular one as her arch nemesis. "I can't play it because even moving that bench way in, I can't reach the pedal. I hate this organ. I hate the sound of it, I hate the feel of it. They were looking for help to fix it, and I said, 'I'll get you a stick of dynamite.'"

Eric had told me that both Bill and Ginny would be performing today, and I asked whether they would use sheet music. Ginny said sometimes she did.

"Me, I could never read music," Bill said. "I'm dyslexic, so there's no way I could play by reading music. I'd get it all backwards." To underscore his challenge, he recalled that during a flying lesson back in the early 1970s "the instructor said, make a gentle left turn.' I pushed the right pedal in and made a beautiful turn starting right, and he said, 'Left!'"

"Well, at least you don't keep losing your place," Ginny said. "I'm getting partway through it, then I say, 'Where am I?'"

"I'm no professional," Bill said. "I play for the enjoyment of it. It's the sound. And there's no instrument more versatile than the organ."

"No, there isn't," she agreed.

Bill moved to warm up the C-2, and Ginny reluctantly sat down at the X-66. She demonstrated, sure enough, that she could barely touch the foot pedals, which sound the instrument's deep bass notes, and played a few bright verses of "Just Because" before declaring again, "I hate this thing."

Much to their relief, Eric and Elizabeth arrived. Eric, who was seventy-two and wore glasses and a fuzzy gray beard, sported a navy baseball cap that featured an eagle in front of an American flag and a tie with Bugs Bunny, Daffy Duck, the Tasmanian Devil, and other Warner Brothers characters. He seemed relieved to be here and was clearly ready to get to work. Ginny gladly slipped off the bench, and Eric tested the keys.

"It's a beautiful room for making music," he told me, gesturing to the tall ceiling and the way the sound filled the cavernous space. "It's just our good fortune." He said he knew of another organ group that used to meet in the basement of a church, with a carpeted floor and low ceiling. "Everything sounded terrible. It was one of the most uninspiring music places I ever played in. And the instrument that they had was real crap. It definitely wasn't a Hammond." That group disbanded a few years ago, he said. "As recently as ten years ago there were probably five similar groups around here. And this is the only one now. This group was going to disband until I took over. I ran into a lot of flak initially because they had been doing things a certain way for years. And I knew that they were dying. They wanted to have a board of directors meeting every time they made a decision. And I'm going, 'How can you have a board of directors meeting if the whole group is only twelve people?' So I dispensed with all that. I pissed off some people. I insulted people — not on purpose — but I did. I was adamant that, you know, if we're going to get people interested, we're going to have to have talent on the bench. When you're playing live you always make a mistake here or there, but I mean, you've got to have it so that people are sitting on the edge of their chairs all excited about what's going on. Some of these old people will fall asleep just like that."

Eric added that within the group, which hovered between forty-five and fifty members, there was not a great level of talent. "He's an exception," and nodded to Bill. But Bill shook off the compliment.

"I don't feel confident enough," he said. "I've been playing 'Moonlight Sonata' for over ten years. You know — Beethoven's 'Moonlight Sonata.' I know that like the back of my hand. But there are times when I'm playing it, and all of a sudden, I can't remember. I have to start all over again, and then I don't even remember where I had the problem. DBS is setting in. Dead Brain Syndrome."

Eric nodded, given his own challenges. "I tell you, I always get nervous when I play for the first five or ten minutes or so. I'm sweating and shaking. My fingers are tingling. Sometimes I even feel like puking. It's a scary thing to get up there and play in front of a group of people, even if it's a small crowd. So I always start off with something I know really, really well—I don't have to think about it. For instance, 'Cabaret,' 'Tea for Two,' some of the numbers I've been playing for the last fifty years or so. Well, 'Cabaret' is not fifty years old, but songs I've played for years and years. Whereas I save my real flashy, fancy stuff for later on in the afternoon."

I sat down at the one table set up in front of the organs; most everyone else would sit on the long benches on either side of the room. I felt like I was one of the judges for America's Next Top Senior Organist.

Albert Zaino, who had been a member of the group for thirty years and had a suspiciously low-riding head of hair, sat next to me. He told me there used to be eight Hammond groups in Massachusetts alone. "They just drifted away," he said. "And there were maybe twenty organ stores in the malls, all over. They're all dead." He and his wife had belonged to all of the clubs, he said. He remembered that one, in Hyannis, on Cape Cod, "at the end of the year they'd have a big ball. It was about 180 people!" One group used to meet in a Chinese restaurant in Danvers, "but the people were just dwindling down, down, down. Oh, we used to have renowned artists come, and we could afford to pay them and everything."

Finally, when all the equipment was set up to Eric's satisfaction and the last of the members had trickled in and found a seat, Eric sat on the X-66 bench and addressed the group. He said that usually he liked to start a performance with some jokes, but this time, Elizabeth, who would sing today, would tell the joke. She proceeded to the microphone and told a Catholic joke about a nun who asks her students what they want to be when they grow up and then becomes alarmed by what she thinks one of her students, Susie, says when she announces she is going to be prostitute. "And the nun said, 'What?!' And [Susie] said, 'I want to be a prostitute.' And the nun said, 'Oh, I thought you said Protestant.'"

The group offered an appreciative laugh.

"OK, anyway, I don't know what we're going to do yet, but it will be interesting," Eric said. "And this is sort of our Christmas program, so I guess we'll play some Christmas songs."

He began with "Tea for Two," a 1920s song that has been performed by everyone from Frank Sinatra and Thelonious Monk to Smokey Robinson and even Alvin and the Chipmunks; it bounced along pleasantly for two minutes and received warm applause. Next came the romantic sweep of "Spanish Eyes," a midtempo number that climbed into the upper register of the organ before Eric finished with an arpeggio.

Then Elizabeth, who wore a red top, her blond-gray hair in a ponytail, moved to the microphone to sing "Winter Wonderland." At seventy-eight, she had a warm, husky voice, and she stood very still while Eric took a couple of choruses as the bass rhythm thunked along. After that she sang "White Christmas," and when Eric took an instrumental stroll it was impossible for me to not think back to Christmas shopping at the old department stores in Fayetteville—like the Capitol and Belk's, most of which had closed long ago—and the easy-listening music that was piped in as men who had worked in the tie department for twenty years straightened their offerings and older women behind the jewelry counter shifted their weight from one foot to another, scanning for the next customer they could help.

Eric switched to the C-2 for "Nola," one of the earliest examples of ragtime. He announced that he'd start off playing it slower so that we didn't miss the nice intricacies of the song. Toward the end, he drove the melody to a dizzying tempo, his fingers flying over the keyboard faster and faster with each verse. When he brought it to a sudden finish, he looked as if he had just gotten off the treadmill. "A few more of those, and I won't have any fingers left," he said. But he got even more of a workout on "Tico Tico," a composition that plays like a cat chasing a mouse before Eric let it give way to a full sprint. At the end, he said, "Who says you don't work hard at this stuff?"

After he'd caught his breath, Eric called out, "Hey, Bill, you want to do a few Ken Griffin things?" and the group clapped. "Ken Griffin died in the late 1950s," Eric told the group, "but he still lives on through people like Bill who play his music."

Bill sat at the C-2, and he and Eric played a duet of Ken Griffin's "Cruising Down the River," Eric staying more in the background as Bill carried out the main melody. Then Eric left Bill to himself as he indulged in a selection of Griffin tunes — "I've Written Your Name on My Heart" and the melancholy waltz of "Roses" among them. His playing was animated and direct, and also assured, despite what he had proclaimed earlier. The performance was a study of Ken Griffin's style, but it was a study of Bill's as well.

I could appreciate the lovely playing and the clear articulation of melodies — though sometimes they were a little mawkish, by my standards — but they couldn't bring me back to the same era that they did everyone else. And it was hard not to conclude that after the people in this room were gone, this music would be gone, too.

During intermission, the group got up, slowly, and wandered over to a room set up with refreshments. This was also the slot Eric had given Ginny to play, and she promptly positioned her binder of sheet music over the keys of the C-2. There was a halting quality to the first song — as if she were stepping over broken glass — but most people were socializing and not paying full attention. She slipped into "Blue Christmas," with a tempo akin to a taffy pull. And she worked in the "Merry-Go-Round Waltz," which alternated between sure-footed and the sound of a record that was slightly warped. She moved through "Too Fat for the Chimney," "When Christmas Comes," "Acapulco Polka," and "Wonderland by Night."

I was impressed with how Ginny managed to segue from one song to another, creating her own musical bridges. Sometimes she kept the melody going with the bass pedals, and with her left hand she would change the settings for the next song, then slide into it. I pointed this out to Eric, who had come over, and he said that was from her training—she had played in skating rinks, where that talent was essential.

Elizabeth came over and said to him, "You'll have to drag her kicking and screaming off the bench."

Eric shrugged. He didn't relish telling Ginny it was time. I asked him what he was hearing in Ginny's playing, and he considered that carefully. "Let's just say there are various degrees of efficiency," he said.

Hearing Eric's comment about Ginny's skating-rink days, Albert, who had settled back into the seat next to me with a piece of cake, told me he remembered when one regularly encountered organs in pizza parlors. But he knew he was describing a different world. "Young people want the wild stuff," he reasoned, though not with bitterness.

The woman next to Albert asked him, in a voice like a rotary engine, "Do you like the rock and roll?" She asked this with the curled-lip disdain of a parent watching Elvis on *The Ed Sullivan Show* for the first time and concluding that the American way of life was officially in ruins. Before Albert could answer she put in, "Because I don't."

When the concert resumed, Eric told the group, "A very, very important announcement from our treasurer: Dues are due next month. So keep that in mind. So if you don't want to find yourself with four flat tires, make sure you pay up."

"I was going to play 'The Petite Waltz,'" he continued, "but I think I'll hold off and do something different. Actually, when I was playing that last song I thought of something else to play, and now I forgot what it was."

A woman from the audience called out, "You're getting old."

"Yeah yeah, I'm seventy-two," Eric said.

"Wow, you're a kid," another woman said.

Eric announced "Sleigh Ride." Through the presets he found a metallic timbre for the piece and even a whip-cracking key to hit at the end of each verse. He followed that with "Jingle Bells" and proceeded to stick his car keys in between two white keys set for high frequency, which produced a constant sleigh-bells effect.

"Amazing what you can do with a Hammond organ and a set of keys," Eric said after the song. "Anyhow, it's that time when I ask my wife, Elizabeth, to come up and lead us through the last song of the afternoon, which will be 'America, the Beautiful.'" Everyone stood up and crossed their hearts as Eric and Elizabeth led a bellowing sing-along. After the last note from the X-66 hung in the air, more than two and a half hours after the meeting began, a hush settled over the room before the Hammond loyalists put on their coats for the walk to their cars.

You'd be forgiven for assuming that an instrument as complex and innovative as the Hammond organ was created by a musical genius. But Laurens Hammond wasn't a musician. He was an engineer who, after graduating from Cornell, had his first success as a clock maker and founded the Hammond Clock Company in 1928. Like many industries during the Great Depression, Hammond's suffered hard times. He next created an automatic card shuffler, but at a time when more than ten million people couldn't find work, that invention wasn't exactly a tonic for the age. Undeterred, his mind roamed in new directions, and his next idea was heavenly.

Hammond believed that there could be a market in churches for simpler, more affordable organs compared to the traditional, behemoth pipe organ. The Hammond organ, which he debuted in 1935, was momentous, in part, because Hammond had envisioned so many newfangled features. One was his pedal board. Pedal boards had been in organs for centuries, but Hammond saw his pedals as doing more than producing a drone; instead, he conceived the pedal board as a true bass instrument; players would just need dexterous feet. Most Hammond models came with twenty-five pedals, and one of the challenges was to play them without looking down. Not unlike dancing.

Then there was the array of presets that gave the organ its vast range of sounds. And the creation of the drawbars was entirely novel.

The original Hammond had nine drawbars for each keyboard, horizontal levers that the player could slide in and out to blend sounds further than the presets — essentially creating new sounds. Depending on the settings, the drawbars could also control the sound level beyond the volume pedal. But perhaps the most significant achievement by Laurens Hammond was what made the organ go in the first place. Drawing on his experience as a clock maker, he built a tone generator containing tone wheels (metal wheels with teeth), which produced electrical impulses of various frequencies as they spun at predetermined speeds powered by a small motor and the alignment of gears. As the wheels rotated, they passed near a magnet; the resulting variations in the magnetic field created a small voltage in a coil wrapped around each magnet, producing a note. And that note's pitch, or frequency, took shape based on the number of teeth passing the magnet each second.

All these complicated inner workings produced an extraordinary new sound, and Hammond had been right: churches embraced the organ immediately, particularly in Chicago, where the company was based. They got a great reception in funeral homes, too. The Hammond organ was a musical marvel, but on its own, its sound wasn't entirely complete. For the first seven years, what amplified the Hammond organ was a separate speaker made by the company. Donald Leslie, a Los Angeles radio repairman who was fascinated with the organ, thought the sound itself could be improved, so he created a speaker cabinet in which the speaker itself spun in a circle. A treble driver and a bass driver rotated by way of electric motors, and as each speaker rotated toward the front of the cabinet, then back again, the sounds become louder and brighter. Leslie demonstrated his innovation for Hammond, but Hammond dismissed the idea. Maybe it was just resentment, or maybe he truly couldn't appreciate how the Leslie speaker brought out the best in his organ, but as players got wise to the obvious improvement with Leslie's creation — which became available in 1941 — having a Hammond without a Leslie was like having pasta without the sauce.

The Hammond's technical achievements notwithstanding, a

major part of the Hammond Organ Company's success was the expansive vision for how it was sold and marketed. From the beginning the organ's image sprung from the association with good old American family values. In ads, the consistent message was, *Gather the entire family around your Hammond!* These ads sometimes showed three generations of Hammond lovers — Grandpa and Grandma, the parents, those lucky kids Millie and Theodore — watching a family member play as the others grinned in a state of delirium. The Hammond was the musical equivalent of Coca-Cola. Why not have one?

For many years the company published a bimonthly magazine called the *Hammond Times*, filled with playing tips, miniprofiles of players, and features about some aspect of the Hammond experience. (One cover story was about Miss Idaho, Kristine Phillips, who for her talent portion of the Miss America pageant played the organ and later went on a tour of military hospitals to play her Hammond spinet — a smaller version of a typical Hammond organ, with fewer keys — for servicemen wounded in Vietnam. The first number at each of her stops? "Tico Tico.")

The *Hammond Times* also promoted stories about the Hammond Organ Society, which, in 1967, had up to 300 chapters and 22,500 members. The most enterprising chapters didn't just settle for regular recitals and use the meetings to talk shop and technique; some provided student scholarships for promising young Hammond players.

As the Hammond's popularity spread, whole organ dealerships — some of which were owned by the Hammond Organ Company — sprang up in cities and towns all over. Dealerships were also meeting places for organ enthusiasts and sites for private lessons. As Scott Faragher writes in his exhaustive study *The Hammond Organ: An Introduction to the Instrument and the Players Who Made It Famous,* "When a new Hammond dealership opened in the 1950s or 1960s, it was usually a gala event, well publicized and celebrated throughout the city." A Hammond dealership was remodeled and reopened in Quincy, Massachusetts, in 1961, and, Faragher notes, "the event was attended by the mayors of both Boston and Quincy, as well as the guests of honor: conductor Arthur Fiedler and recording artist Ethel Smith."

Known as the First Lady of the Hammond Organ, Smith was a notable star of the Hammond, releasing dozens of albums starting in 1947. She was also known for her colorful hats and high heels and was an appealing, enthusiastic ambassador for the instrument. As the 1950s rolled on, the Hammond organ became more associated with other genres besides church music. In jazz, it was Jimmy Smith who revolutionized the instrument. Where previously the organ had been an afterthought in jazz, Smith, soon after the Hammond B-3 made its debut, put together his trio, bypassing a bassist altogether and handling the bass lines through his pedals. With his first release for Blue Note Records in 1956, his smoky B-3 sound made the organ cool and seductive and ushered in a slew of new jazz organists.

Booker T. Jones, who had played on nearly all of Otis Redding's recordings for Stax Records, formed Booker T. and the M.G.'s with the rest of Redding's backing band in 1962. Washington's bubbling organ work fueled the slow-burning instrumental "Green Onions," along with Steve Cropper's slinky guitar. With that hit, Booker T. helped the Hammond step from the soul world to the larger pastures of rock and pop, where it became more commonly pushed to the forefront. The Hammond supplied the main, fervent riff of the Kingsmen's riotous take on "Louie Louie" the next year, and in 1966 teenager Steve Winwood's organ in the Spencer Davis Group's "Gimme Some Loving" wailed with the force of an air-raid siren. The following year the haunting moan of Procol Harum's "Whiter Shade of Pale" would prove to be one of the most epochal demonstrations of the Hammond in all of popular music. Jon Lord, the keyboardist for hard-rocking Deep Purple, which formed in 1968, produced some of the heaviest Hammond sounds heard so far—pulling his Hammond not through the Leslie cabinet, but through Marshall stacks— the popular guitar amplifiers—which gave his organ a sound bordering on menacing.

In progressive rock, whose earliest efforts began in the late 1960s, the Hammond organ was a critical element. Its possibilities in one of the most dominant — and musically adventurous — forms of rock in the 1970s were further showcased by Tony Kaye of Yes and his replacement, Rick Wakeman; Keith Emerson of Emerson, Lake and Palmer; and Rick Wright of Pink Floyd, among many others. By then, however, the popularity of the keyboard in rock had inspired new innovators, and their keyboards had become increasingly visible. The Mellotron, which relied on tape loops and created the dreamy flute sounds on the Beatles' "Strawberry Fields Forever," and the modular synthesizer the Moog (and later the Minimoog) were in great demand by musicians looking to modernize and multiply their sounds. But as the decade gave rise to punk, which tended to have no keyboards at all, and new wave, which relied on the latest synthesizer sounds, the Hammond suddenly seemed like an antique.

The Hammond Organ Company, which had created a copious series of organs — from the original Hammond A to the B-3, the CV, and the E-300 to the H-100 to the X-77 — was closed in 1986. It was later revived by the Suzuki Music Corporation of Japan, which, in 1991, would eventually rechristen the division responsible for the organ Hammond USA. It even returned to its Illinois roots and located in Addison, near Chicago. The company built new Hammonds with careful respect for the original design, but, inevitably, with the latest digital technology. Not all the changes were welcomed by purists.

Many of the famous organists kept playing their Hammonds and still routinely hit the road with them — Steve Winwood and Booker T., for example — playing to smaller but no less adoring audiences. But as the Hammond inched past its eightieth anniversary, its devotees grew that much older, too. With today's keyboard market dominated by such brands as Yamaha and Korg, the Hammond organ's biggest challenge is simply to keep surviving.

In the months that he and I had been talking, I understood plenty about how Eric made the music he did. The Hammond is a complicated instrument, but I grasped, basically, how you went about playing it. What I wanted to better understand was, why was it the organ that had so shaped his life? Why not the trumpet or the guitar? The theremin or the marimba? Why Ken Griffin versus, say, Chuck Berry? And I thought I could get some answers by watching Eric play at home.

The first thing you see when you walk through the front door of Eric and Elizabeth's ranch house, in Ipswich, is a pipe organ. It's set in a white wood console, with one set of keys a few inches above the other, and a row of preset switches above the keyboards. It was built in 1928, and Eric bought it from a friend who collected theater organs. But the pipe organ, whose pipes were in their garage, wasn't working when I visited because one of the air-supplying pipelines from the blower system had a leak in it.

In the same room, right by the front door, was the Steinway that belonged to Elizabeth's grandmother, and Eric's upright piano was in the adjoining kitchen. In a bedroom down the hall Eric had a Hammond X-66 and a Wurlitzer Electrostatic organ. Sitting down at the X-66, he said, "Even though they came out with other models, this was actually Hammond's most versatile and most advanced instrument." The X-66 was a gift from Jim Gregory, the club's vice president. "He had about eleven or twelve of these things," he said. "Jim is particularly devoted to the X-66 model."

When I asked Eric how he came to be drawn to the organ in the first place, he began by explaining that as a boy growing up in Boston, he had perfect pitch. "I didn't know at the time what that meant, but I could hear any sound and I would know what pitch it was. I could memorize pitches—I didn't know they were called names like C and F-sharp and so forth. One of my high school teachers had a piano in his house, and I was picking [songs out], and he told my mother, he said, 'Your son has some definite musical abilities, and he needs to have a piano.'"

This was in the late 1950s, when Elvis Presley, Buddy Holly, and the Everly Brothers ruled the radio, but the early days of rock music held little interest for Eric. He liked older, instrumental music.

Eric was thirteen when a piano arrived, and he started taking private lessons from a teacher on the staff of the New England Conservatory. That following summer, for vacation his parents rented a cabin in Gloucester. A friend of Eric's mother was staying in a nearby cabin, and Eric's family walked over for a visit. From the kitchen Eric heard music drifting over from the woman's record player in the bedroom, and that music would change his life. The song was "You Can't Be True, Dear." He'd heard organs before—as a child, he was afraid of organs because in church he found them to be so loud. But now he wanted only to get closer. "What is that?" he asked the woman. He went to the bedroom to listen, and she showed him the album: *Ken Griffin at the Organ*. On the cover was a black-and-white picture of Griffin next to his Hammond, holding one leg he's pulled casually up onto the bench and wearing a shirt open at the throat and a carefree smile. Eric's mind was racing.

"I was thinking: The piano basically had one sound, and it was either loud or soft, depending on how you played it. And here was an instrument that has so many vastly different sounds." He spun around on his bench to demonstrate. He played the opening chords to "It Had to Be You" and pointed out that on the piano, you use your left hand to play both the chords and the bass, but with the organ, the left hand was freed up, because of the bass pedals, to add a counter melody to the melody played with the right. With three musical layers at your disposal, he was saying, the opportunities were limitless.

After that camping trip, "I instantly wanted an organ," Eric said. "And as luck would have it, the church we went to had a Hammond organ in the chapel." The minister and organist of the church—First Parish in Brookline—encouraged Eric as he employed different sounds, flipping preset keys and experimenting. "I knew my life's direction right then," he said. He made a vow to himself: "Whatever else I'm going to do, I'm going to learn how to play this thing. I'm going to try and be as good as I can be at it. So that was my all-consuming passion."

Eric completely lost interest in the piano and started taking organ lessons under the supervision of a woman named Doris Tirrell, who played the Hammond for several radio stations in Boston. And when he wasn't taking lessons with her, he went to the chapel several days a week—he wasn't playing church music, but no one minded. When he wasn't in the chapel, he went around to music dealers who sold organs. By the time he was hitting the stores for practice opportunities, he had become quite a proficient player, and because he was so skilled, the salespersons at the organ showrooms were happy to have him turn up as potential buyers perused, taking in his music. His playing led directly to several purchases by impressed customers. Between the organ showrooms, lessons with Tirrell, and the chapel sessions, he was playing seven days a week.

Then he began a new quest. One day Eric and some friends went to a roller-skating rink called Wal-Lex Rollerway, in Waltham, which featured a live Hammond organ player. The musician was set up on a small stage, near the halfway point of the rink, with a large mirror angled at forty-five degrees so that skaters could see his hands roaming the keyboard. "I said, 'Wow, Jesus, here's something I'd like to do best, and you're getting paid for it, too! I've got to do this!' So I applied for a job at this roller-skating rink."

The problem was, in the audition he had to play along with a metronome, which he had never done before. "I failed miserably," Eric said. He immediately wrote the manager a letter declaring he knew he needed more practice.

The metronome was an essential element in skating-rink music because many couples went to the rink to skate-dance—waltzes, fox trots. "And the playing had to be extremely precise to maintain the rhythm of the dance," Eric explained. As soon as Eric sent his letter off, he bought a metronome. For two weeks he practiced relentlessly with it until he could follow it without trouble. Still, he knew he wasn't yet ready for Wal-Lex so soon after his stumbling. Instead, he went to the Skating Club of Boston, an ice rink that also had an organist. "I went there at the end of the summer, and the guy who had been playing the organ there for about ten or twelve years, he wanted to quit. So they auditioned me. They had several skaters listen to me, and I was following the metronome *exactly*." He got the job. It was 1963. And at eighteen, his professional career had begun.

Eric played three nights a week as he finished high school. Within a year he had saved six hundred dollars to buy his first Hammond—a Hammond BC. After high school, he attended nearby Wentworth Institute and studied electrical engineering, but he dropped out during his senior year. He planned for a career in the power industry and utilities and intended to earn money on the side through his organ work.

By twenty-one he started playing in area clubs, restaurants, lounges. In his free time he would slip over to Wal-Lex—to skate, to listen to the organist. There he met a pretty skater named Ginny Pratt, though she went by Peggy then. Ginny was a terrific skater and a regular at the rink. "She was actually going with someone when I appeared on the scene, and she sort of liked me better," Eric said. One thing they had in common was that they both had their eye on the Wal-Lex organist's job.

Eric eventually got hired at Wal-Lex and worked weekends. Wal-Lex had an excellent sound system, and the reception he got from skaters was a great boost to his confidence. He and Ginny dated for several years, but in time Eric ended the relationship. "It wasn't working out as far as I was concerned," was all he would say.

By that time he was making a full-time living playing clubs at night and tuning pianos during the daytime. Eric's interest in the Hammond had gone beyond just playing it; he wanted to know how it worked, too. "I made a very careful study of it. I wrote to the Hammond Organ Company. Back then they were quite generous about supplying service manuals, so I got the service manual, and I read about it, and I figured it out little by little. I would tag along with some of these musical instrument technicians when they went out on jobs." Before long he was servicing organs himself.

At twenty-four, Eric had saved enough money to buy his first house—around twenty-four thousand dollars—and he had his mother move in with him. (His father had died two years earlier.) It's the same house he lives in today. Part of the house's appeal was the roomy two-car garage. Eric knew that one day he wanted a pipe organ of his own, and those pipes would have to go somewhere.

He added servicing pipe organs to his résumé—a lucrative though greatly time-consuming project. But the nightly organ gigs were becoming harder to come by; times were changing, and having a solo organist was starting to become passé. Now he was down to two or three gigs a week. His work during the day went through a transition, too, and he set up a woodworking business, where he made flooring, wall paneling. That prospered for many years, but when the economy struggled in the late 1980s, Eric closed the business and went to work for a power plant.

While there were hardly any gigs for a solo organist by then, Eric, now in his early forties, was ready to stop being a solo act in his personal life as well. Elizabeth, who was fifty then and living in nearby Norwood, was divorced with five children. She put a personal ad in a publication called the *Dating Page*, leaving out her age and declaring her desire for someone "stable, solid, and sweet." Eric was intrigued and wrote her a letter. What drew Elizabeth to his reply, in part, was that he didn't include a picture of himself. In her experience with personals, she was used to getting pictures of men showing their muscles.

Their first date was in Walpole, at a Chinese restaurant. They married five weeks later.

Eric joined the North Suburban Hammond Organ Society in 2007, and a few years after that, when the president, Evelyn, was ready to step down, she asked Eric to take over for her and for Ginny to serve as vice president. The group had dwindled to a dozen members by then. Elizabeth, who never played the organ because she hasn't been able to work out how to play the pedals, became the club's secretary. "I don't have to do much," she said. "I just send cards to people when they're sick or someone dies."

Ginny's tenure as vice president lasted only about a year. "She had been hounding me to play a concert, so I finally said OK," Eric said. He scheduled her for a particular day, and it just happened that Jim Gregory, whom Eric didn't know, had seen the club's website and was intrigued, so he came down with his family. "During intermission he asked if he could try the instrument, and I said, 'Sure, go right ahead.' So he got on there, and after I heard him play for about thirty seconds I thought, *Wow, this guy's fantastic. This guy really knows his stuff.* So I asked him right then, I said, 'Would you like to do a program for us?' Because when he started playing, people were just milling about, having refreshments, and they came flocking in to see what was going on. I actually felt sorry for Ginny because after the intermission, when Jim stopped playing, she had to follow him."

After Jim joined the group and the next time a vote on officers rolled around, members voted to replace Ginny with Jim. In the years since, Eric managed to get membership up to much healthier numbers, though fewer than ten play at meetings. He sometimes managed to bring in outside performers, and part of the new momentum came from a remarkably extensive website he created. There are profile pages for members most likely to perform, and a slew of links to articles, mostly written by Eric, on technical aspects of the Hammond such as vacuum tubes, sine waves, and reverb units. Eric often writes postconcert notes on the society's website that are remarkably detailed. "The X66 performed flawlessly with no more 60 or 120 Hz power humming since we replaced the defective wiring that had been the cause of several previous problems and also a few nasty shocks when we'd inadvertently touch both any metal on the X66 and also a microphone, for example."

The group has taken up a fair amount of his time, but the turnaround has been personal for him. In a given year, Eric plays a few concerts a year for the group; otherwise there are few if any calls for him to perform elsewhere.

I had to wonder: despite the total adoration from the North Suburban Hammond Organ Society, had an artist who recorded more than two dozen albums and sold close to ten million records ever been more forgotten than Ken Griffin? He enjoyed considerable success in a decidedly short window of time, yet his name didn't register with anyone I asked outside of the enthusiasts in Massachusetts. Griffin's music has never undergone any period of renewed appreciation (though quite a few of his original records are still in print), and there's no biography that makes a case for his unappreciated genius. If I was putting together a band of the musically expunged, there's no question who I'd put on the keys.

Griffin was born in 1909 in Columbia, Missouri. The violin was the first instrument he played with purpose, but he ultimately gravitated toward the organ, though he was self-taught and never had any formal lessons. His biggest gift, perhaps, was his feel. After serving two years in World War II, he began to play in the nightclubs and restaurants around Aurora, Illinois, where he'd relocated, and an AM radio station there, WMRO, began to broadcast those performances.

In 1948 Griffin hit the big time with the song that seized Eric as a kid—"You Can't Be True, Dear," written by two German songwriters. Griffin reimagined it without words, and the result reached number 2 on *Billboard*'s Most-Played Jukebox Records chart and was the best-selling song by a solo instrumentalist at that time.

In 1950 he recorded his first album for Columbia Records, where Griffin was heavily guided by label executive Mitch Miller to play in a more straightforward style to appeal to as large an audience as possible. Griffin was prolific. But to scan even some of the album titles is to understand why his music seems frozen in time: *Anniversary Songs* (1951), *Skating Time* (1953), *The Organ Plays at Christmas* (1955), *Plays Romantic Waltzes for Listening, Dancing, Skating* (1959). Regardless of the integrity of his playing, that output could easily get you inducted into the National Squares Hall of Fame.

When he wasn't in his studio, Griffin kept up a relentless touring schedule, driving the country with his Hammond in a trailer behind him. He was one of the most visible solo organists of the era, and his success even ushered in a short-lived TV show in 1954 called *67 Melody Lane*, which didn't exactly remake his image. Griffin plays himself on the show, filmed in black and white, and it takes place mostly at Griffin's TV-set home, with a Wurlitzer Electrostatic center stage; various guests drop by, most of whom play duets with him. Also appearing on the show are Griffin's manager, secretary, and housekeeper. Oddly, there is also a duck that the camera pans to sometimes as Griffin plays. Griffin's gee-whiz voice is so clear and wholesome he could have been just as successful selling viewers Swanson TV Dinners. But he was uncomfortable with the format of the show, and with its stilted mix of lighthearted banter and earnest, if unexciting, music, *67 Melody Lane* made *The Lawrence Welk Show* seem like brash, avant-garde theater.

Bill Reid discovered Griffin's music as a teenager growing up in Aberdeen, Scotland, in the late 1950s, and after a lifetime of listening to and reading what he could about Griffin, Bill created a sweeping smorgasbord of a website in 2001 called the Ken Griffin Memorial page, which features web-only articles about Griffin's style and recording technique, fan remembrances, and also pictures of people posing next to Griffin's gravesite just south of Aurora. Bill told me that one of the intentions of *67 Melody Lane* was to promote the Electrostatic, and that, similar to the situation at Columbia Records, Griffin was directed to play with a simplicity that made viewers believe that anyone could play the instrument. Bill felt that was unfortunate, since the Electrostatic was "very watery" compared to Griffin's rich Hammond organ sound, which was the hallmark of most of his recordings. In fact, as Eric had stressed to me, Griffin was pioneering in his recording techniques because he experimented with reel-to-reel tapes to overdub additional parts, produced nuanced but notable background echo, and created reverberation effects, all of which contributed to the unique Ken Griffin style.

As the records poured out, most of them failed to please music critics, but then, you didn't record an album and call it *Lost in a Cloud: Music to Relax To* if that was your chief motivation. Griffin's legacy is further complicated because he died tragically young—of a heart attack, in 1956, at age forty-six. The posthumous albums would roll out for several years, since Griffin had recorded so much material in the studio. His fans were elated to buy them, but his music has never been discovered by a younger generation. And that's the surest way for a music to disappear.

In the 1960s the music, like American society, was moving in radically different directions from the Ike years. Free jazz and the

Civil Rights movement. The British invasion and, after Martin Luther King Jr.'s assassination, riots from coast to coast. Folk rock and Vietnam. Psychedelic rock and Nixon. By 1970, the solo organist was the musical equivalent of the coonskin cap. Soft, comfortable, and part of an entirely different frontier.

As soon as I met Bill Lambert, he was talking about Ken Griffin, so I understood that that music meant everything to him. How had Bill managed to play Ken Griffin's music so distinctively without ever having had a single lesson? We'd get to that, eventually, but in my first visit to his home, he sketched out the arc of his musical progression.

When I pulled in to the dimly lit trailer park in Alfred, Maine — a small town not far from the New Hampshire border — Bill was, despite the cold, standing outside his mobile home, waiting for me. His older brother, Jim, and his wife of two years, Jane Ann, lived next door, and they came over to watch Bill be interviewed. In the main room was Bill's Hammond A-100, which he liked, in part, because it sounded more like a theater organ. He'd bought it five years earlier from a fellow club member. In a room he called the parlor room was his Hammond spinet.

Bill said that his parents had a piano when he and Jim were growing up, and I asked the brothers if they played it.

"I didn't," Jim said. "He did."

Bill said he really only fooled around with it. "All I wanted was an organ."

Like Eric, Bill came to his love of organs through hearing Ken Griffin for the first time. His mother had a 78 record that featured "When I Lost You" on one side — "which I fell in love with," Bill said — and "Are You Lonesome Tonight" on the other. It was released in 1950. He still had that very record and got up from the couch to retrieve it.

"Ah, there it is," he said, the sense of awe washing over him again. He handled it like a piece of china. "This is very breakable." The record was released before vinyl was the standard format and was coated with a shellac resin.

So what was the power of "When I Lost You" for him, I asked.

"The beautiful sound of the organ, and the beautiful melody," Bill said.

"He basically fell in love with Ken Griffin," Jim said.

Bill began to pull out the many other Ken Griffin albums he bought as a teenager — *Love Letters in the Sand, Skating Time, Moonlight and Roses, Plays Romantic Waltzes, Hawaiian Magic.* And what did his teenage friends make of his obsession with Griffin's music, I wondered. "They thought it was corny," Bill said, but that made no difference to him.

He didn't get to play an organ until 1963, when he was in his late teens and working at Oscar Hillman and Sons, a jewelry and retroplating company in North Attleboro, Massachusetts. A coworker had a spinet, and Bill went over to his house and tried it. He was fascinated with the sound but unsure how to play it, exactly, since the bass pedals were new to him and he wasn't used to his left hand being freed up. What he did know, though, was that the connection he felt was profound. Two years later he was able to save up enough to put a down payment on his own — a Lowery spinet. Bill showed me a picture his mother took of him playing it. In the black-and-white image, the twenty-year-old Bill, a shock of hair falling over his forehead, had the same studious look in profile that he had when he sat at the organ now. He said the picture only made it look like he knew what he was doing, and he laughed, thinking of all he still had to learn back then.

Two years after the picture was taken, Bill had his first professional gig, at the Shamrock Club in Wrentham.

"My parents knew the owners of the place, and they had a country band," Bill said. "Right around Christmas the band had to go into the National Guard — they were called in. And they had no entertainment. They asked me if I'd like to have the organ moved up there. It was just a bar room, more or less. But I know one thing: I filled that place with people in their forties and older." That made him laugh heartily.

He was twenty-two and "nervous as hell," he said. The gig was for

Friday and Saturday nights for two months. Afterward, he had a few
nights at a place called the Golden Anchor, in Plainville. For those
shows, Bill kept his organ at home since the Golden Anchor had a
Baldwin spinet. He played with a saxophonist and drummer. "They
had an old woman playing the organ, and a lot of times she didn't feel
good, and they'd call me," he said.

"Now he doesn't feel good sometimes," Jim said, needling him in
only the way a brother could.

"That was the end of it," Bill said of his evenings playing out. "After the late sixties, nobody wanted it." For many years almost no one
heard Bill play, until he joined the North Suburban Hammond Organ
Society around 2006.

Bill lived at home for his first thirty years, got married briefly
and divorced, and worked at Plainville Stock Company, in which
he set casts for rings and earrings and set the stones, when "after
thirty-six years, they moved to Mexico, like everybody else," he
said. He managed to get a job at as a custodian in the North Attleboro
school system for the next ten years before retiring and moving to
Maine, along with his two tarantulas and a cockatiel, to be closer to
his brother. He had more time to play his organs now — and the accordion, which he picked up twenty years ago, and also the guitar, a
newer pursuit.

Sometimes, though, he still thought about that brief period when
he had his own gig playing the organ.

"A professional told me one time — he was smiling while I played
a nice waltz — he said, 'I can't help laughing.' He says, 'That was beautiful, but your fingering is *way* off. You never took lessons, did you?'
I says no. He says, 'Don't start.'"

Bill shook his head at the way he had made his musical life.

On another visit, Bill and I got to talking about Ken Griffin's
"When I Lost You" again, and, sitting at his A-100, he demonstrated
how, when he was twenty and his Lowery had been delivered, he set
to learning the melody one key at a time. After he had that figured
out, he moved on to finding the right chords to play it properly. It
took him a full month, several hours a day, to learn the song, and

during all that time he never tried another one—no "Twinkle Twinkle" or other musical baby steps. "But I didn't have any rhythm or style," he said. "That came later, when I was familiar with the notes and chords."

He played the slightly ghostly melody again; fifty years later, the pull of "When I Lost You" on him was the same.

Once he had that song down, he said, he moved on to the next Ken Griffin song, then the next. When he was playing the Golden Anchor a few years later, he was advanced enough to play with other musicians, but there were potential pitfalls for someone so entirely self-taught. If one of the musicians had said to Bill, "Let's play this in the key of B-flat," Bill would have had to respond, "I don't even know what B-flat is." He marveled at how vulnerable he'd been in that situation. "I do now, but then I only knew C and G and F." So sometimes Bill would have to sit out as the saxophonist and the drummer played a song on their own. No matter. He was still otherwise playing for a room of people there to listen.

If the Golden Anchor was the apex of Bill's brief performance career, it also represented a study of constraints versus persistence. There was no musical discourse interlaced with Bill's growing up; he had no obvious, innate talent, and the resources for his musical advancement didn't go beyond his own head, heads, and feet. Those realities might have defined the role Bill envisioned the organ having in his life, but they didn't hinder the development that came from his deep drive and dedication—and also his patience—nor did they set the limits on the pleasure and satisfaction the organ would give him.

As Eric wrote on the group's website, "Bill Lambert never took any music lessons at all, nor does he read music at all either." But "neither of these facts is a limitation as far as what Bill can do musically. Bill has managed to learn all kinds of things on a Hammond organ."

There was music in the house that Ginny Pratt grew up in, but it created tensions, too.

"My father hated it," she told me. A couple of days after the December concert, we were sitting at her kitchen table in the large federal house, built in the 1820s, that she and her family moved to in Reading, Massachusetts, when she was around nine. "He didn't care what, he didn't like it. My mother liked it. Mostly the big band music. So I kind of got used to hearing things from her—radio, records, and things like that. She liked Benny Goodman. She liked Guy Lombardo."

Ginny was born in 1937—on Halloween—in Medford, a Boston suburb. As a little girl she became sick with rheumatic fever and was bedridden for six months. Despite her parents' attempts to keep her calm and amused, she soon grew restless being bound to the bed day in and day out. "Bring me the record player," she would tell her mother. "I'm tired of paper dolls."

Her mother would oblige her by bringing in some records, "and that's the way I got involved in it," Ginny said of the music in her life. She got particularly hooked on Francis Craig and His Orchestra's "Near You" and the long piano intro anchored by Craig's bouncy, left-hand bass work, which is followed by his full band stepping in for the main chorus before returning to Craig's solo piano. After that, she declared, "I want a piano."

"Maybe," her mother said.

"Well, I nagged and nagged," Ginny told me, "and the more I hounded, the less I got. So I went to my grandfather one day, when I could get up, and I said to him, 'I want a piano. They won't let me have it.' And he says, 'Well, we've got to do something about that, don't we?'"

That conversation led to her parents getting her a piano, but Ginny said it drove her mother to distraction.

"You should be out in the yard playing with the kids," she would tell Ginny when she parked herself on the bench.

"I don't want to play with the kids," Ginny would respond. "I want to practice."

And she did, constantly, but her playing life became more diffi-cult when, as a teenager, she developed an infection in her ring and middle fingers on her right hand. The infection led to blood poisoning. In trying to treat her, a doctor, Ginny said, cut too deep into the tendons. To make matters worse, afterward he wrapped her fingers in bandages in a bent position. When the bandages came off, roughly a month later, her fingers wouldn't straighten — and never have. She adjusted the way she could play, with eight fingers, and kept at it.

By the time Ginny was eighteen, she was taking piano lessons in Waltham. And in Waltham one day she went to the Wal-Lex Roller-way, where she spotted the Hammond organ. "I said, 'Oooh, I like that.'" She skated there as often as she could, always paying particular interest to the organist.

"That's where I met Eric," she said. She remembered him trying out for the organist job because she was skating during his audition. "We were all groaning," she said, and cackled ruefully.

One of the managers, who knew Ginny played piano, asked her about learning to play the organ. Ginny explained that her father would never permit her to have an organ in the house to practice on.

"Well, go get some lessons, and we'll arrange for you to practice on this," he told her. "You learn to play it, and you've got the job."

At the time she was dating a young man named Doug, and being supportive was not one of Doug's chief attributes. He told her, "You'll never do it. You'll never play that."

Ginny, who was born feisty, got mad. "Do you want to bet?" she said.

Despite his skepticism, Doug offered to lend her the money to buy an organ. He would cover the down payment, and she would pay him back as she could from her secretary's salary. The plan was for her friend Jerry to keep the organ at his house. But when Ginny, who was around twenty-two at the time, announced this development at the dinner table, the news wasn't greeted warmly. It didn't help that she began by declaring, "Don't look for me too much around this house anymore."

Her father didn't like the idea of her being away to practice, and despite his feelings about music, told her to have it delivered to the house and to put it in her bedroom.

After dinner, her mother told her, "I don't like this."

"Well, Dad said to bring it in here," Ginny replied. "Are you going to cross him?" And that was the end of the discussion.

By her late twenties, she got to know the new Wal-Lex organist: Eric, who'd finally prevailed. They would sometimes skate together on his break, and before long they were a couple. Their dates often centered on going to places to see live organists—restaurants, lounges—and sometimes they traveled to the beach on the North Shore, often bringing Eric's mother along.

I asked her if she thought she and Eric were headed toward marriage. "I really didn't know," she said and pointed out that marriage wasn't at the top of her priority list. "I always said, 'Nobody's going to be under my feet!'"

Eric was a teacher as well as a steady boyfriend, so when they broke up, the loss for Ginny was significant. "Eric was the teacher that walked out and left me," she said.

But staying focused on getting the Wal-Lex job herself, she sought out new teachers. She studied under Ken Wilson, the music director at the radio station WHDH, in Boston, for thirty-six years. "I got a lot from him, but he didn't have the rink beat," she said.

So she found a teacher named Paul Gagnon, who managed a rink in Lunenburg and also played the organ there. She studied with him for several years, practicing songs such as "(I'll Be With You In) Apple Blossom Time," "Tea for Two," "Lover," "The Cuckoo Waltz," and "Fascination." And they struck a deal: she wouldn't seek the organist job at Wal-Lex until Gagnon said she was ready. She did, though, zero in on a rink in Lowell called the Hi-Hat Roll-a-Way, where Gagnon also played sometimes. Occasionally he would call her and say, "I want a day off. Want to come play?" Ginny always did.

The organist at the Boston Skating Club also gave her pointers as Ginny kept tabs on the organ situation at Wal-Lex. One afternoon she walked into Wal-Lex and saw that no one was at the organ. She was friendly with the manager, Louise, and Louise knew that Ginny had been studying with Gagnon. Louise told her to give the organ a try.

"I can't touch it," Ginny said, and explained her agreement.

But Louise persisted. "We won't say anything," she said. "Just go up and play around with it. The kids aren't going to know the difference." So Ginny sat and played it.

The experience was as disorienting as it was thrilling because she was so used to being on the Wal-Lex floor, skating and watching the organist from below; still, she relished sitting on that bench. On another night, when the organist who was scheduled to work wasn't coming in, Louise encouraged her to try it again.

"I don't even have any music," Ginny said.

"There's a metronome in the bench," Louise replied. "And he usually leaves the music in the bench. Let's see what's there."

They pulled out the music, and one of the songs was "Paper Roses," which Ginny knew. Remembering playing that as the first piece, Ginny said you've never seen someone change the beat so many times in one song. "Poor 'Paper Roses.' It was a march, a waltz, a tango."

Gradually Ginny became a fill-in organist at Wal-Lex, sitting in forty times or more and fulfilling her promise to herself from ten years ago—and to her terrible boyfriend. "Don't tell me I won't do something," she told me. In total, as she worked various office jobs during the day, she played skating rinks for eight to nine years. But "they kept phasing us out," she said, still a little wounded all these years later.

For ten to fifteen years, she didn't play the organ at all, in fact, but when she was in her early sixties she decided to get back into it, so she joined the North Suburban group. Around six months later she became vice president to Eric's president.

Through the years, she's had some frustrations with the group. "I always felt that everybody else got to play, and as soon as I sat on the bench I was told someone else needed it," she said. "The ones that sit there are the world's worst critics. They tell me, 'Oh, I used to play.' They'll criticize any of us. 'You missed this,' or 'Hit a lot of notes today we didn't like.' 'How come you played that piece that way?' Oh, you'd be surprised at what some of us get." Sometimes Ginny gives it right back: "'I don't see you up there, so if you haven't got the gumption to get up here and play, and you don't read music, you're no critic. And you should keep quiet.'"

Ginny agreed to play for me, so we went downstairs to what used to be her bedroom but is now called the music room. And for good reason. Here was her Hammond BCV, a Conn organ, a piano, and three smaller, more modern keyboards. She warmed up the Hammond, then looked in her bench for sheet music. She found "Jingle Bells" and worked her way through the beginning. It was a little wobbly, as she missed notes here and there. "Sometimes I get through it, and sometimes I don't," she said, and started over. She was much more in command with the second effort; the sound was bouncier, more up-tempo, until some missed notes crept in, but this time even they came across more as intriguing little curveballs. Now it slowed to a glacial pace as she transitioned into the next song, which had a strident oomph to it. She was dealing with more complicated chords now, but she played more capably, more fluently.

Next she glided into "Merry-Go-Round Waltz"—which she'd also played during intermission. She hit a snag in the middle and redirected herself, rescuing the melody. She brought out a new harmony with her left hand, then missed some notes before coming to the main verse. Yet she was utterly unbowed. Ginny was never guided by dreams of playing to captive audiences or recording her own albums; her goal was playing at the rink, and she achieved that. Her music was more paint-by-numbers, and it brought its own satisfactions—or frustrations, depending on the day.

As the tune filled the room, it was easy to imagine young skaters—the women in plaid skirts and cat-eye glasses, the men with crew cuts—gliding by as Ginny, who would never go on to marry or have children of her own, played the Wal-Lex Hammond, staying on the beat and having proven that no one was going to keep her from her organ.

Eric was still with her, too: over the piano, on the opposite wall, was a painting she had made of him. He sits at the organ, his hair neatly parted; he's wearing a smart red dinner jacket, and his hands are fixed to the keys as he smiles and stares straight at the viewer.

She painted it from a picture of Eric playing in a restaurant called the General Edwards Inn, in the early 1970s, in Revere. The restaurant, like so many things from her long life, was no longer there.

The members of the North Suburban Hammond Organ Society had survived another New England winter, but it hadn't proven to be a particularly productive time for playing their Hammonds. As Bill told me when he arrived for the April concert, he hadn't been playing his organ as much because it needed repairs. "It sounds a little distorted. Eric says it's either a capacitor or a tube." Ginny told me she'd been sick for eight weeks and had barely touched hers. "I went to the stupid doctor," she said, her voice reduced to a whisper, but the stupid doctor hadn't been of any help. Of the three musicians, Eric had had the roughest time of all. As Elizabeth informed me when she walked in, she'd recently suffered from atrial fibrillation, a heart arrhythmia. She was feeling much better now, but because her heart hadn't responded to medicine, the doctors had to reset the rhythm of her heart by essentially shocking it. That procedure had come with its own high risk. "I haven't really done any practicing," Eric told me as he was plugging in cables. "With Elizabeth being sick it's kind of knocked me on my ass emotionally. I mean, I'm feeling a lot better now. I didn't tell her because I didn't want to worry her, but six weeks ago I was afraid I was going to become a widower. It just blew me away. I didn't feel like playing at all."

So it was just as well that none of them were scheduled for today's concert. The entire show belonged to Jim Gregory, the group's vice president, and there was great anticipation about what we were all in store for. Members referred to Jim as Lightning Feet, and Karen Powers, who sat next to me, said as he started up the performance with "Miserlu," "Watch his footwork. His footwork is marvelous." But I still wasn't prepared for the spectacle. In the up-tempo songs he appeared to be tap dancing. His legs swung over the pedals— often violently—like they were being manipulated by puppeteers. Throughout the performance none of us could take our eyes off his legs.

Almost everything about Jim's performance felt entirely different from the concert back in December. For one, at fifty-three, Jim
was far and away the youngest member of the group. Too, he brought
a portable Korg keyboard, which he and Eric set atop the X-66. And
while generally the organs were turned so that the audience could
see the backs of the players and watch their hands, Jim was turned
to face the crowd. As he played, his body swayed from side to side,
and sometimes it looked like he might fall backward.

His range of songs was decidedly different than the more traditional 1950s pop standards and roamed decades. He played the
disco anthem "The Hustle," the schmaltzy "The Wind Beneath My
Wings," the Ventures' "Wipe Out," "Blue Moon," "Love Theme from
'Romeo and Juliet,'" "Baby Elephant Walk," the country tune "Make
the World Go Away" (which was recorded by Elvis, Donny and Marie
Osmond, and Mickey Gilley), and "God Bless the USA." He trotted
out a couple of originals and frequently deployed a percussion ac-
companiment from the Korg, and also the sound of strings. He sang
a few of the songs, too.

Jim began playing the organ professionally at age twelve and
managed a schedule of six gigs a night — restaurants in the New Jersey area, mostly, and around the New York waterfront — until around
1992. "I caught the tail end of that, more or less," he told me during
intermission. Then, a new mindset took hold about hiring organists
for entertainment. Those who had been booking Hammond players
forever began looking at their spaces and asking themselves, "Why
do I need that seven-hundred-pound beast in here?" Because, as Jim
explained, "restaurant owners don't want to give up six tables." Portable keyboards got smaller and lighter, "and to the untrained ear,
they *sound* like a Hammond, so: 'What I do a need a Hammond for?
I'd rather have a table and seat another six people and make money.'"

While Jim had come into that scene later than most, he also lasted
longer than most, too.

After the performance and as members were saying their good-
byes, I told Jim I was struck by how varied his repertoire was. That
was for good reason, he said.

"There's not enough new young blood coming in, and therein lies the problem. Which is why I do what I do. I take a different path," by which he meant that he didn't rely on the old standards that Eric and Bill and players of their generation performed. His eclectic mix, as he saw it, had a particular objective. "I want these folks to get excited to the point where they go home and tell their nieces and nephews and grandchildren, 'Hey, you *gotta* come next time.' That's the gift that I can give back."

That was, I suppose, an admirable notion, but Jim had been performing for the North Suburban Hammond Organ Society for years now, and clearly the younger people hadn't been turning up. And they weren't going to be. That had nothing to do with the quality of the playing or the passion—either from the performers or the audience. Or the wonders of the Hammond organ, for that matter. The solo organ had had its moment—plenty of them, in fact. But as Lorenz Mühlemann, the zither devotee in Switzerland, knew all too well, a lifelong devotion wasn't enough to keep the sound of some instruments from growing fainter.

As it turned out, Dave "Baby" Cortez hadn't disappeared entirely. He'd just stayed gone for a really long time. My search for him led me to Norton Records, which Miriam Linna, a drummer who spent her formative years in Cleveland and who briefly played with the punk band the Cramps, and her husband, Billy Miller, started in 1986. Before Norton, they'd created a fanzine called *Kicks* to tell stories about artists and records that interested them but that they knew nothing about. "Obscure, crazy records," Linna told me. Later they went from writing about music to being in the business itself. "Our bag was always putting out recordings that we thought should see the light of day and just be heard." Their wide-ranging roster includes rock guitarist Link Wray, jazz luminary Sun Ra, rockabilly legend Gene Vincent, and pioneering garage rockers Question Mark and the Mysterians.

Around 2009, Linna thought to turn their attention to Cortez, whose records she'd always loved—especially "Rinky Dink," a sly, more sedate organ-driven romp than "The Happy Organ" that hit number 10 on *Billboard*'s Hot 100 chart in 1962. She was curious about why he hadn't released any more music in the ensuing decades. Where had he gone?

Based on her experiences with tracking down other artists who had disappeared, Linna figured there were a few possible explanations. "People get religious, and they just don't want to have anything to do with the music that made them famous," she said. "Or they got really shafted in the business and just wanted to get away from it." Or maybe Cortez was simply ailing. "So we really didn't know, but I had to make a valiant search for him."

Finding Cortez bordered on an obsession. For years she'd kept a picture of him on her desk, in which he was standing on top of a piano, perched on his tiptoes, in a red Zoot suit and "glistening." A cascade of pearls around his neck. "He just looked like he was the ultimate cool, rocking guy who just wanted to make people dance," she said.

Linna and Miller knew that Cortez's real name was David Cortez Clowney. They did extensive internet searches and made phone calls but got nowhere. They reached out to Cortez's son, David Cortez Clowney IV, who played for the New York Jets for several years, through his website. Nothing. Then one day, more than a year after their search had begun, Linna's phone rang while she was in her neighborhood hardware store. It was Cortez—his son had passed on Linna's number. She learned that he had been in Ohio for many years; he was married and lived a religious life. And his days of working as a musician were long behind him. Linna told him that she would love to get him back in the studio and release an album, but "he was not interested in being involved with the rock and roll world," she said. He had, though, just moved back to New York, to the Bronx.

Despite his lack of interest in stepping back into the spotlight, the conversations continued, and he finally agreed to meet with Linna and Miller. Gradually he began to reconsider. Or maybe they just wore him down. Linna and Miller had mentioned musicians they could hook him up with, including their friend Lonnie Youngblood, a saxophonist who had played with James Brown, Jackie Wilson, and Jimi Hendrix. Over time a new album now seemed like it might actually happen, but there was one looming question: Could Cortez still play?

He told them he'd been playing in his church, but that wasn't exactly the stuff of "The Happy Organ" and "Rinky Dink."

"Maybe it was a leap of faith for some people," Linna said of the risks going into the session without having seen if he could still play, "but that's the way we've always done it."

One of the key decisions was getting guitarist and producer Mick Collins involved. It didn't hurt that Collins, like Cortez, was from Detroit. Collins and Cortez hit it off immediately and collaborated on the new material. The resulting 2011 album, *Dave "Baby" Cortez with Lonnie Youngblood and His Bloodhounds*, taps into that classic Cortez sound, and, just as any fan might hope, it sounds like it was recorded in 1958. The all-instrumental album is a collection of resilient organ jams, with Cortez's trademark Hammond sound front and center throughout, his solos flittering through with the darting grace of a hummingbird.

Sales were modest, but everyone was pleased with the record. Now Linna's big hope was getting Cortez to play a show. So Cortez, at seventy-three, agreed to perform a set at the Norton Records twenty-fifth anniversary party, at the Bell House, in Brooklyn, that same year. In the studio he'd shown he still had the goods, but the prospect of an actual show had its own questions.

"We didn't really know how he was going to be in a live situation," Linna said. But from the minute Cortez walked onstage, dressed in a tracksuit and sporting a big, gold medallion, she said, "he was mindboggling!" He played standing up, spinning around in circles, "with one hand waving over his head. He was like everything you would have dreamed of but wouldn't have dared to dream." His energy, Linna said, was astonishing. "He put all of the backing musicians, who were mostly younger than him, to shame. He was just a ball of fire." By the time he broke into "The Happy Organ," the crowd was insanely happy.

Afterward, Cortez was mobbed by fans. They told him how great he was and asked for his autograph; they posed with him as friends snapped pictures on their smartphones. It was a lifetime away from his last concert, like a time warp—snippets of the show now posted on YouTube, pictures instantly posted on social media. After all this time, Dave "Baby" Cortez was back!

Except, "that was pretty much the end of the story," Linna explained.

Cortez's return to the public eye had been so joyous and heartening that it was only natural that Linna and Miller started thinking about what might come next. When they started to talk future plans with him, "He was like, 'Yeah, yeah.' Very encouraging," Linna said. But then they struggled to reach him. They tried his phone number and couldn't get an answer. Then the number became disconnected. They wrote him letters. No response. They drove over to his place in the Bronx and knocked on the door, but inside it was still. Had he moved back to Ohio? Had something else happened? They were pretty sure he wasn't dead. It was all a mystery.

"He just vanished off the face of the earth again."

CHAPTER 5

Going for the One

As a GOP political strategist, John Brabender had been on countless conference calls in countless conference rooms like this one. On a late Halloween afternoon in 2013, he was at the National Republican Club occupying an oatmeal-colored room. He had a dozen political heavyweights on the line and was pacing with the steady rhythm of a tiger in captivity.

John was best known as the top strategist on Rick Santorum's 2012 presidential bid, though he had helped run campaigns in almost every state. Clients included senators Tom Coburn and David Vitter and former Pennsylvania governor Tom Ridge. But this time the client wasn't a politician. The cause wouldn't affect the economy or the environment; it had nothing to do with tax reform or healthcare legislation. John was leading the charge to get Yes into the Rock and Roll Hall of Fame. The band had been eligible for induction since 1994 but had been shut out every year, though just a couple of weeks earlier it was announced that they'd been formally nominated for the first time, and the group John had put together, Voices for Yes, was trying to seize on that momentum.

It seemed to me that this was the only Washington campaign in modern times that was a true across-the-aisle effort — avengers bringing the full weight of political strategy to correct an injustice. And though I was here in a journalistic capacity, as a lifelong Yes fanatic there weren't many causes I could have cared more about.

Those on the phone included Tad Devine, senior strategist to Al Gore and John Kerry's presidential efforts; Sara Fagen, White House political director for President George W. Bush; Ed Goeas, the pollster; Vinny Minchillo, who worked on presidential ad campaigns for Mitt Romney and the Bush-Cheney ticket; and Leslie Gromis Baker, chief of staff for Pennsylvania governor Tom Corbett. There was Steve Capus, head of NBC News for nearly eight years, along with Steven Sullivan, a senior research scientist at New York University, who on the side ran a website called Forgotten Yesterdays, the mother lode for information on Yes's forty-five years of live performances. "He is sort of our on-staff historian," John told me.

John threw out ideas to the group. He was creating a short film to tout Yes's impact and would aim it at Hall of Fame voters. There was the suggestion to get Yes fans to replace their Facebook profile photos with the Voices for Yes logo. The group could reach out to artists who already had been inducted — John had heard that was the best strategy. He was thinking about Bono. "He's somebody that, if he tweeted, 'It's time for Yes to be in the Rock and Roll Hall of Fame,' would indeed have quite a bit of influence," he told the group.

Tad Devine broke in. "I'm on a plane, and the flight attendant is waving at me, so I'm going to have hang up right now."

Maybe, John wondered, folk singer Donovan could help. Donovan's big hit was "Mellow Yellow," a song many believed to be about smoking dried banana skins. "Is Donovan in the Rock and Roll Hall of Fame?" John asked. "He toured with Yes in the seventies and was their opening act. Was that in the early eighties? Whenever it was, I'm pretty sure Donovan was an opening act." "Yeah, he was," said Sullivan, who was phoning in from Scotland. On any Yes question, he chimed in with the urgency of a *Jeopardy!* contestant.

Eventually the conversation turned, as does any campaign conversation, to the competition. The list of nominees included Nirvana, Peter Gabriel, Linda Ronstadt, Hall and Oates, the Meters, the Replacements, N.W.A., the Paul Butterfield Blues Band, the Zombies, Link Wray, Cat Stevens, and LL Cool J. A few bands on the ballot had been nominated before — Chic, Deep Purple, and Kiss. Five to seven of the sixteen would get in.

"I think most people believe that the group that is automatically, *probably* going to get in is Nirvana," John announced. "The assumption also is, that's probably not Yes's competition. Probably Yes's competition in this thing is probably more likely to be Deep Purple."

Deep Purple had produced one of the most ubiquitous songs in all of rock music with its 1972 anthem "Smoke on the Water." The simple riff was like sex itself: at any given time, somewhere, somebody was doing it. In 2007, more than 1,680 guitar players gathered on a baseball field in Kansas City to claim a world record for the most people playing the same song simultaneously, and that song was "Smoke on the Water."

John reminded the group that on the Hall of Fame's website, the public could vote. Currently, Yes was running fourth. "Moving the needle on the popular vote is important," John told the group. "I'm not sure it's critical that Yes wins the popular vote. But I sure would like to see them ahead of Deep Purple."

Sullivan noted that Deep Purple had been running consistently ahead by about ten thousand votes. John couldn't hide his bewilderment. "If you look at the body of work that Yes has done compared to Deep Purple, I mean, I just . . ." He left the thought unfinished. John had helped Rick Santorum go toe-to-toe with Mitt Romney for the Republican presidential nomination, but in the end, Romney proved too formidable. This time, John worried, Mitt Romney just might be Deep Purple.

I had spent years focused on various pieces of musical equipment and the larger stories they told, so in a narrative centering on the Rock and Roll Hall of Fame, in Cleveland, I was dealing with, quite literally, instrument heaven. The Hall was the afterlife for an almost inexhaustible list of famed instruments — Pete Townshend's Les Paul Deluxe, Jimi Hendrix's Gibson Flying V, the ZZ Top drummer's furry drums, and on and on. The Hall didn't feature any instruments belonging to Yes, but even if it had, they couldn't have illuminated much for me. That's because I'd spent an obscene amount of my life reading every Yes article I could find, pouring over any interview with a present or former band member, studying every Yes videocassette — cassette! — like it was the Patterson-Gimlin Bigfoot footage. I knew Yes's history better than my own family's. But in chronicling Voices for Yes's crusade, this time I was as interested in what the music meant to the fans and the outside institutions as I was in the musicians themselves, though I wanted to understand that, too. And I was eager to see if the payoff to all the phenomenal music Yes had made would, at last, bring them to the most visible destination of rock and roll success.

Of course, I didn't really believe the Rock and Roll Hall of Fame was the ultimate arbiter of who was great in rock. But if the Hall wasn't, who was? Did the verdicts of rock critics mean more? Did album sales? Or was the money made on tour the most convincing proof of an artist's excellence? Was it the perspective of other musicians? (And if so, who?)

Yes's music had taken them plenty far going on five decades. They'd toured the world, produced gold records and hit singles, and sold more than thirty million albums. They got airplay on MTV, won a Grammy, and in 1980 held the record for most consecutive sellouts at Madison Square Garden — sixteen. During the months I spent talking to John about his Yes mission, I couldn't help but wonder:

did getting in the Rock and Roll Hall of Fame mean as much to Yes, or was it possible that, as two devoted fans who had spent our lives listening to Yes music more than any other music in the world, it meant just a little bit more to John and me?

There is a certain paradox in Yes having such a short, simple name because everything about the band has always been complicated. They recorded an entire album side inspired by Tolstoy's *War and Peace*—*The Gates of Delirium*—and had a tour in which they played under a stage design meant to resemble the Crab Nebula. They released a concert film that showcased the band through slow-motion shots and footage of Venus flytraps. And when it came to equipment, Yes had a kind of Howard Hughes approach: Rick Wakeman used more keyboards on stage than a typing pool; drummer Alan White had toured with a kit that included robotic arms to play drums he couldn't reach himself. Every time the band performed "Awaken," Chris Squire pulled out a triple-neck bass. And capes! No band ever used capes like Yes. In his early days with the band Wakeman took the stage decked out like an Egyptian god, his long-flowing, spangled garments sweeping the ground; other times the look was more Royal Magician. In the late seventies his capes got shorter, more befitting a superhero. For a few years Chris Squire preferred the pleated-style cape. And Jon Anderson spent much of the seventies in a white tunic. Collectively, no rock band came closer to the look of *The Magic Flute* than Yes.

Yes also had a surreal visual identity on their albums, thanks to Roger Dean, who created much of the artwork; some of the central images associated with the band are floating islands and rock formations that twist out of iris waters, fish lazing on toadstools like bored retirees. But for me, all these unusual, sometimes bizarre elements were part of Yes's appeal. Everyone likes Spiderman; sometimes it's more satisfying to choose Doctor Strange instead. Carlo Rotella pinpointed the band's "otherness" in a column he wrote about Yes and the Rock and Roll Hall of Fame in the *Boston Globe*: "To my ears, Yes's maximalist tendencies always made them sound not just other-worldly but cosmically ill, as if the band's members could not abide the musical conditions that prevail on this planet."

Certainly their individual backgrounds were unique by rock standards. Rick Wakeman studied at the Royal College of Music with the intent to be a concert pianist; Bill Bruford's influences were the great American jazz drummers; guitarist Steve Howe was heavily influenced by classical guitarists but could easily conjure country picker Chet Atkins or jazz maestro Django Reinhardt; Chris Squire was a student of church music; and singer Jon Anderson, who could hit notes as high as weather balloons, sang in skiffle bands. His lyrics were ethereal, with lots of references to the sun, rivers, mountains, dreaming, Mother Earth, love. They also tended to be inscrutable. But as one musical force, Yes was equipped to create a symphonic form of rock music that had never been heard before.

Yes formed in 1968, in London, starting out with Peter Banks on guitar and Tony Kaye on organ. They were signed to Atlantic Records, and their first two albums' sales were scanty. But starting with their third release, *The Yes Album*, in 1971, Yes put together an astounding string of groundbreaking records that still provide the bulk of material they play in concert today. On *Fragile*, *Close to the Edge*, and *Going for the One*, songs such as "Roundabout," "And You and I," and "Awakening" showcase their high-flown talents both in their sophisticated compositions and in their virtuosic playing. The songs shift moods — one moment thunderous, another soft as clouds. The music is consistently buoyant, sometimes blistering. It contains razor-sharp shifts in tempo and intricate solos. If there is an aural equivalent of quantum physics, Yes music is it.

In the 1970s, there were many great rock albums released by many great rock bands, but no one sounded like Yes. Which is all the more notable because through it all they've switched lineups more often than the Harlem Globetrotters.

As a preteen still sorting through what music I did and didn't like, everything about Yes's music spoke to me. In my high school geometry class I spent more time drawing Roger Dean's bubbly, iconic

Yes logo in my notebook than I did the Pythagorean theorem. I've spent much of my life driving to Yes music and belting out some of the strangest lyrics in all of recorded music. *Dawn of our power we amuse redescending as fast as misused expression.* As if the title of that song, "The Revealing Science of God (Dance of the Dawn)," isn't hard enough to remember! And then there's this: My youngest son, Anderson, is named after Jon Anderson.

Yes has been my favorite band as long as I ever thought of having a favorite band. In that way, John Brabender and I spoke the same language.

I first met John in Washington's Union Station. We found a table in the downstairs food court, and here we were, a *Washington Post* journalist and a Washington political operative blathering for hours about a British progressive rock band whose keyboardist, after the first of many times he left Yes, once staged a set of concerts telling the story of King Arthur and the Knights of the Round Table — on ice.

When I asked John about his beginning point with Yes, he unfolded his own involved backstory. Every teenager's life changes when he or she starts driving, but for the sixteen-year-old John growing up in Erie, Pennsylvania, the keys to his older brother's Pontiac GTO ushered in more consequences than he could have imagined. His brother, he said, had an eight-track cassette of *The Yes Album* in the car, and the music took a powerful hold. John was knocked out by the sheer complexity. A Yes song "might be a ten-minute piece of music, and it had movements," he said. "And you could literally isolate different instruments and listen to them."

He bought the rest of the band's catalogue and gave Yes's triple live album, *Yessongs*, to his girlfriend for her sixteenth birthday. In his freshman year at the University of Richmond, John went through a phase when he couldn't stop playing Yes's *Relayer* album. A hallmate finally knocked on the door and begged: "Can you *please* put another album on?"

As he became an adult, being a Yes fan got more complicated. In 1980 he read that Jon Anderson and Rick Wakeman had split from the band but that Yes was continuing on. "It was like finding a singles ad written by your wife," he said.

Because we loved Yes so deeply, we wanted other people to love Yes, too. But as John pointed out, "Yes music is not something that you're going to listen to and think, *I'm not sure if I like this.* You either get it or you don't. And they're a lot of people, believe me, that don't get it. In fact, a lot of them turn out to be rock critics."

When I first started to hear about the Rock and Roll Hall of Fame, I always imagined it as the Smithsonian on acid: wild characters, outrageous costumes, a sense of enchantment all around. By the time the museum was erected, in 1995, I took a deep interest in who got inducted. Early on, it was quite a few bands or artists I idolized — the Beatles, the Kinks, the Who, Little Richard. In the ensuing years, there were also a few performers who got in that I could only shake my head over. But I understood that musical politics was surely involved, and I figured that the other great bands I had followed my whole life would get in at some point. And I looked forward to the time when I would make my way to Cleveland and spend a full day luxuriating in electric guitars, original lyric sheets, and vests with fringes.

But the years ticked on, and every time the new nominations were announced I became increasingly livid. Yes was repeatedly passed over. But the Animals? the Hollies? Oh, the Hall had room for them. The Dave Clark Five, too. Bill Haley's *backing* band. And who was Clyde McPhatter?! Until the Rock and Roll Hall of Fame recognized Yes for its influence and illustrious legacy, it was official: I was boycotting it.

But then in 2010, Genesis, another band I love, got inducted. Genesis was the first progressive rock band — a strange, glorious genre of music that I'll say more about directly — to make it in. A lot of people were surprised that Genesis went before Yes, but then, Genesis had only gotten bigger as their career continued, selling out stadiums and scoring massive pop hits to the very end. I took their induction as an encouraging sign. And then came another good omen: Rush got in as well.

True, Rush, a Canadian power trio that formed in the early 1970s, had mostly shed their progressive rock inclinations long ago, and they were another band who had only gotten more popular as their career sailed on, unlike Yes. But Yes was a kindred spirit to Rush, who had been eligible for fourteen years before being inducted. Yes's influences were all over Rush's early albums. Besides, what Yes had achieved in the 1970s alone should have made them a lock. But with Rush in, surely Yes should be next. So I decided to drop my ban, and my son Anderson, who was twelve at the time, and I drove to Cleveland the summer of 2013. I understood that there were items in the Hall from bands who hadn't been inducted, so I was sure there would at least be a lyric sheet from Jon Anderson to placate me, or maybe they would have one of Rick Wakeman's capes.

In our long, enjoyable visit, we came across the towering, demented teacher puppet from Pink Floyd's *The Wall* tour. Here was the suit John Lennon wore for the *Sgt. Pepper's* cover shoot. Here were glasses worn by Janis Joplin and Kurt Cobain's death certificate. The lyrics to Otis Redding's "Mr. Pitiful," written on the personal stationery of cowriter and guitarist Steve Cropper. I stared dreamily at Greg Allman's Hammond organ.

When we got to the Rush display—Rush was one of Anderson's favorite bands—I had Anderson pose for a picture in front of Alex Lifeson's double-neck guitar and a snare drum from Neal Peart. Peart had one of the most massive drum sets in all of rock—during his lengthy solos, it mechanically rotated so that he could get to all the many pieces. ("He don't have as many as me," Bill Allen pointed out to me with great pride.)

And on every floor we scoured the place for any Yes memorabilia, but there wasn't a single artifact, not a speck of evidence that Yes had ever existed. Even the docents I asked about this couldn't explain it. "I like Yes," one of them told me. He agreed that Yes belonged in the Hall, considering its broad spectrum of inductees.

"Personally, I think there's room here for 'Little Deuce Coup' *and* 'The Gates of Delirium.'" What I didn't know then was that as I carried on in my passive torment, back in Washington someone was actually doing something about the situation.

As the years rolled on, John, too, had become focused on how the Hall of Fame kept passing over Yes. And as a man used to channeling ideas into action, he was piecing together a plan. "You start to realize: *You know what? Maybe I can have an influence on something,*" he told me. "I never got involved with Save the Whales or anything else. This became sort of my wanting to do something to change the world." So he hatched a plan to "bring in these top Republicans and top Democrats and even some of the news media to some extent and work together to try and do this." But could the two parties unite over a rock band that released a double album based on a footnote in *Autobiography of a Yogi*?

Tad Devine was the first guy he reached out to. John paid a visit to the offices of Devine Mulvey Longabaugh and made his pitch. Devine wasn't close to John's record of thirty Yes concerts. In fact, he had never seen Yes live, but he was intrigued by the unusual nature of the work itself. He was in. "You use the skills that you have in one context and transplant them into another," Devine told me during the Voices for Yes campaign. "Political consultants get involved in all kinds of projects that are not quite political. This is unusual, though. This is definitely different."

Early on, John was tipped off about Steve Capus's renown as a Yes fan. Capus, of NBC News, had seen the group twenty times. He also played bass and loved running through Chris Squire's commanding bass lines. "Who could forget the first time you hear the bass guitar on 'Roundabout'?" Capus asked me. "I mean, nobody ever played the bass like that before."

So John tracked him down, "told me about the project, and I said, 'I'm a big fan of Yes, and I've got some time on my hands, so sure.'" Capus, who had left NBC News and was more or less in between jobs, told his wife about the project. "Look, I'm not going to do this as my *career,*" he explained. Just like John and me, each year Capus had followed the Hall of Fame nominations and been outraged by Yes's continual exclusion. "It was absolutely a sore subject," he told me. The work he was doing with Voices for Yes came from a deep conviction. "The day that it happens, it's not going to be because of this effort. It's going to be because they're incredibly deserving."

How high could Voices for Yes go? Was it possible that Secretary of State John Kerry was a Yes fan? Al Gore? President Obama? They knew where Rick Santorum stood, at least: He was a Styx man.

With the core team assembled, the research stage began. Over several months, a researcher produced a thirty-thousand-word document that listed everyone who had been inducted into the Hall—and some key acts who hadn't. It revealed who had been on the nominating committees. It highlighted every scrap of positive press on Yes and reported how high each Yes album peaked on the *Billboard* album charts. It noted that *Guitar Player* magazine readers had voted Steve Howe best overall guitarist five years in a row, from 1976 to 1981. It cited favorable concert reviews and quotes by such luminaries as Led Zeppelin's Jimmy Page and U2's the Edge. It mentioned that Pulitzer winner Michael Chabon liked to write while listening to Yes—no matter that it was partially because "the lyrics don't really make a lot of sense." It stated that director Joss Whedon named his production company after a Yes lyric: Mutant Enemy. There were quotes from writer and director Cameron Crowe reflecting on the beginning of his music reporting: "I wanted to write about the music that mattered to me. I wanted to write about Yes."

Feeling confident and focused, John arranged for a meeting with Yes when the group played the Sands Casino Resort in Bethlehem, Pennsylvania. (A sign of the times: the band that in 1976 played for about one hundred thirty thousand fans in Philadelphia's JFK Stadium—along with Peter Frampton—was booked into a venue where you can also get a facial.) John met the band backstage and told them he could help their cause—strictly pro bono. Although responsive, Yes made it clear that they didn't want to be perceived as promoting themselves. Also, "it was very important to them that this was not seen as a political ideology fighting for Yes," John told me. "I'm a consultant. My role was not to bring any ideological perspective whatsoever. It's simply to say, 'From a campaign tactical standpoint, ultimately there's a vote, and our job is to improve that vote.'"

Yes gave their blessing. The band even let John and Steve Capus travel with them and film them on tour. Now it was time for Voices for Yes to be heard. The official website received thousands of signatures for a petition. The group gave interviews, sent emails, and released a media statement, and the campaign was mentioned on CNN, NPR, and the *Atlantic*'s website. Whether Yes belonged in the Rock and Roll Hall of Fame was debated on Fox News. Still, John put the group's odds at fifty-fifty. The campaign would be ambitious, tough-minded but ethical. "The one thing we've absolutely sworn off is negative campaigning," he told me. "You're not going to see any anti–Moody Blues ads."

To understand Yes's long-standing snub from the Hall of Fame, you have to understand the peculiar world of progressive rock. The overwhelming majority of prog bands hailed from England, and the biggest were Yes, Genesis, King Crimson, Jethro Tull, and Emerson, Lake and Palmer. But if you ever owned *Brain Salad Surgery* or *Tales from Topographic Oceans* or *Larks' Tongue in Aspic*, you already know this. For the uninitiated, here is a brief run-through on a form of music whose core principle was the antithesis of condensed.

In 1967, the Beatles' *Sgt. Pepper's Lonely Hearts Club Band* came through like Dorothy opening the door to the strange, blindingly colorful Land of Oz. With the album's dreamy swirl of carnival organ, abstract lyrics and images, and highly melodic compositions, the Beatles had showed that the boundaries of rock could be limitless. The songs explored and combined different genres not typically associated with pop music—music hall, classical music, psychedelic—and featured just as many unexpected instruments: sitars, tablas, the clarinet, the harpsichord, timpani, the alarm clock. With that album, the seeds of a new kind of musical expansion—of prog—were sown.

Prog took the blues-based rock of Cream, Hendrix, and the Rolling Stones and divided it by 3.14. The disparate influences were like a musical buffet: here was jazz, here was a symphonic structure, a little folk passage here, and right here a big slab of rock. Lyrically, prog wasn't much interested in love or sex, but often immersed listeners into fantasy worlds: places where giant hogweeds would have their revenge; tales of man versus computer; a conflict between species of trees. It was as if J. R. R. Tolkien, in his seventies, declared: "Listen up, lads. To hell with it. I'm forming a band."

The musicians were more likely to be inspired by classical composers like Igor Stravinsky and Modest Mussorgsky than they were rock pioneers such as Chuck Berry or Buddy Holly. They saw no reason their songs had to clock in at three minutes, so they composed longer pieces with sections, motifs, recurring musical themes. They experimented with counterpoint. Song titles had subheads and chapter titles. If you were a prog band and you hadn't cut your teeth on at least one twenty-minute, full-album-side song, maybe it was time to consider a career in haberdashery. (That track by Rush, for example, was "2112," about a world controlled by something called the Red Star of the Solar Federation and the priests of the Temples of Syrinx.)

But it wasn't just the length of the songs that prog reimagined. Hear the shrill mockery of prog rockers as they consider the standard 4/4 backbeat of rock. Prog produced songs with time signatures that seemed as complicated as calculus: 7/4, 15/8, 21/16. Songs changed directions more often than a scurry of squirrels crossing the road.

Then there was the visual aesthetic. If, in its early days, rock was the tough kid at school, wearing a leather jacket and smoking in the bathroom, prog transformed that kid into a nerdy math whiz who was flourishing in Drama Club. So take the tight trousers of Robert Plant and the open shirt of Roger Daltrey and replace them with the rental costumes for a Renaissance festival. Add capes and codpieces. Or in the case of Peter Gabriel, the original singer of Genesis, bat wings.

To a certain kind of male in the 1970s inclined toward the novel *Hadon of Ancient Opar* and T-shirts of wolves worn under corduroy sports coats, the results were high-fidelity euphoria. For females, the music held as much appeal as the novel *Hadon of Ancient Opar* and T-shirts of wolves worn under corduroy sports coats.

Prog relished excess. At its peak, prog resembled a cross between a circus and a house party at Liberace's. Jethro Tull's Ian Anderson played smokin' flute solos — while balancing on one leg. Carl Palmer played a stainless steel drum set — outfitted with electronics — that weighed two and a half tons. Not to be outdone, in concert Keith Emerson would take a solo turn at the piano, which seemed rather sedate until it began to lift and spin upside down, with Emerson still pounding away.

Prog didn't attract the traditional type — or number — of groupies. Instead, it found frequent companionship with orchestras.

All of this might have been horrendous if many of the musicians hadn't been innovative composers and highly skilled musicians. They could play at blinding speeds, but they could also produce exquisite, moving passages that built with grace and eloquence. Soloing was an essential element. At its worst, it was like being around a drunk who wouldn't stop talking. Bassists had their turns in the spotlight as well; drum solos sometimes lasted as long as childbirth.

Prog bands sold millions of albums and played for legions of zealous fans throughout the decade. Not surprisingly, American rock critics, particularly as prog wore on, often went after the music like a band of marauding pirates. *Rolling Stone* wrote of Yes's "overreliance on the amateur mysticism and pseudo-orchestral maneuvers that made them famous." The magazine summarized Yes's 1978 album *Tormato* this way: "Rotten."

Critics winced at prog's indulgence, the silliness. They resented that prog had stripped rock of its dangerous essence and had essentially turned it into Doug Henning's World of Magic. In an otherwise admiring 1972 review of what is routinely cited as the greatest album in progressive rock — Yes's *Close to the Edge* — one *Rolling Stone* critic offered: "Most progressive rock has a drastically limited appeal, its initial glitter proving in the long run to be more technical bravado, and its lyrics some of the emptiest 'poetry' ever."

The conventional storyline is that by the late 1970s, punk bands, with their barely discernible three-chord songs, brought about prog's extinction. The truth isn't so neat. Some prog bands were put in deep freeze; others, such as King Crimson and Rush, embraced more modern sounds and tighter arrangements. After Phil Collins replaced Peter Gabriel as the singer in 1976, Genesis got immensely more popular with simpler songs and without the bat wings.

The surviving bands tried to fit into the MTV culture. They cut their hair into mullets, ditched the silk kimonos and Jedi robes, and suddenly looked like characters in *Miami Vice*. Similarly, Yes roared back to life in 1983, streamlined and harder-edged with new guitarist Trevor Rabin. Their "Owner of a Lonely Heart" would hit number 1 on the *Billboard* singles chart. But not all the diehard fans were thrilled. Whatever you thought of what the music had become, it wasn't the prog of old. Maybe that was inevitable, but it was also a shame because at its best, prog, with Yes leading the way, was responsible for some of the most joyful and transfixing music ever produced.

As Voices for Yes was playing out in Washington, I got in touch with my all-time musical hero, Chris Squire. Squire, talking to me from his home in Chandler, Arizona, was the only member to have played on every Yes album. So what did he think of the nation's capital trying to get the band into the Hall of Fame?

"I thought it sounded real corny at first," he said in a sleepy British accent. "But then I kind of thought, *Yeah, it's kind of cool.* In reality, we should have been inducted into the Rock and Roll Hall of Fame a long time ago. As we all know, the bias from [*Rolling Stone* editor and publisher] Jann Wenner towards progressive rock has always been there." (Wenner never responded to my attempts to speak to him.) Squire was talking about Wenner because Wenner is cofounder and vice chairman of the Hall of Fame, as well as an inductee for lifetime achievement. "Obviously, it's been quite

an effort to make sure that progressive rock in general wasn't acknowledged," Squire said. "I could be cynical about it sometimes
and say, 'Well, we know *four* chords, so we're probably not eligible.'"
He laughed. "Maybe more than four chords."

Mostly, Squire focused on the band's durability. "The idea of a
forty-five-year-long career was not even conceivable at the time [the
band formed]. So I think that's quite an achievement." And he didn't
give the band's snub undue thought. "I didn't pay much attention
to it at all, really, until, of course, people started coming to me and
saying, 'Why the hell aren't you in there?'" When he did think about
it, he wondered who, if the band ever did get inducted, of the many
members that had come through Yes would make the cut. "Obviously,
it's not a problem in my case, in the bass player's seat." Then he went
down the lengthy list of current and previous members, reasoning
why they should all be included. "I'm always trying to build what
Yes is," he said, "and, of course, it has had many different members.
At some point in the future, I'm sure there'll be a time when I won't
be in it—apart from some magnificent medical miracle that comes
along." He laughed. "It's very possible that there could be a Yes one
hundred years from now, or two hundred. In a way, Yes has always
been in existence to honor its music from the beginning until the
present day, so I've started to look upon the Yes idea that it's more
like a city symphony orchestra that could still, you know, be around
in a couple hundred years. Assuming we all are."

The next day I reached Jon Anderson at his home in Arroyo
Grande, California. (Confession: When I got these calls lined up,
I wrote in my day planner for Monday "Call Chris Squire" and on
Tuesday "Call Jon Anderson," with their phone numbers below.
When I realized the personal magnitude of this, with the precision
of a surgeon I removed that page, and then I framed it.) Anderson
expressed some similar feelings as Squire did, and more complicated ones. He left Yes in 1980, rejoined a few years later, left again
before decade's end, and rejoined once more in the early 1990s,
staying on through 2008, when he had a severe asthma attack and

was unable to tour. The band replaced him with a singer from a Yes tribute band that Squire saw on YouTube, then later replaced that singer, too.

"It's not easy," Anderson told me of the split. There's "not a day that I don't think about it. I still remember and revere the times I was with Yes. And I hope there's going to be another burst of energy coming. You never know."

Anderson, too, had some mixed reactions to Washington's trying to get Yes into the Hall "It's awfully bizarre, yet wonderful at the same time. You know, when we were really going through the sort of realization of the music we were creating in the early seventies and how we were followed by *so* many people around the world—especially in America—we would come here and perform, and we were on cloud number nine all the time. So in a way, I felt there was a reason for our music. It wasn't anything other than, I don't know, an awakening in my mind, that the music we were doing was something a little bit different than the norm, and life needs that. It needs change."

If Yes were inducted, it would be expected that the band would reunite to perform at the ceremony, with Anderson back on vocals. So getting into the Hall not only represented, for him, a chance "to be part of that whole recognition, that whole energy that, obviously, when you walk around the Hall of Fame, you see all that music and all the people that created the music that I wouldn't be creating but for them," but it would also offer a chance at reconciliation. "It's a unique possibility for everybody to let go of the past and move on with the future."

"Again, it wasn't on my radar," he explained. "This management company kept mentioning it. And I said, 'OK, when it happens it will happen.' That's my mantra. You know, by the beginning of the 2000s Rick was in the band. We were traveling, touring, performing all around the world, and you do forget about anything like the Hall of Fame. You're being a musician, creating new music, and you carry on with that." But when he found out the band had been officially nominated, " I went, 'Oh my gosh, maybe it's our time to be presented with this wonderful gift.' We will see."

When I was at the Hall of Fame, other genres such as heavy metal, punk, and hip-hop had their own exhibits, but there was no similar acknowledgment of progressive rock. So how, I wanted to know, did the Hall explain the relative absence of prog?

"The status of different genres in music shifts over time," Lauren Onkey, then vice president of education and public programs and a member of that year's nominating committee, told me. "I think when we make our distinctions about art, they're fluid. They're a product of where you're standing in history and how things change."

Onkey was well aware of Yes fans' bemoaning its exclusion—and the exclusion of a whole genre of commercially successful music that helped define the 1970s. "Prog rock music was not particularly well reviewed in the seventies, even at the height of its popularity," she said. "I think for some critics it might have been considered pretentious, or for some critics, they might have felt, like, maybe it's even anti-rock, in a way. It was almost like, 'Well, if you feel the need to progress past rock, it's almost like you're insulting rock,' you know? For other people prog maybe strayed too far from rock's African American roots. It was reinforcing a stereotype that associated European music with the intellect or African American music with the body. As we think about the music historically, it got saddled with a lot of those concepts. And I think that's changing."

The induction process is run by the Rock and Roll Hall of Fame Foundation, based in New York. For nomination, you have to have released your first record at least twenty-five years earlier. A rotating committee of thirty or so puts forth the list of nominations. According to Voices for Yes, the committee—artists, journalists, industry executives, and museum officials—has included David Letterman's band director, Paul Shaffer; rock critic Dave Marsh; Robbie Robertson of the Band; Jann Wenner; Atlantic Records founder Ahmet Ertegun; Clive Davis; and Phil Spector. (The Hall wouldn't confirm who had served on committees.) A ballot is sent out to a voting body of nearly six hundred industry folks. Inductees can vote as well. And for the second year, the public could also vote, and the five top selections from that process would be counted as a single ballot. Onkey insisted that no one voter has more influence than another. So it was hard to tie Wenner's supposed attitudes toward prog to Yes's exclusion.

"Jann Wenner's not on the nominating committee [this year]," she said. "So that's not a factor. People have a lot of ideas, and people freely lay them out there, and then we try to reach, through voting, a kind of consensus on the ballot. Nobody's blackballed, nobody's mocked."

Onkey said one thing that separates the Rock and Roll Hall of Fame from the sports halls of fame is that a lot of it is simply subjective. If a baseball player had a career batting average of, say, .393, that player is a shoo-in for Cooperstown. Not so with the Rock and Roll Hall of Fame. Kiss, for example, had sold more than one hundred million albums, but that hadn't gotten them inducted. "I mean, that's the interesting thing about talking about standards for artistical excellence as opposed to sports excellence, right?" she said. "Because you can't really reduce things to numbers." She also made the comparison to literature, how some writers go through immense popularity, then fall into obscurity until they get championed once again. And she wondered if this was simply prog's time. The nominating committee had even formed a subcommittee on prog rock just to make sure the genre wasn't being left out of the conversations. There was something intuitively prog about that—the separate section, the splintering off. But would that be enough to get Yes in?

When the news came out shortly after my conversation with Onkey that Yes had been nominated, John Brabender was ecstatic. It was, he believed, time to be in "the war room. We just won the primary election, and now it's time to win the general election."

In the weeks that followed, Voices for Yes stayed on task—more meetings, more interviews, more tweets. More members of the team,

Democrats and Republicans, trying to get the word out. The video eventually made its way to voters and the public. Meanwhile, the rest of political Washington went about its work in the usual partisan ways: the noise without harmony.

In a few months, Jon Anderson would go on tour—just he and his acoustic guitar—for mostly East Coast gigs. Like Yes, he was still looking to make new connections on stage. But the chief draw for Anderson would always be based on what he did with Yes. He couldn't escape it, and he didn't want to. "I nearly died in 2008," he told me of his severe asthma attack. When his doctor walked into his hospital room "he knew I was really in a bad way." The doctor grabbed his hand and said, "I must tell you, I'm a big fan." Anderson laughed at the memory. "And I thought: *We obviously touched a lot of people.*"

While Anderson would be on his solo tour, Yes would be playing shows in Europe, performing three of its classic records: *The Yes Album, Close to the Edge,* and *Going for the One.* The band was talking about getting into the studio and producing a new album. They were also hosting their Cruise to the Edge enterprise, in which they and other prog bands shared a luxury liner and performed. Maybe there was something odd about the notion of oceanic travel in 12/8 time, but to me, the ocean seemed the perfect place for this music. Whales sing a pretty unusual song themselves, but lots of people really love it.

When the Rock and Roll Hall of Fame officially announced the inductees for the class of 2014, Yes's name wasn't on there. I was particularly pained because I was sure that if they couldn't make it this year, given all the efforts in Washington and the publicity that Voices for Yes had drummed up, they were never going to get in. John was disheartened, too, but given the nature of his work, he was used to the wins and losses. And he was resolute that there was still a chance.

Voices for Yes decided to scale back their efforts the next year, since they had accomplished—at least partly—what they had set out to do: bring awareness to the situation and get the band nominated.

And also because John worried that too much promotion could cause a backlash. The next year Yes was left off the nomination list. Before long Voices for Yes's website and Facebook pages stopped being updated. The way I saw it, it was like the idea of fighting even harder for Ralph Nader's second presidential campaign, after he'd gotten so trounced the first time. If you really believed in a candidate, your faith didn't waver, but there were simply limits to how you could make people vote. (Unless you were in Russia.)

For the class of 2016, Yes was nominated again, but they got another no. A year or more passed without John and me checking in with each other. What was to say? We'd always have the Paris sessions (those troubled times in the studio in 1979, when Yes, burned out and uninspired, tried recording the next album in France, ultimately leading Jon Anderson and Rick Wakeman to quit the band). Groups such as Green Day and Joan Jett and the Blackhearts had no problems sliding in. Deep Purple got in, too. So did Steve Miller and Chicago. The fact that those last three acts — all of whom had been eligible for so long — had just now gotten inducted suggested it wasn't completely over for Yes. But mostly I tried not to think about it.

And then came Yes's third nomination, for the class of 2017, along with fellow nominees such as Electric Light Orchestra, the Cars, Journey, Pearl Jam, Joan Baez, J. Geils Band, Steppenwolf, Journey, and quite a few others. In Yes circles, the chatter returned once more to the question, if the band got in, which members would make it? In coverage of the latest group of Hall-of-Fame hopefuls, Yes members past and present were asked yet again what getting in would mean to them after all this time. Would there be a reunion? Some inducted bands had blown off the ceremony completely — only half of Van Halen performed in 2007, without brothers Eddie Van Halen and Alex, and singer Axl Rose was a no-show when Guns N' Roses took the stage in 2012. Other bands who had long ago split, such as Talking Heads, put aside their differences for a few hours and gave the fans what they wanted.

Finally, in December, the list of the latest inductees was announced: Journey, Pearl Jam, Joan Baez, rapper Tupac Shakur, Electric Light Orchestra. And Yes! Eight members: the original band, minus Peter Banks, and then Steve Howe, Alan White, Trevor Rabin, and Rick Wakeman. But a full reunion was no longer possible, since Chris Squire had died from a rare form of leukemia in 2015, at the age of sixty-seven. His passing broke the hearts of Yes fans everywhere, but the band had carried on without him, tapping Billy Sherwood, who had been the Yes's second guitarist for a few years, to replace him. Still, it made the news of Yes getting in a little bittersweet.

I was happy for the band, though, and I was happy for myself. The vindication was a little personal, sure, but it was also bigger than that. I cared about rock music, and Yes — and all the great prog bands — was an important, influential player in the story of rock and roll. Without Yes in there, the Hall of Fame was like a natural history museum without a stegosaurus.

John and I exchanged notes of celebration — "Big day indeed!" he wrote in an email. (Steve Capus told the *Los Angeles Times* that the news was his "birthday and Christmas morning rolled into one.") John planned to be there for the ceremony but at the last minute couldn't make it. I couldn't make it, either. I was attending a different concert the same day — the April concert for the North Suburban Hammond Organ Society. That evening, after I'd come in from dinner with a few of the members, Rush's Alex Lifeson and Geddy Lee were taking the stage of the Barklays Center, in Brooklyn, for the Rock and Roll Hall of Fame concert to formally induct Yes.

Lifeson spoke first. He described the awe he felt as a teenager listening to *The Yes Album* and told the crowd, "Yes helped give me the gift of music, which is everything, as you know, and made me want to be a better musician, and that provided some of the determination to one day stand on this stage giving tribute to this amazing band." And he added, "I'll leave you with this: the musical choices we make in our youth help to mold who we become."

The Yes men, sitting at tables near the stage, applauded. Next up was Lee, who had similar memories of being blown away by hearing *The Yes Album* for the first time, which he described listening to with his friend Oscar. "We both sat there open-mouthed as the songs rose around us and our musical world shifted and fell from its axis. I might've been a young musician jamming to basement grooves in Toronto, but through Yes, I was tuning into a wider world of possibilities. One where music seemed to have no limitations."

Lee then talked about the first time he saw Yes live. "It's not overstating things to say it changed the way I played and listened to music forever. So here we are, decades later, and the music of Yes is still showing me that music truly is a continuum. On behalf of Oscar, my good friend and Alex's, Neil, who's not here tonight, Alex, and myself, I say, 'Thank you, Yes.' It's our great, great privilege and our great honor to right a total wrong and to finally welcome Yes into the Rock and Roll of Fame."

Six of the eight Yes inductees, seated in front of the stage, then came up to accept the honor and offer some speeches. But when it was time to perform, it wasn't hard to pick up on the tensions. By this point, there were two camps touring and performing Yes music: long-timers Steve Howe and Alan White in one, continuing under the Yes banner; and Jon Anderson, Rick Wakeman, and Trevor Ravin, performing as what sounded like a law firm, Anderson, Rabin and Wakeman. (Shortly after the ceremony, they would rechristen themselves Yes Featuring Jon Anderson, Trevor Rabin, and Rick Wakeman.) Geddy Lee was handling bass on the first number. Still, it had been many years since the various members had shared a stage, and interviews in the weeks leading up to the ceremony hadn't much concealed ongoing resentments and slights. But now the first haunting note of "Roundabout" moaned to life until Steve Howe plucked those supernal, classical-style opening notes, and the unease immediately gave way to rhapsody. Over the years, as he was asked about Yes getting into the Hall, Rick Wakeman typically scoffed at the perpetual indignation and suggested that if they ever did get in, he would likely skip the ceremony. "I might be washing my hair that night," he told *Billboard* magazine in 2016.

CHAPTER 6

Into the Darkness

On one level, at least, I was prepared. I reached into my shirt pocket and pinched two foam earplugs into my ears, then, out of nervousness, twisted them further in, like screws. Seconds later, Scott Hull launched into a crushing riff on his seven-string guitar, and drummer Brian Harvey whaled a beat on his snare as rapid-fire and ear splitting as a jackhammer. J. R. Hayes, on vocals, was outside smoking a cigarette.

We were in the basement of Scott's immaculate three-story home in Bethesda, Maryland, that today was being christened as the new practice space for the band Pig Destroyer. After eleven years of playing in Brian's parents' basement, in Herndon, Virginia, the band had to relocate. (Brian's parents wanted a home theater.) Scott was worried about the noise here—not inside the basement, but how it was leaking out. Though he had warned neighbors that his band would be playing this Sunday afternoon, it was unlikely that any of them could fully imagine just how loud the music might be—or what kind of music it was. This was no garage band, in which case a startled neighbor might quickly turn forgiving as the feel-good classic rock of "Jumpin' Jack Flash" or "Bad Moon Rising" wafted through an open window. Pig Destroyer plays what is arguably the most extreme form of heavy metal music—grindcore—which, Scott told me, "almost by definition has to be rough." With the intensity of heavy metal shot through with the attitude of punk rock, the songs run, on average, less than two minutes; the guitar and drums are played at a relentless speed. Grindcore is all but indistinguishable from death metal, though aficionados point out that death metal is more technically accomplished, whereas grindcore is looser, more raw. In both genres, the vocals are not sung but screamed, generally in a deep, guttural growl (though in grindcore, there is room for more shrieking). "Cookie Monster vocals" is how they are commonly referred to, conjuring up the low, throaty pleas of the famed *Sesame Street* Muppet. But that barely gets at it. Instead, imagine a gym teacher who has returned from the fires of hell, barking ferociously in your face, not ordering you to do more sit-ups or demanding to know why you're not dressed out but instead shouting all the ways in which he is going to inflict bodily harm. At least that's what it *sounds* like; with grindcore and death metal vocals, it's impossible to understand the words.

I was as far away from Yes music—its harmonic uplift, the structural complexity, its lyrical hope and optimism—as it was possible to be.

The volume coming through Scott's amp was pulverizing. I could feel the vibrations in my fingertips. When Scott and Brian's jam came abruptly to an end, even though I had earplugs, I had the sensation of having been slapped on both sides of the head.

"It probably needs to be louder," Scott said.

Blake Harrison was standing just inches in front of the huge speaker. "Well, yeah," he said. "It's Pig Destroyer, dude." Blake was an anomaly in the world of grindcore-death metal, in that he played what was seen as a decidedly unmetal instrument: the electronic sampler, which produced preprogrammed digital sound effects—

bits of spoken dialogue and static textures (with names he'd be-
stowed such as "Lake of Fire" and "Psych Ward"). Oddly, the band
didn't have a bassist. Few major bands have gotten by without
bassists—the Doors and the White Stripes being two of the most
notable examples—but such a minimalist approach was even more
rare in heavy metal. But I was particularly grateful to be spared one
more instrument delivering auricular annihilation.

Blake, who'd joined the band a few years earlier, pressed a few
large buttons per song; otherwise, he pumped his fist and sipped
beer or water as the rest of the band played on. Most of the band's
set featured songs Pig Destroyer had recorded before he joined, but
Blake said he had figured out some noises he could add. "I mean, part
of that is just me not wanting to stand there and do nothing."

On Pig Destroyer's site for online posts, fans urged the band to "keep
it brutal," and I was spending time with the guys in Pig Destroyer to
try to understand why anyone would want to listen to brutal music. The band understood that I was not only uninitiated but baffled.
And that was before I even considered the lyrical content and overall imagery of the band. On the cover of its 2001 release *Prowler in
the Yard*, a figure is hard at work sawing his limbs off. On 2007's
Phantom Limb, a woman holds a severed arm. (Did the band just not
like arms?) Most of the songs were about anguish and death, heartbreak and retribution. Violent images abounded. I came across this
summary: "The lyrics paint loathsome, frightening images of pitch-
black, self-hatred and the frailty of the human experience." And this
was a promotional statement from the band's own label!

So what was I doing here? Why did I care? There were plenty of
genres of music for which I had no deep affection, but that didn't
mean I couldn't understand their general appeal. For example,
I didn't go out of my way to listen to polka, but that didn't mean I
couldn't admire the rhythmic bounce and sunny nature of the music.
I most definitely didn't listen to New Country, but why people did
wasn't lost on me. It was for people who liked their pop music with
a twang, the occasional violin solo, the jubilant chime of the mando-

lin, perhaps, and lyrics about hangovers, heartbreak, and the beauty of the open road seen through the windshield of a pickup truck. I could love music and not love *all* music, of course, just like I could love sports and not care the slightest about international handball. But wanting to understand this world of extreme metal had become unexpectedly personal.

When a man imagines the pleasures of fatherhood, he might focus on the image of taking his children camping for the first time, or tinkering with engines with them or showing them how to hit a ball or build stuff. When I thought of having children, I tended to focus more on what would be the first Beatles album I'd play them. In fact, I didn't wait until my sons were born to introduce them to music. When my wife, Katherine, was pregnant I'd position one of my kalimbas — also known as a thumb piano — next to Katherine's pregnant belly and cull gentle melodies. As we got closer to the due date with our firstborn, I spent many more hours putting together a mix tape of songs for Katherine to give birth to than I did reading *What to Expect When You're Expecting*. I was determined that our children would revere great music the way I did, and while I wanted them to make their own discoveries, in time, I certainly didn't mind putting them on a path of musical stops quite similar to my own.

And both sons did love the Beatles. How could they not? As they got a little older, I expanded the canon to some of my other favorites. Early on, Anderson gravitated toward the Kinks, Rush, and Queen. Griffin liked Led Zeppelin and U2. But I kept a steady rotation of the Beatles going, and one day I played them "Helter Skelter," a Beatles tune so raucous it doesn't sound like the Beatles so much as the band that just beat the Beatles up. There are the wild, churning guitar lines, Paul McCartney's primal vocals, the chaotic chorus. After that, mellow fare such as "Something," "For No One," and "Across the Universe" mostly bored them. By the time Anderson was eight, whenever I played him something new, if the first few seconds had the slightest suggestion of midtempo, he would shout from his car seat, "When is it going to get rocky?!"

Around this time, Griffin, at twelve, became fascinated with

Metallica, the once-underground metal band that went on to sell more than one hundred fifty million records and made thrash metal appealing to the masses. He'd discovered Metallica on his own. Pretty soon he had a Metallica sticker on his school binder. It wasn't hard to see where this was heading. If he liked Metallica at twelve, how heavy would the music have to be for him as a teenager? And how quickly would Anderson follow?

It wasn't that I begrudged them developing their own preferences—another pleasure of parenting is seeing what moves your child and what doesn't. But if Griffin and Anderson were going to end up listening to music much heavier than my own—and there was every indication that they would—I just wanted to understand the appeal. And if I could do that, I believed, we could keep music as a bond between us.

I needed a tutor that could give me an appreciation of the music, who could break it down and help me discern its essential elements: I needed Pig Destroyer. When I got in touch with Scott, I told him exactly where I was coming from musically and that, in all honesty, I couldn't fathom the appeal of their music. From doing some preliminary research and (painful!) listening, I had developed some stereotypes about what a group like Pig Destroyer might be like in person. From my first communication with Scott, however, those ideas quickly fell away. As I would come to see, Pig Destroyer lived a striking duality. It played a blistering and scary music, but the members happened to be particularly friendly and sweet individuals. They were also quite successful, considering the band's part-time status. Pig Destroyer has sold nearly one hundred thousand albums, and it earned about twenty thousand dollars each year from merchandising, album sales, and live appearances, which, when the band wasn't playing a festival, was generally in front of crowds of three hundred to eight hundred. Though the band had, over its twelve years together, performed in such far-flung countries as Japan, Australia, Germany, Belgium, Mexico, and the United Kingdom, it played only a handful of shows a year because its members were fiercely protective of their lives outside the band. Scott, for example, was the devoted father of two small boys and a frequent volunteer at his older son's school. He worked for the Department of Defense, though that was all he could tell me for security reasons.

In a week, the band would be playing at the three-day Maryland Deathfest in Baltimore, America's biggest extreme metal festival, and that would be my test. On the bill were more than fifty death metal and grindcore bands from all over the world, with names such as Venomous Concept, Cattle Decapitation, Napalm Death, Despise You, Kill the Client, Rotten Sound, and Destroyer 666. About twenty-five hundred concertgoers from all over the United States — and more than a dozen other countries — would be descending on Charm City. Watching Pig Destroyer rehearse was a way to ease me into the fire. The band members had wondered out loud how a suburban dad like me, who was raised on classic rock and ten years older, was going to handle a festival like this. I had, too. Only Blake planned on attending more than just the one day; three days of extreme metal, the others said, was too much even for them.

In the basement, they were about to run through the set they would play at Deathfest, and Scott's wife, Lisa, was fleeing from rehearsal with their six-year old son and toddler. She worried about what I was in for. "I went to one show," she told me, "and I couldn't hear for two weeks."

J.R. had brought his brother along; Josh did construction, and he was here to help Scott figure out how to convert the basement into a permanent studio and jam space. Scott had given him a decibel meter from Radio Shack, and as the band played, he wanted Josh to get readings from inside and outside.

As the full band ripped into the first song, I had the sensation of standing inside a building as it was being knocked down. And then J.R. came screaming over the demolition like a possessed foreman. At one point, I got up and went to the glass doors. I was sure I'd see someone looking out a window or pointing from an adjacent back yard in horror. Instead, the only person I saw was Josh, who was taking a reading from the upstairs patio. He waved. I waved back.

When they finished their last song, Josh took Scott through the trouble spots. The noise was seeping out the windows, he said, and the glass doors would probably need to be replaced with metal ones. Scott said he'd probably have to redo the ceiling. But this was about what Scott expected. Now it was official. Pig Destroyer had a new home.

A few weeks earlier, I met Scott for the first time so that we could start up my crash course. He pulled up in his driveway in a black SUV with six-year-old Preston. Scott looked like any other suburban dad, save for the skull tattoo on his leg and the kaleidoscope of tattoos on one arm. He grew up a military brat, the son of an Air Force officer. His parents divorced when he was ten, he told me, and though he was mostly raised by his mother and stepfather, it was his father who was the musical influence. He bought Scott his first guitar at age seven and shared his Beatles records with him, which Scott loved. Later, he took Scott to his first rock concerts — AC/DC, but also Judas Priest and Iron Maiden. Around the time Scott was in middle school, he was listening to hard-hitting underground punk and metal bands. He liked the rush the music gave him. But he started getting into trouble. He grew his hair long and skipped class frequently, experimented with pot and alcohol. His teachers knew that he was smart, but he wasn't applying himself, so his family sent him to a boarding school in New York. There, Scott got focused. He joined a band with the headmaster's son. By the time he was enrolled at Lynchburg College, in Virginia, he was "a complete nerd," he said. "I was just really interested in learning about how stuff worked. I'd read Stephen Hawkins's book and think that I wanted to study elementary particle physics. And on the other side of the brain I'm reading William Burroughs and Henry Miller, and I want to be the next writer — I want to go to Paris. It was all very exciting to me."

After Lynchburg, where he played in a couple of bands that covered classic and contemporary rock, he was working on his PhD in physics at Boston College. While in Boston, he learned about a local band with the charming name of Anal Cunt. "The music was just totally noise," he said. "I mean literally, Anal Cunt was noise. It was not playing anything. And I saw them live, and I was like, *This is fucking amazing.* First, it was so absurd. And then you have to think to yourself: *Why are they doing it?* Then you realize, *Hey, this is actually pretty funny.* I mean, it's not music, but something about it I really liked."

He ended up recording a CD with them, but he stayed for only a couple of months. "I couldn't take off and do all the touring that they wanted to do," he said. But that wasn't the only problem. He began to realize: "*Hmmm, I'm the only one with a credit card. I'm the only one with the ability to rent a car. I'm the only one with any sort of education.* A lot of things were starting to come into focus. And I thought, *I'm not sure I want to follow this path. This is fun, but I'm eventually going to want to have a family. I eventually want to be comfortable. I want to have a future.*"

He got tired of life as a teaching assistant making twelve thousand dollars a year, so he relocated to Washington and started up his career. He was working at Lockheed Martin in the IT department, which put to use his skills as an analytical thinker. After stints with other bands, he started up Pig Destroyer in 1997. "We tried to be as noisy as possible," he said. "I just wanted us to sound almost like a car wreck, you know? Just really fast and really, really obnoxious." But from the beginning, Scott saw the band as offering something to do on the side. His main interest was writing and recording rather than performing on the road.

For Scott, the pleasures of both making and listening to death metal–grindcore come down to "the sheer aggression about it," he explained. "It sort of titillates that part of you that likes to go on roller coasters. That's all it is. It appeals to your desire to have your adrenaline gland squeezed a little bit." He added, "Even though death metal is all blood and gore and stuff, people are very, very normal."

In 1998, Pig Destroyer released its first full album, *Explosions in Ward 6*. Among extreme metal fans, it was a sensation, due in large part to Scott's pummeling guitar work and J.R.'s poetic lyrics. The reception was heartening to Scott, but it didn't make him rethink his priorities. And the future that he had envisioned for himself years earlier became further realized when he met Lisa Scappa through an online dating service that same year. They were married eight months later.

"People, when they first see him, they're kind of intimidated because of the tattoos," Lisa, who worked as an executive recruiter, told me. "But then as soon as they talk to him, they realize that he's probably the nicer of the two of us."

Scott enjoyed the careful balance he had set for himself. "I like being in my own house, and I like having my family around. On the road it's like: 'Where are we going to find ourselves tonight? Oh, no hotel? Okay, we'll just get back on the road. Who's going to drive?' It's just an endless array of problems you have to solve."

When Pig Destroyer did play a show, the preference was for weekends, which let Scott save as much vacation time as he could for his family. "Ultimately, this is not a career," he said of Pig Destroyer. "Bands typically fall apart after a while. And then your ability to want to continue to do this sort of wanes, and then all of a sudden you're stuck in a position where you've professionally chosen to do this for your livelihood, and all of a sudden you *have* to do this, and it's a job. That's why we choose to keep a lot of the pressure off. That's why we don't tour so much. All of that just tears people apart."

Some days later, I drove to Baltimore to meet Blake Harrison. He lived in a redbrick rowhouse with three roommates, one of whom, Aaron Kirkpatrick, was Pig Destroyer's lone roadie. Blake wanted to talk outside on the porch since it was noisy inside. As Aaron, who played bass in a doom metal band called Oak, and I sat on an old, weathered couch, I noticed a copious number of empty beer cans corralled in one corner.

Blake dropped out of Towson University in 1996 and taught himself drafting. He now worked as a drafter and designer for an audio engineering company that did large-scale sound-system installations. Blake looked just a few years removed from a fraternity; he was clean-cut but jittery and talked quickly as Aaron sat cross-legged and remarkably still, which seemed apropos, since doom metal incorporates some of the slowest tempos in all of metal. We were discussing the various subgenres of metal when Blake told me that he had a side band. He and a friend put it together, each playing bass and guitar and using a drum machine. Then he told me about the third member.

"We use a parrot for a singer," Blake said. He took a puff on his cigarette, and I waited, sure I had misunderstood. "It's a death metal band called Hatebeak." The parrot—a Congo African Grey whose stage name was Eyeball—mostly just squawked. But then, that was why he was in the band. "There's really no overhead on Hatebeak," Aaron added.

Blake had hung out with the guys in Pig Destroyer long before they made him an official member. He had been their roadie and started to manage the band's affairs. For Blake, playing a sampler was ideal. "It's kind of drunk-proof," he said. "I drink a lot." He said that at his first performance with the band at Deathfest, he drank what he figured was a case of beer before they went onstage. "I mean, it was bad. I don't remember it. And I'm glad I don't."

Inside the apartment, which I could see was decorated with posters of metal bands such as Biohazard and Motörhead, another roommate and a friend had cranked up Def Leppard, and the occasional empty beer can pelted against the screen door. I explained to Blake and Aaron that I was trying to understand why anyone would want to listen to music characterized chiefly by its brutality and bleakness. At first Aaron was stumped. "I don't know—you just do," he said.

Blake had always enjoyed a broad range of artists. As a teenager he liked the Cars, Prince, Steely Dan, and the Beach Boys, but he also got into Metallica and Slayer. And he had a surprising affection that surely separated him from his metal contemporaries: "I love Hall and Oates," he said. "Music should be raw, no matter what you play." I said I didn't think there was any way you could describe the smooth, even polite soul of Hall and Oates as raw. "But they mean what they do," he said, "and it's raw."

Aaron was still thinking about how to illuminate extreme metal for me, and he began to connect his love of the music to how he saw himself as a teenager — and how people saw him. "I was never, like, the most popular kid in school," he said. "I was kind of a geek. I was into comic books and stuff." He said that there had been some bullying issues in middle school and high school. "I'm sure a lot of people into extreme music probably have a kind of similar experience of being an outcast, so to speak. And then as an outcast, you see what the popular kids are listening to and what's being played on the radio, and you kind of go as far away from that as you possibly can."

We all considered that for a moment. And then another beer can hit the screen door and jolted us out of our reflection.

Drummer Brian Harvey knew a few things about parrots himself. He and his girlfriend of eleven years, Amanda, had two Nanday Conure parrots that flew around their comfortable townhouse in Sterling, Virginia. In fact, when Blake mentioned his plans for recording with a parrot a couple of years ago, Brian was hopeful his would get the call. "Blake was like, 'Can they scream?'" he said. "I'm like, 'Yeah, they can scream.'" But for reasons still unclear to Brian, Blake went with another bird.

Like Scott, Brian grew up as a military brat. There wasn't a lot of music played in the house and no siblings to pass along discoveries to, but when a childhood friend played him Metallica for the first time, he was mesmerized. He was still a little unsure why. "I've been trying to pinpoint it, and it's hard," he said. "I was a little hyper. Maybe that had something to do with it."

Brian persuaded his parents to buy him a drum kit, and he set up in the basement and taught himself rock beats by playing to tapes of metal bands. He got better, but drums weren't yet a burning passion. Another influence, however, might have helped pave the way for a love of death metal. "Horror movies, and blood and guts, and all of that," he said. "My parents kind of exposed me — they let me watch *Friday the 13th* and *Texas Chainsaw Massacre* when I was a little baby. A lot of people might not agree with that, but I loved it. I would sit there on the couch and be enthralled." The action was exciting and gave him the same adrenaline rush he would later get from the music. "Not that I necessarily, you know, advocate killing people."

After high school, Brian tried his hand at Northern Virginia Community College, but his heart wasn't in it. He quit school and took on odd jobs—telemarketing and stocking shelves at the local grocery store. A coworker at the grocery store named Rich Johnson invited him over to listen to metal music that was even more hard-core than Metallica: Napalm Death. "I loved it right off the bat," Brian said. "I sort of laughed the first time I heard the really guttural vocals. I was hearing insane drumming. As a drummer it blew me away." Johnson was a guitarist, and he wanted Brian to start up a band with him, but he wanted Brian to pick up the bass because he wasn't sure Brian was up to the ultrafast drumbeats that death metal requires. They'd rely on a drum machine for that.

The band was called Enemy Soil, and Brian stayed with it for a couple of years. Eventually, he did switch to drums after learning what is known as the blast beat, a hypersonic combination of bass, snare, and cymbal or hi-hat. It's grueling work, and Brian said there were times when he was so exhausted by a Pig Destroyer show that he collapsed to the ground immediately afterward.

"When you're playing that fast for that long, it takes a toll," he said. "And I'm getting a little older." He didn't believe he was too old to be playing this music, but since the tour in Australia, in 2008, he had experienced pain in his fingers, and he wondered how much harder playing drums this fast would become in the years ahead.

Brian, who paid the bills by working as a surveyor and taking construction jobs on the side, was keeping his drums at Scott's studio, but he had an electronic drum set, which dominated the living room; he could program various sounds that came through his headphones. Real drums, he said, would be too disruptive to his neighbors. He then demonstrated the blast beat. The sound was turned off, but between his feet flying on the double-bass pedals and riding the rubber cymbal and snare, it sounded like the entire town was banging on the door. When he finished, a hush fell over the room. Then, in the corner, a ruffle of feathers briefly rattled the cage.

Outside the modest Sterling, Virginia, ranch house that J. R. Hayes rented with two other roommates, two menacing gargoyles stood watch. J.R. grew up in a house just a few blocks away, where his mother played her beloved country artists—George Jones and Conway Twitty—while his dad put on albums by Cream, the Animals, and Jimi Hendrix.

In person, J.R. looked more hillbilly than hell raiser—well fed, with a scruffy beard and a shaggy haircut. His path to writing lyrics, he explained, started as he spent a couple of miserable years at George Mason University. Before he dropped out, he was introduced to the poet Charles Baudelaire, and then later, at Scott's urging, he delved into beat writers such as Charles Bukowski and William S. Burroughs and their angry alienation. The discovery was a revelation. "Finally, I was reading something like, 'I can relate to this. This speaks to me,'" he said. "Most of the stuff that I had read before that made me never want to read again."

Back in the mid-1990s, at the local Tower Records, J.R. ran into his friend Rich Johnson, who was looking for a new vocalist for Enemy Soil. J.R. knew he wasn't a singer, but then, when he showed up at Brian's parents' basement, singing was not what they wanted to hear. For the next ten minutes the three of them played, with J.R. attempting his version of vocal bedlam. Brian and Johnson then met on the other side of the basement and talked it over. J.R. was in.

J.R. met Scott when Enemy Soil came to Boston to have Scott engineer a few tracks. Later, after J.R. left Enemy Soil and Scott relocated to Washington, the two were ready to create their own band. After their first drummer didn't work out, they called Brian, who had also moved on from Enemy Soil. And they made the decision to go without a bass player, an unorthodox direction that left some fans scratching their heads. But the threesome had a chemistry that felt right, and Scott played his guitar through a bass-heavy amp, which gave their sound plenty of low-end heft.

Scott wrote the music, and J.R. wrote the lyrics; in metal magazines and album reviews, and particularly among fans, J.R. was revered for his startling literary sketches. The imagery deals with all kinds of emotional and physical pain. On "Lesser Animal," he writes:

Got no use for psychiatry
I can talk to the voices in my head for free
Mood swings like an axe into those around me

On the single-stanza "Murder Blossom," it's the foretelling of violence—and resignation to it—that is so chilling:

Dyed red hair, a forest green dress and a pair of kitchen knives
It was the last time I ever saw a rose.

In imagery so rampant, J.R. said he was simply following a well-trod path. "Go back to Shakespeare," he said. "Are you going to find a bigger bloodbath than *Macbeth* or *Hamlet*? Violence is a part of art." It's also part of a long-running fascination in popular music, whether it's Johnny Cash's "Folsom Prison Blues" (*But I shot a man in Reno just to watch him die*) or Jimi Hendrix's "Hey Joe" or the chart-topping rapper Eminem and his track "Kim," which lays out a sadistic fantasy about killing his ex-wife (he didn't even bother to change her name).

"Violence is kind of the language of the heart," J.R. said, "the emotional language. It doesn't always take into account morals or laws or what's right and what's wrong. And I think that when I'm writing I'm trying to convey emotion, and sometimes emotion is extreme."

J.R. liked contrasting dark images with beautiful ones. "I learned that from Charles Beaudelaire," he said. "He could write a whole poem about a dead body, and it's just the most beautiful poem you've ever read, you know? And it's not even necessarily the imagery as much as the words that he chooses or the emotion that he puts into it."

On the musical side, J.R., like Scott, was pretty much instantly drawn to death metal and grindcore. "I just love the attitude of it, the noise of it, the intensity." As for the vocal style, he remembered first hearing the tumult of the band Cannibal Corpse—a pivotal death metal band in the late 1980s. "It scared the crap out of me," J.R. said. It was so new a sound he didn't have any precedent to put it up against. "And there's a curiosity about that. Like, why is this band so different? How is he even singing like that? The beautiful thing about grindcore is you don't have to carry a tune. You have to make a lot of noise. If you can stay in rhythm with the song and you can sound really mean, you can be in a grindcore band."

Like the others, J.R. didn't think about trying to make the band a more full-time pursuit, so when the band did convene, he said, it was always special. "So much of life is just not fun. So the band is what we live for."

But being the singer in Pig Destroyer has not come without hardships. Once, while headbanging during a rehearsal, J.R. bashed his head on one of Brian's cymbals. He lifted his hair and showed me the scar. Another time, while in England, he jumped into the crowd from the stage, and no one caught him. He spent that night in the emergency room.

Unlike Scott and Blake, J.R. didn't have the security of a salary. Some months ago he'd been laid off from his job as a surveyor, and he took construction jobs where he could get them. Then he picked up night shifts driving an ice-resurfacing machine over the two rinks at a nearby ice-skating pavilion. "I've never been in a position where I wasn't living paycheck to paycheck or I wasn't worried about paying bills or how I was going to eat next Tuesday," he said. But despite financial struggles, he was grateful not to have to depend on playing more shows. "If I go out on the road for six or seven days," he said, "I've had enough."

It wasn't that I was fully ready for Deathfest, but the time had come. Pig Destroyer had done its best to prepare me. I still had plenty of questions, but the foremost question on my mind now was: Was I about to die?

As the gates opened up, the crowd of black T-shirts all around me was so unbroken by color that watching it move about was like observing a giant, roiling tar pit. The attendees were overwhelmingly white and young, and the males' long hair, beards, leather vests, and spiked belts wouldn't have looked out of place at an eighth-century village plundering. Many of the females presented themselves as metal babes — long, blue-black straight hair parted down the middle, Morticia-style; ripped or ultra-short dresses; fishnet stockings.

Metal heads like to let their T-shirts make a statement, and there were plenty of them to read at the festival. "The Time to Kill Is Now," read one. Another depicted the lovable stuffed tiger Hobbes mauling his best friend, Calvin, into a bloody pulp. And this one: "I'm already visualizing gaff tape over your mouth." I, on the other hand, as a journalist, was wearing a white dress shirt and a navy tie.

First I stepped into the club Sonar, where some of the acts would perform, with trepidation. Ceiling, columns, curtains — all black. As the volunteer crew shuffled around out front, I checked out the venue like a prisoner having a tour of his torture chamber. Outside, vendors were busy getting their merchandise ready to sell as fans lined around the block to get in. Tristin Campbell had come from San Francisco just to give out CDs he had made by himself as a one-man death metal band. When I asked him what the appeal of this music was, he said, "It's like, why do people want to jump out of a plane?"

At the booth for Relapse Records — Pig Destroyer's label — Bob Lugowe, director of advertising and promotions, was busy getting ready for a long, productive day of sales. He had just graduated from Northeastern University a few months earlier, and he described this as a dream job. He was wearing a T-shirt that had a picture of the serial killer Jeffrey Dahmer, notorious for eating body parts of his victims. Underneath his image it said, ". . . let's do lunch."

Lugowe told me there was a danger in reading too much into all the dark images and violent references that surround death metal. "I just like seeing people's reactions," he said. "It's funny. It's totally tongue in cheek. I mean, I'm fascinated with serial killers." To prove his point, he rolled up his sleeve to show me a tattoo of the masked marauder, Michael Myers, from the *Halloween* movies.

Logowe's partner in the booth, Eli Shaika, had been listening and tapped into the same explanation Aaron Kirkpatrick had given me. "There's a lot of anger, too, man, from people who have been ostracized in high school. They just want to lash out, you know? This is a cathartic kind of thing to a wear T-shirt like that."

On the other hand, Lugowe added, "Like, I was the homecoming king in my high school."

Hero Destroyed, from Pittsburgh, was the first band of the day. I sucked in my breath and walked inside Sonar, but a couple of songs in I felt genuine relief. This was like listening to Van Halen compared to the onslaught of Pig Destroyer. I could even pick out some of the words here and there. But after twenty minutes, Hero Destroyed was done, and the next band, Triac, shattered my newfound confidence completely. The diminutive singer shrieked a blood-curdling yawp, like a classic horror-movie scream broken down into its own musical language. The room was filling up, and the response from the crowd was enthusiastic until the singer, in between songs, stymied everyone by asking, "Does anybody have any questions?" No one did.

The Czech Republic's Jig-Ai (without the hyphen, the term refers to the ritualistic suicide of Japanese women) raised the bar for challenging vocals. Bounding around shirtless, the bassist-vocalist emitted distorted, high-pitched bleats. It was the sound used in movies by aliens disguised as humans to signal to their kind that they've been found out. Were they going to explode? Were we?

After the set, I stepped into the blinding hot sunlight, reeling a bit. I picked out one of the few spots of shade in sight, and an emergency medical technician gave me a double take. "No offense," she said, "but you *definitely* look out of place."

From the moment I'd arrived I understood I was a curiosity, since I had the look of a beleaguered guidance counselor. But this had its advantages, too. While some people were content to stare or chuckle as I passed, others sought me out and wanted to know what I was doing here. Frequently the folks who stopped me and got my story would say, "OK, so what do you want to know?" Brandy, a thirty-six-year-old graphic designer who had come from California for Deathfest, was one of them, summoning me with her finger. As I approached I noticed an upside-down cross around her neck—an overt shout-out to Satan, or maybe it was just a prop. As a comely female, Brandy was only too aware of how male oriented the experience of Deathfest was. "It's a sausage fest," she said. "It's all dudes. As a woman you have to protect yourself." She explained that the mosh pit was the trickiest part. "Some guys will drag you in and fuck you up. It gets really frenetic." But as a woman, she was drawn to the music for most of the same reasons as everyone else. "It's really cathartic," she said. "You can get out all your aggression."

She was most excited about seeing the band Mayhem, which would be playing on the outdoor stage. Mayhem played yet another subcategory of heavy metal called black metal. Along with a steady stream of other black metal bands, Mayhem hails from Norway; as Garry Sharpe-Young writes in *Metal: The Definitive Guide*, "Not since the Viking longboats set out from the fjords has Norwegian culture imposed itself so harshly on the world." Black metal is known for, among other things, its vehemently anti-Christian lyrics and imagery, band members painted up like corpses, and its link to dozens of churches being burned down in Norway.

Even by extreme metal standards, Mayhem had a grisly backstory. The band's vocalist, Per Yngve Ohlin, who went by the name Dead, killed himself in 1991, shooting himself in the head with a shotgun. His suicide note was brief: "Excuse all the blood." Founding guitarist Oystein Aarseth, who went by Euronymous, discovered the body and, the rumor has always been, before police arrived, gathered up pieces of Dead's brain to put into a stew. Two years later, a fellow black metal musician named Varg Vickernes, who briefly filled in on bass, murdered Euronymous with a knife. Mayhem may have been the only group at the festival whose name *undersold* the band.

Brandy let me in on a secret: Mayhem was going to come onstage from a womb! "I read it on the internet," she told me. "This is their first big tour here, and it's like a *rebirth*." But for a band also known for destroying Bibles onstage and performing with pigs' heads impaled on stakes, this sort of entrance seemed modest. Sadly, when Mayhem took the stage that evening, there was no womb. Not even any pigs' heads lining the stage. (This didn't surprise Scott Hull. He told me that when Pig Destroyer briefly toured Japan with Mayhem last year, the band's singer, Attila Csihar, was complaining about the price of pigs' heads.)

As I stood in the crowd listening to Mayhem, scribbling notes, one towering young fan, in a leather vest and thick, scraggly sideburns, sized me up with some disgust. "Like, what — what is your *deal*?" he demanded. "Are you a *narc*?"

This guy was sharp. Because if you were going to try and blend in with this crowd as an undercover agent, carrying a notebook and wearing a tie would have been the only way to do it.

When Mayhem finished, the crowd moaned in approval. As Csihar exited the stage, he growled, "See you in hell."

While prog had taken flight from the whimsical dream that was the Beatles' *Sgt. Pepper's*, heavy metal was the malevolent spawn of Black Sabbath. But Black Sabbath wasn't the first rock band to dabble in heaviness: The Kinks' "You Really Got Me," in 1964, with its frenzied, buzzing solo, was arguably the heaviest that rock guitar had ever sounded. On the lyrics side, there was the Doors' spooky Oedipal opus "The End." Then Led Zeppelin came stomping through the gates in 1969 with its first album and the anguished rocker "Dazed and Confused," whose ghoulish, descending riff would come to be a kind of template for those who wanted to traipse into the gloom. But Black Sabbath, based in Birmingham, England, and fronted by a young singer who christened himself Ozzy Osbourne, set out to own the darkness completely. With the release of its self-titled first album in 1970 and the ominous riffs and chords that fueled tracks like "Wicked World" and "Black Sabbath," the band created a kind of rock music intended to play like a soundtrack to horror films.

Throughout the decade, other bands probed the sound Black Sabbath had ushered in, but mostly heavy metal, as the music was coined, remained a singular, consistent genre of rock. It was largely unpopular with rock critics, and a range of other rock acts drew considerably more interest, whether it was the prog bands, rock heavyweights like the Who and Pink Floyd or the cartoonish Kiss, modern blues-based bands such as the Rolling Stones and Led Zeppelin, or the softer, more folkie sounds of Fleetwood Mac and the Eagles. Heavy metal bands, such as Judas Priest and Rainbow, played to far fewer, though no less loyal, fans.

By the 1980s, metal was snaking around in different directions. Spurred on by the raw power of the British punk scene and a new wave of British heavy metal groups, such as Iron Maiden and Angel Witch, some bands created a new signature sound by playing faster and more intensely. Thrash metal, as it was called, featured lyrics and imagery pushed to new extremes—some of it overtly Satanic. In 1985, the San Francisco–based band Possessed released what is generally acknowledged as the first record to have the traditional growling vocals of death metal. As Albert Mudrian, the author of *Choosing Death: The Improbable History of Death Metal and Grindcore*, writes, the band's singer, Jeff Becerra, was preparing to record the vocals, and the guitarist said, "'Just go rrrooaarr!' So I pretty much yelled my guts out." The last song on their first album was called "Death Metal," and the new sound and moniker paved the way for what was to come.

The sunny state of Florida became the country's leading scene for death metal bands, with the seminal acts Death and Morbid Angel emerging there. In England, Napalm Death became the first grindcore band. The vocal sound was similar, but the lyrics were more leftist and social-conscious punk. The famous British DJ John Peel became fascinated with Napalm and their debut, *Scum*, and he championed them over the national airwaves.

The death metal scene was underground, which helped keep it from attracting greater controversy than it might have, given the times and the grisly content. The small labels releasing the music weren't even trying to get these albums into traditional record chains. Most of the music's coverage was through word of mouth, a network of tape trading and shoddy-looking fanzines made by devoted teenagers. One of those teenagers was Matt Jacobson, in Colorado, who started his own label, Relapse Records, in 1990, and brought out his first release a month after his eighteenth birthday. "The first couple of years, it was all hot dogs and macaroni and cheese," he told me. "But then we started actually to generate a pretty good amount of income because our overhead was so low." He soon relocated Relapse to rural Pennsylvania and signed a lot of national acts. Jacobson was happy if a band could sell five thousand or ten thousand copies, and often part of those sales were based on the label alone.

He signed Pig Destroyer in 2000. He was hopeful about what was ahead for the band, but he didn't forget that, ultimately, heavy metal had remained an outsider's music—and likely always would be. "Metal heads really have a bad name," he said. "I think that people are really just afraid of what they don't understand."

Here was one thing I could definitively say a full day into Deathfest: metal is not pretty in the early morning. On day two of the festival, the parking lot smelled of urine and vomit, and suddenly the name Deathfest felt truer than ever. The gates wouldn't open for a couple of hours, and some of the concertgoers had slept on the few patches of grass outside the chain-link fence, the sunlight slowly forcing their eyes open. Others, such as Jason Keyser, had started their day by drinking beer.

Keyser was in a band called Skinless, but this weekend he was just another fan. He was philosophical about the life that being in a death metal band afforded him. Skinless had traveled to Portugal, Denmark, Austria, Ireland, Switzerland, Sweden, Germany, and New Zealand, among other places—and he pointed out that someone paid for the plane tickets every time. The band was on the road more often than it wasn't, he said, but when it wasn't, he picked up a job to put a little more money in his pocket. This was how it was for all the death metal bands he knew. You could make money, but making a living was too much of a stretch.

Keyser had an original take on the appeal of death metal vocals. He *liked* not being able to understand any of the lyrics. "I don't want to hear somebody's stories," he told me. This was particularly striking, considering that he was the band's singer and chief lyric-writer.

Before Deathfest kicked off for the day, inside Sonar I found Ryan Taylor, who was trying to finish his breakfast while dealing with the latest production details. Taylor cofounded Deathfest with Evan Harting. The two best friends were unabashed metal heads at Parkville High School in Baltimore County and worked together in a restaurant after graduation. They were on their way back from a death metal festival in Ohio in 2002 when it occurred to Taylor that the two of them could put together something better. A year later, with no experience and no industry contacts, they managed to put on the first Deathfest. It had been growing every year since.

Stepping out and watching the bands and the nearly twenty-five hundred attendees was like "a year of work unfolding right in front of my eyes," Taylor said of the festival's first day. He had been a fan of heavy metal since he was twelve, and though it was unclear to him how much bigger this kind of extreme music could get, he wasn't worried about it ever fading away. "Metal music—it's like once you start, you can't stop."

Eventually, bands took the stage; bands came off. The music didn't sound much different to me than it had the previous day, but it never stopped being jarring when, after screaming his lungs out in a demonic growl, the singer would say, in a neighborly, does-your-lawn-need-cutting kind of voice, "We're selling T-shirts and CDs over here if you're interested. Check it out."

The guys from Pig Destroyer turned up in the afternoon. They listened to a couple of bands, then stepped into the club to get ready for their set. The backstage area grew more crowded in anticipation. Onstage, the band Birdflesh, from Sweden, was finishing up. It introduced a song called "The Flying Penis."

Afterward, Pig Destroyer hustled to set up its gear onstage as fans looked on. Scott was hitting a stray chord, J.R. stalked around the stage, and then the lights went down. One of Blake's lengthy samples began to play. It was Larry King reading from Henry Miller's classic *Tropic of Cancer* (". . . I will sing while you croak, I will dance over your dirty corpse."). The crowd waited quietly, ready for release. Then Scott dug into the menacing riffs of "Scarlet Hourglass," dropping almost to his knees as J.R. put the mic to his mouth and wailed the first lines.

The band chewed off songs from the list and spit them back into the crowd. J.R., wearing an expression of pure anguish, lurched like a man torn between destroying everything around him and destroying himself. It was the same set they had run through at Scott's house a week earlier, but the difference was like a careful test run around the block versus jamming your foot to the gas on the open highway. Scott's and Brian's speed was stunning, but it wasn't just musical athleticism. There were grooves within the maelstrom, and I was catching them now. Most everyone around me was bobbing his or her head up and down—headbanging—but my head just went side to side, in awe.

After twenty-five minutes, the crowd had been hammered into an exhausted bliss. I sat closer to the stage than anyone, but I was outside of it all. It wasn't my music, and it didn't need to be. But it also wasn't so alien to me anymore.

Pig Destroyer came out of the building as Napalm Death got ready to play on the outside stage. Every member of Pig Destroyer had mentioned to me encountering Napalm Death's music for the first time and being riveted. When Blake Harrison saw the group on MTV's "Headbanger's Ball" one night, he told me, "It changed my fucking life."

Now here they were—most of the original members having moved on long ago, true—but this lineup was attacking the music with vital energy. The longtime singer, Mark "Barney" Greenway, was pogo-ing on stage with an exuberance that surpassed what any singer had been able to muster since the festival had started. Besides being innovators, Napalm Death had the distinction of producing what may be the shortest song in recording history — .75 of a second, according to the *Guinness Encyclopedia of Popular Music*. The song is called "You Suffer," and considering its length, the fact that it has any lyrics at all was a marvel. "You suffer, but why?" it goes, all grounded into one mordant yelp. As the sky darkened, the band played the song, which came through like an electric bolt. It didn't slip past the crowd, though, which threw up its arms in salute.

J.R., his girlfriend, Rachael, and Brian's girlfriend, Amanda, and I climbed to the parking ramp rooftop to watch the rest of Napalm Death's set. A mosh pit had formed maybe twenty feet from the center of the stage. Young guys pushed and knocked each other into an almost perfect circular path, their arms and legs flailing. From up high, it looked like a whirlpool. Amazingly, no one fell down, and the circle kept swirling, sometimes widening and picking up people who meant to stay out of it but couldn't escape the pull and were swept in. It seemed to have little relationship to what was happening onstage, but I was struck by what trust you had to have to be in that mosh pit. Though no one was throwing an actual punch, it was extremely physical, and it would have been easy for someone to have stopped and pushed back, which could have led to trouble.

As I watched from above, it wasn't impossible to think that my sons could, many years from now, be down there, spinning amid the heavy riffs. Even after what everyone had told me about the appeal of this music, I wouldn't understand it completely. But then, no son listened to rock music in the hopes that his father would understand. My father never paid any attention to the music I listened to, and it never once occurred to me that he should. Or that I would want him to. For now, the love of a lot of the same great rock songs was something we still shared, as Scott and his father had. Maybe this wasn't going to last a lot longer, but there were memories linked by rock music that I — and they — would always have.

In the swirl below, the crowd stayed on its feet, moving, colliding, and the circle kept flowing, contracting, and expanding, as the band tore into each song with abandon. Howling, snarling, but in no way suffering.

In the years that followed, Anderson, now sixteen, had mostly stayed with the music he'd liked when he was younger. Movies were more his passion now. But music had become a much bigger part of Griffin's life. He loved hip-hop and listened to jazz as well. He had a newfound appreciation for some of my bands, too — Yes, Genesis, Pink Floyd. At twenty, he was constantly going to concerts, and he reviewed shows and new releases for his college newspaper. And sure enough, he loved heavy metal. One of the two posters on his dorm room wall was of Iron Maiden's venerated *Number of the Beast*. He wore a Slayer *Reign in Blood* sweater (a sweater!) and a Mayhem shirt, too. He was into Pig Destroyer.

I had kept tabs on Pig Destroyer, and I wondered whether Blake Harrison's unusual role in the music had evolved. Could you grow as a sampler player? It turned out that Blake had left Baltimore and we lived just a few minutes apart, so we met for drinks and caught up. There had been a lot of changes with the band since I'd seen them last. One, they had parted ways with drummer Brian Harvey. "He wasn't putting forth any effort," Blake explained. "If you don't practice your stuff, you can't play it in the studio." He was still a little bewildered, remembering all the turmoil seven years back. "It nearly broke up the band," he said. But they found a replacement and made a new record, *Book Burner*, back in 2012 to what had now become typical acclaim for the band. (The album cover is sedate by Pig Destroyer standards: a ghostly image of a small girl staring pensively at the viewer. And she has both arms!) They were playing more shows. J. R. Hayes had married Rachael and spent his days working on a farm.

Blake was busier than ever, he said. On the side, he had put together his own music of samples and sounds for a project he called *Tentacles of God*. Also, Hatebeak was still going and still fronted by Eyeball, the parrot. The band had released *Number of the Beak* a couple of years ago and had another recording ready to go, featuring songs by Hatebeak and by another band that used guinea pigs for the vocals. I said I didn't even know what sound guinea pigs made. "It's like a weeping," he said.

Perhaps most significantly of all, Pig Destroyer had added a bassist—a cousin of the new drummer's. Blake said that the music they were recording was probing some new sonic territory and that Scott had felt it was time to add that extra dimension.

Though having a bassist complicated Blake's contributions somewhat since he had previously occupied some of that lower range, he felt more secure about his role in the band than ever. Currently, Scott had demos for about seven songs for the new album they were writing, and "we're stepping up what I do a lot more," Blake said.

I asked him if he thought he had become a better sampler player.

"I feel like I have," he said. He also believed he had a better handle on the technology, on the rhythmic possibilities of sound, but, he added, "I don't practice—there's no practicing." Instead, his time went into composing, searching out new samples. And he did more coordinating with J.R. about where these samples could come in so that they wouldn't compete with the lyrics. A couple of weeks later I visited him at the apartment he shared with his girlfriend so that I could get a better handle on his process. On the walls were, rather reassuringly, creepy posters and artwork—skulls, images of death. And a map that showed the geographic activity of the murderous activities of the Zodiac Killer.

Blake opened up his laptop and showed me the software that accessed all his sounds and its complex editing tools. There were snippets from TV shows, movies, podcasts, YouTube videos, noises he'd recorded himself—a merry-go-round that he would distort to sound sinister, a creaky elevator. He pointed to a shelf that held all his DVDs, covering one end of the apartment. Mostly these were horror movies, from slasher films to Bela Lugosi movies. When he watched, he was conducting fishing expeditions, and sometimes a new sound stood out to him, but just as often he came away with nothing.

To illustrate, he played a demo for a new track that Scott had given him, which had guitar and programmed drums and bass. So what could Blake add to it? "Like, I'll take a sprinkler, and I'll stretch it, shift the pitch down or shift it up, put stuff on it, different effects," he said. But the sprinkler was rejected. Scott told him it sounded "too chirpy."

He played samples from a documentary about Betty and Barney Hill, who claimed that in 1961 they were abducted by aliens; we listened to Barney drone on. "The dialogue here is not important to me," Blake said. "It's just really weird sounding—it's just a total aural thing." He listened some more. "That evokes a mood to me."

He said that if he was using a speaking passage with Pig Destroyer, he didn't want anything familiar or trite, like Arnold Schwarzenegger's "I'll be back," since that would go against the vibe he was trying to build. Plus, the band didn't exactly gravitate toward the mainstream. Instead, a sample might be a random snippet from an FDR fireside chat. And even then he might layer it in other sounds he'd manipulated. Among players of conventional instruments, Blake was the mad scientist in the laboratory. He didn't work with notes or chords but created his own musical language, however mangled, from wayward elements. And this helped serve the band's mission: Pig Destroyer's music was noise, but the noise was still music.

He searched through more folders on his computer, where he had voluminous variations of static, of ominous humming. He pulled up the sound of a generator. It was the kind of discord he might use for his own soundscape or a Pig Destroyer track. "I'll let that go for two minutes or ten seconds," he said. "It just depends on what I feel."

If Blake was the king of static, he was no slouch when it came to screams, and he played me some bone-rattling examples from his extensive collection. "You can never have enough," he said wistfully.

A car alarm went off in the distance, and for a couple of minutes he went on talking. Then he stopped to acknowledge it—in a way that, given the world of harsh clangor he lived in, surprised me. "This drives me up a wall. All night. *All night*."

CHAPTER 7

"You May Have Never Heard Nothing Like This Before"

It was Fourth of July, and CanJoe John's fuse was lit: someone had just canceled his appearance at the annual Celebrate Bristol! festival. He had been booked to perform for a few thousand people gathered in Cumberland Square Park, in Bristol, Tennessee, and yes, he was only supposed to play a couple of songs, but it was a chance to be seen again by friends and make new connections. CanJoe John was all about the new connections. Most important, it was one more way to promote the odd contraption in his hands. As musical instruments go, the canjoe is the epitome of minimalism—a stick of wood, one string, and a can at the bottom of the stick that acts as the resonator. (Like *banjo*. Get it?) It offers ten notes. You can't play chords, of course, which is one of the instrument's chief constraints, but CanJoe John had been making his way with the canjoe for nearly twenty-five years, and this little sea biscuit of an instrument had taken him plenty far in bluegrass. The problem for CanJoe John—at least one of them—was that his career highlights were in the long ago.

He was scheduled to play between two acts—Fritz and Co., a name perhaps better suited for a bratwurst kiosk—and Virginia Ground, known for its bluegrass-inflected, hard-hitting Americana music. But earlier in the day Jon McGlocklin, one of Virginia Ground's singers, the manager of both bands, and an organizer of the day's concert, had called with some news. Apparently, the sound guys said they couldn't set up for Fritz and Co. and have the sound system also be ready for Virginia Ground and accommodate CanJoe John, too. Considering that CanJoe John, whose real name is John VanArsdall, was going to play into an open mic and needed just two lines in the sound system, this was not entirely convincing.

"That's bullshit," John told me at the edge of the gathering crowd. All around us families were arranging their chairs and coolers and settling in for an evening of snappy music, patriotic reassurance, and fireworks; children were working their way through barbecue, ice cream, and pork rinds bought at the row of food trucks, and old-timers who'd wandered over alone searched for a corner of unmoving shade. Over his long career, John had had his share of bookings—deals made over the phone, without signatures—fall apart at the last minute, so he always believed that "it ain't happening unless it happens." He was upset, then, about the day's developments but not exactly floored.

At the corner of the stage he ran into Logan Fritz, the wild-haired eighteen-year-old leader of the opening band. John had had Fritz and Co. on the weekly radio show he hosts and explained to Logan what was going on; he said to me that while Logan was an excellent acoustic guitarist, he could also really rock. Logan smiled appreciatively, then said in a leery voice, "I don't want to be in a box," as if I might be one more music journalist looking to typecast him.

"I want to be in a can," John said.

He still thought he had a chance to turn the situation around if he could find McGlocklin, so he went over to the tent selling Virginia Ground CDs and shirts as a singer took the stage and warbled through "God Bless America." No luck. The more John searched, the more he simmered. The whole scene here, he declared, was "cliquish. If you're not in that Bristol circle, if you're not in their little group, you're an outsider." He said he resisted any attempts from the Bristol insiders to get him to "fit their peg. I'm not one of them."

Suddenly he became aware of some revelers eyeing him, which was understandable: outfitted in his overalls, Civil War–era gold-rimmed glasses, and Australian duster hat with real snakeskin on the band, and with his silver beard, he looked like he'd just stepped out of *Huckleberry Finn*. He stooped to address the small boy in the group. "You got a birthday?" he asked, his voice now bright, grand-fatherly.

"My mama just had one," the boy replied.

"Everybody has a birthday," John said, "so here you go." He strummed a quick version of "Happy Birthday" on the canjoe. The boy's family smiled in surprise. *How did he do that with that thing?* "How about a little bit of 'Black Mountain Rag'?" John said of the bluegrass staple and played that, too. The canjoe is not a loud in-strument, and through the ruckus of the crowd it was easy to miss it entirely if you weren't standing right in front of it. "I'm CanJoe John, and I'm the man who fit the can in the plan," he told them. He explained a few things about the canjoe to the boy's father and said, "Check it out: canjoe.com. C-a-n-j-o-e.com." He added that he custom-built all his instruments for sale, which meant that you se-lected the type of can (Coke? Bud Lite? Yoo-hoo?) and picked the wood — poplar, say, or maple, walnut, oak. And if you wanted it out-fitted with extras — special inlays or elaborate carvings — he'd be glad to oblige. The extras were where the real canjoe money was. The instruments started at a hundred dollars and could run up to a thou-sand. The man and his boy nodded with interest, then John took two steps over and another family got its own show. Their two children were in strollers, and John bent down farther this time. He held the canjoe in front of them.

"Pretty cool, huh? Ten frets, a tuning key. I do a tour of children's hospitals for kids his age and up"—he told the parents as he mo-tioned to the boy, who looked to be about two. Then he said to the girl, slightly older, "Would you like to hear '(Somewhere) Over the Rainbow'?" Before she could respond, he fired off the prominent notes, his right hand furiously vibrating the pick against the string—a technique he called "candolin" style, which made the sound fuller, closer to the richness of a mandolin. The adults made clear their approval. When he turned around to get back to searching for Mc-Glocklin, more interested attendees were drawn to the hubbub. He went through his spiel again, gave another demonstration, but now Fritz and Co. was starting up its direct, retro-influenced guitar rock, leaving the canjoe as audible as a bug.

Time was running out. "I've got to find Jon if I'm going to get on," he told me, "but if I don't, what we're doing here"—playing his canjoe for interested folks, explaining how they could order one from him—"is really how I maneuver, and you can see how that's a marketing skill. So you don't just give up and go home."

He caught side of McGlocklin's cowboy hat behind the stage at last, and we cut a straight path through the crowd. After they exchanged pleasantries, McGlocklin explained again about the response from the sound guys and that "Maggie from Believe in Bristol"—the executive director of the nonprofit organization that promoted the downtown area—"was like, 'If he wants to come out and busk around through the crowd or whatever, then good.' I'm like, well, that's their call, I can't make changes."

John reminded him he was only going to play two songs.

"You'd have to talk to them—I did my due diligence," McGlocklin said.

"We'll figure it out," John told him. And then he said to me, "I'm going over to that sound engineer and show them what they're missing." But he continued to be interrupted by calls for a performance. By the time he finally made it to the mixing board, Virginia Ground was taking the stage. Now the mission was just a matter of principle. John explained to the two sound guys who he was and the message he'd been given, but they said they knew nothing about it. "I would have been glad to," the first guy said about setting him up.

"Not me," said the other about having John scratched.

John nodded—he never really believed they were behind the

cancellation. He suspected the event director wasn't sold on him being right for the festivities. "I played the Grand Ole Opry," John told them—not to brag, I didn't think, but more to make clear: *I'm not nobody.* In the days before, I'd heard him tell plenty of folks this fact, and I'd keep hearing him tell it the rest of the week. It was, by any measure, a prodigious accomplishment. There was probably no one in this crowd who could make such a claim. As I was starting to learn, though, John had his admirers, but he also had his detractors, which provided an extra challenge in his attempt to push past the limitations of an instrument that was inherently limited.

In truth, John wasn't an outsider—he was a Tennessee-born bluegrass musician who looked and sounded the part. The canjoe, however, was a different matter. It was an untraditional instrument in a music bound by tradition. And John had tied his legacy—personal, musical—to the canjoe. It was an exceptionally simple instrument, and yet, in these parts, it sure brought its share of complications.

When it comes to music and fantasy, no one really pretends to play a keyboard or mimes the position of a contrabassoonist. No, the real image of musical power lies in holding a guitar. I love the drums, and they've always felt like a natural fit, but it's miraculous that I haven't developed carpal tunnel syndrome after the incalculable hours I've spent pretending to play a guitar solo. I've forever yearned to coax just a few melodies out of the guitar. My trouble is, every time I pick up a guitar it feels like I'm at the control panel of a nuclear reactor. Too many places to put my fingers.

But I continued to stay alert to some manageable string instrument that could address my occasional craving, and one evening, while searching the internet for instruments from India, I came across CanJoe John playing a stirring, countrified instrumental version of "Over the Rainbow." I was struck by the ineffable musicality of the performance, given that he looked like he was playing a fishing pole. Mostly what I'd heard were jazz covers of the beloved song—lush, romantic—and I was surprised to be so swept up by the heavy-hearted *ting* coming from this mysterious instrument. Before long I was on the phone with John and ordering a custom canjoe for myself. When it arrived that Christmas — a gift for my wife to give to me — I began to navigate my way through "Over the Rainbow" with the halting uncertainty of a beginning chess player. Five years later it's just one of a handful of songs I can play, still in some piecemeal fashion, but this was all I really needed. So when I'm not playing my steel pan or my kalimbas or my udu drum or seated behind the drum kit, somewhere in the house I'm playing the same simple notes to the same song on the canjoe. In those moments, it occurs to me that my family would, given the choice, prefer that instead of musical instruments I collect shrunken heads.

Over the years I wondered about John and his exploits in musical reductionism. His was, in ambition and scale, on the opposite end of the spectrum from drummer Bill Allen, but in my early conversations with him, I learned that, as was true for Bill, tragedy and struggle were parts of his story. There were also echoes of Felix Rohner, in Switzerland, in CanJoe's story and in others producing their versions of the instrument. In John's Antebellum-style house, which sat on five acres, in a room where canjoes were huddled together like old golf clubs, John took me through the arc of his life in music.

He was born in Knoxville, the middle child between two brothers and two sisters. His father, who went by J.R., was an ophthalmologist — and a man of few words. His mother, June, who was Irish, loved to tell stories; John, who talks as fast as he plays, was much more like his mother. The records that filled the house came from his father's collection and included such country acts as Minnie Pearl, Tennessee Ernie Ford, Elvis, Patsy Kline, and Hank Williams. For relaxation, J.R. played an old Stella guitar from Sears and Roebuck and sang early country songs with the family gathered around.

John was drawn to the guitar, but in a way that foretold his musical future, "The bottom E string was the only string I could figure out how to play," he said.

After high school he attended the University of Tennessee; by his senior year he decided he was wasting his father's money and went into the navy and its hospital corpsman school. He was active duty for four years and then worked at Camp Lejeune as an ophthalmic medical technologist. Early into his stint, he took a continuing-education program in St. Paul, Minnesota, where he spotted a woman with long, dark hair—seductive, exuding a hippie vibe—walking into a hotel bar. John approached her, and they started up a conversation she wasn't much interested in. Her name was Sissy LeBlanc. She was, he gradually learned, down on her luck. She had a three-year-old daughter born out of wedlock that her parents, devout Catholics from whom she was estranged at the time, were raising back in Louisiana, and she was struggling to get by. At the bar she was thumbing through want ads. That night John took her to dinner at McDonald's. They met several times during his stay, and before John headed back he gave her fifty dollars and his phone number. Two weeks later Sissy called him and said, "Hey, man, I'm on my way." She took a bus down to Camp Lejeune, where they soon started living together.

They married about a year later, in 1979, when John was twenty-three. For a brief time they settled in Alcoa, Tennessee, and his father gave him his first fiddle when he was in late twenties, after he and Sissy had moved back to North Carolina. As John got better on the instrument, he assembled comparable musicians to play with—mostly picking their way through traditional bluegrass—who named themselves New River Grass. But music was still a side gig for John. He was making a six-figure income and drove a Mercedes.

In 1993 the physician he'd served under for seventeen years, Greg Cobb, died of cancer, which left John devastated; Cobb had looked after John, been a mentor to him. John and Sissy returned to Tennessee, choosing the Blountville-Bristol area because "it was the oven of all Old Time"—a term indicating some of the oldest American folk music recordings, which date back to the 1920s—"and traditional mountain music. That's the way it is today. You can't walk out the door and throw a cat without hitting a musician." (New River Grass carried on without him.) On his return, John set to establishing himself as an ophthalmic consultant, but soon he met the fiddler Ralph Blizzard, who inspired in him a new drive to learn Appalachian music and taught him the long-bow technique. With his family close by and music becoming a bigger part of his life, this new chapter should have been a happy one. Instead, within a year, and fifteen years into their marriage, Sissy was diagnosed with kidney cancer.

During that time, a friend of John's named Herschel Brown—a master woodcrafter and dulcimer maker—came across an object in a Boone, North Carolina, gift shop that would change not his life, but John's. It was called the uni-can. It featured one string across a plastic fret board that was molded in the same pattern of the diatonic scale of an Appalachian dulcimer and was outfitted with a dog-food can at one end. Brown didn't think much of the sound, but he was intrigued by the possibilities and went home to make a more substantial version, using a bigger dulcimer pattern and a piece of wood as the backing. He experimented with different kinds of cans to affect the sound, ultimately deciding that the thinner soda can worked best. He called his version of the instrument the Can Joe. When Herschel showed him the creation, John was equally intrigued—it was toylike in one way, but you could play it with serious intent. John didn't strum it by holding it on his lap like a dulcimer, though—he held it as if were a guitar, and the feel of it in his hands sealed a lifelong connection to the instrument right then. Herschel encouraged him to show it around and see what people thought of it.

The next day John shared it with his patients, who were equally smitten. He started carrying it around wherever he went, introducing it to musicians and nonmusicians alike. And he continued to probe the Can Joe's possibilities as a solo instrument.

"I was applying all the principles of the fiddle on the Can Joe," he said. That meant he learned how to slur notes with his finger positioning, which let him turn notes into flats, or mute notes. One of the biggest realizations, though, was an understanding that the Can Joe needed other instruments around it. The Can Joe was quiet, and it could sound thin, too. But with other instruments—a guitar, a banjo, a mandolin—it worked as an appealing alternative. Or, depending on your point of view, it was the runt of the litter.

As Sissy got sicker, John decided to quit work and take care of her full-time. He'd saved up money, but then their insurance was dropped, he said, due to complications with their move to Tennessee, and the money quickly began to drain. John set up a hospital bed for her on the first floor, and sitting by her side one day he asked, "Can I play the Can Joe?" Sissy had no interest in John's musical avocation, but on this day she replied, "If you play what I like." She requested gospel tunes. John started with "Amazing Grace" and carried on with "I'll Fly Away."

"You're getting pretty good on that thing, John," she told him.

"I'll never make it to the Grand Ole Opry on the fiddle," he said, "but maybe I can on the Can Joe." He was only making a joke, but Sissy replied: "Go for it, Can Joe John."

"Then this heat went through me," he told me. "And I said, 'Can Joe John.' Why not? I'm gonna make it to the Grand Ole Opry.'" They laughed, and he was grateful to see her smile for a change. But John's calling going forward, he said, "hit right then and there."

He called Herschel and said he wanted to learn how to make Can Joes and sell them. By that point Herschel had tracked down the maker of the uni-can, Rogers Magee, of Aiken, South Carolina, and, according to John, the two had struck a financial deal in which Herschel paid for the design patent for both the uni-can and the Can Joe—around ten thousand dollars—which lasted for fourteen years. (When the time came to renew it, Herschel was dead, and John didn't have the money, which, he believed, paved the way for imitators.) Herschel and John agreed that after John purchased the materials from him, all sales proceeds would stay with John. (He would later tweak the name when he began to market it himself.)

John had about as much experience in woodworking as he did throwing the javelin, but after borrowing tools from his father, he learned quickly. The original stash of wood was pine, already cut, already fretted, and as John got more comfortable, he began making canjoes from scratch himself. Sissy, however, wouldn't get to see how far he would take his new venture — or her role in it. She died a couple of months later, at the age of thirty-nine. John fell into a deep grief, losing so much weight that friends and family worried about his health. But eventually he was ready to put all his energy into the canjoe. As he saw it, he had a rare chance to take a new and novel instrument that anyone could learn to play and become its ambassador.

In 1994 he developed his website for ordering custom canjoes, an early entry into online music sales. (The most popular can? Cheerwine.) In those peak years, about 80 percent of John's yearly income came from canjoe sales. And the local marketing approach became all-encompassing. "Everywhere I went the canjoe was in my hand," John said. Canjoe sales were always brisker when he could demonstrate it for potential customers. Through his experience with New River Grass and playing in festivals he had gotten to know plenty of promoters in the industry, and he was aggressive in contacting them and getting in as a vendor. But just as important, "Every single event that I went to, bar none, put me on the stage for at least thirty minutes. I would recruit musicians real quick, get onstage, and say, 'Ladies and Gentlemen, I'm CanJoe John, and this is my band. They're known as MB4—because I ain't never played with them before.'" The puns, the corn pone humor, and storytelling quickly became part of his performance style. And his encounters with audiences confirmed what he long suspected: the canjoe had to be seen to be fully appreciated — an odd handicap for any musical instrument.

Through it all, he stayed keenly aware of his goal of getting to the Grand Ole Opry. "But I didn't know how to get there yet."

He continued to network relentlessly. And one musician in his orbit who would play a helpful role in his quest and, later, to hear John tell it, be detrimental, was a celebrated banjo player in the area. Tim White was one of the founders of the Mountain Music Museum, which was originally in Bristol before relocating to nearby Kingsport and was a key player in getting Congress to designate Bristol as "the Birthplace of Country Music," in 1998, because of the famed

Bristol Sessions, a series of recordings that essentially established country music as a bona fide genre of music. "He and I at first became friends," John said. "He loved the canjoe."

In 1995 White had helped put together a show at the Paramount Center for the Arts, in Bristol, and booked John to sell his canjoes in the lobby. On the bill, among other artists, was bluegrass legend Bill Monroe. Once John got set up, he slipped backstage, with a canjoe in hand, and the first person that saw him was Monroe. "He beelined right to me," John said. 'What is that?' I said, 'It's a canjoe, Mr. Monroe,' and I played him a Bill Monroe tune. 'Blue Moon of Kentucky.' And he looked around with the starry wide eyes and said, 'I want one.'" John went back to his table and grabbed a canjoe to present him. Mountain Dew can.

At the end of the show, Monroe and the rest of the evening's acts headed toward the stage for the finale, and John had gotten himself backstage again. "Bill Monroe does this number with his head, like 'Come on.' I look around. I'm the only one there, so I followed him." The group started up "Will the Circle Be Unbroken," the iconic Carter Family tune, and a couple of verses in, the various musicians took their last breaks of the night—in bluegrass, a break is the equivalent to a solo, though sometimes the musician just restates the song's main melody. Monroe dazzled the crowd one last time on his illustrious Gibson mandolin, then he turned to John, indicating for him to have at it on his canjoe. John was ready. "I got a huge applause," he told me. Monroe nodded at him in approval, and when the song was finished, John walked off the stage with the other musicians, giddy and dazed.

Backstage, John said, Monroe told him, "I want to get you on the Opry." But Monroe suffered a stroke the next year and died six months later. Still, that opportunity, the embodiment of a bluegrass dream, "gave me inspiration that if that one comes along, something else is going to come along."

At the Cherokee Bluegrass Festival, in the mountains of North Carolina the following year, John met Doc Watson, the folk and bluegrass legend. After an introduction, John handed his canjoe to him and watched Watson, who was blind, run his fingers up and down the neck, across the string. He was holding it backward, and John gently turned it around for him. "It didn't take him a skinny second to learn to play it," John said. And just like Bill Monroe, he wanted his own. John told him he'd make one for him, and Watson said that in a month he'd be performing at the Carter Fold—the concert venue in Hiltons, Virginia, that Janette Carter, the last surviving child of A. P. and Sara Carter of the Carter Family, helped create—and that John could give it to him there. John knew the Carter Fold well. Even as an attendee there he'd brought his canjoe, and one evening, as Janette was greeting visitors, she spotted the canjoe and had John play it on the spot. "Honey, we're putting you onstage," she told him, and that night she squeezed John in between acts. (He would play there in a similar capacity another ten or so occasions.)

When Watson arrived at the Carter Fold, John presented the canjoe to him backstage. Watson played "Black Mountain Rag" "like nobody's business," John said. Two days later, one of Watson's band members called John and said, "'CanJoe John, I'm gonna kill you, man.' I said, 'What for?' He said, 'Man, Doc Watson played 'Black Mountain Rag' from the time we left the Carter Fold all the way to Deep Gap [North Carolina]. We told him if he played it one more time we were throwing him and that thing out the window.'"

John found ways to keep getting on various stages in various festivals, and canjoe sales were strong. Now it was time to try the instrument in the studio. In 2000 he put out his first CD: *One String, One Can, One Man, and One Band*, made up of bluegrass classics, Americana and Old Time, and a couple of traditional tunes. He self-financed the project, which cost him thousands. It didn't sell well. Three years later he recorded a Christmas album, *An UnCanny Christmas*, but the commercial results weren't much different and gave further evidence that the canjoe was a performance instrument.

A year after Sissy died, John had married an artist and graphic designer named Catharine, from Charlotte, North Carolina. He was forty. The marriage was turbulent and short-lived, but before they separated, John said that one day Tim White, who in addition to being a banjoist was a visual artist, visited them at the house to ask Catharine if she would teach him graphic design on the computer. According to John, she said, "Yeah, that will be seventy-five-dollars-an-hour consultation fee." White, John said, suggested, "How about I trade you? I'll put your husband on stages all over Bristol in exchange for you teaching me." Catharine balked—and she said John "is an artist in his own right. He can do it without you." Then, John told me, White said, "Well, I'll just make sure he doesn't get on another stage in Bristol again."

"And he made good on that," John told me. White hosted a radio show in Bristol, and John said he began to refer to him and his "canjoke" on the air. "He's very powerful in this business, and he was able to maneuver a lot of negativity towards me."

(Tim White told me none of that was true. "That's not the way I operate and never have. I'm not powerful enough to keep him off stages in Bristol. I mean, I appreciate him thinking I had that much power, but I'm trying to help people. I'm the best friend local musicians have." As for the "can-joke" bit, he said, "My bosses at the radio station would have never tolerated me talking bad about him on the air.")

As John's momentum began to falter, he became aware that he wasn't the only one selling a stick, a string, and a can. In my time in Tennessee I witnessed several encounters in which someone told John they had one of his canjoes, only for John to figure out theirs had come from someone else. In New Hampshire, C.B. Gitty Crafter Supply, which owns the brand and website for the American Canjo Company, sold considerably more instruments than John—both as canjo kits and completed instruments. "This guy's outmaneuvering me by his position on search engines," John lamented. "He took the name, the idea that canjoe now relates to anything with a can. He's got the market right now, even though I've owned the website since 1994. I created the CanJoe Company website, created the CanJoe Company name, and licensed it. He's not very ethical, put it that way."

(I spoke to Ben Baker, who owns C.B. Gitty Crafter Supply, and he told me he'd heard all this from John before. "What he has done with it is really remarkable and amazing and commendable," he said. "If he would just drop this whole 'I-own-the-whole-thing-and-nobody-else-can-do-it bullshit,' we could all get along. You know, it's sad. People have been sticking cans on a stick long before the early 1990s." In fact, Baker sent me a picture from a magazine of an instrument that closely resembled the canjoe and was labeled "Canjo," dated 1971. But John, who said he's done more research on the subject than anyone, dismissed it as a piece of folk art and hotly disputes that the canjoe, or canjo, existed as a musical instrument before Herschel Brown created it.)

And then there was Canjo Joe. John said of him, "He's the one who took my head off the caricature"—John had an illustrator create an image of him around 1997, with his duster hat, sunglasses, and canjoe, that looked like a cross between R. Crumb's and Al Capp's Li'l Abner characters—"and put his own head in place. Said he'd never heard of me and got himself into Dollywood and was presenting himself as the world famous Canjo Joe—playing absolute garbage."

(When I reached Canjo Joe—Joe Cutshaw, who grew up in Newport, Tennessee, and now lived in Jessup, Georgia—sure enough, he told me he had never heard of John or his canjoe work until the day John called him with a few choice things to say. As for any similarity in his image versus John's, he told him, "John, I'm sorry—I'm not going to change the way I look." In his three years at Dollywood, he sold around eight thousand canjos, he figured. But after that conversation with John, he switched the name of the instrument to Georgia1Stringer; now he sold a few hundred each year. And like Ben Baker, Joe took exception to any idea that only John should be allowed to make the instrument. Different people make guitars, he pointed out. "If John feels threatened by me," he told me, "then I'm flattered.")

As getting gigs in Bristol became more rare, John found success in other places. There was a greater interest in John and the canjoe in Nashville, which he explained by stressing how different the scene there was from Bristol, with broader attitudes and interests amid a more diverse range of music and styles.

John's friend George Chestnut, a fiddle repairman from Nashville, knew John's dream was to get to the Grand Ole Opry, and in 2006 Chestnut called his friend Mike Snider, a banjoist and comedian who was a regular on the show. Snider had met John before and had once traded him some of his cassettes for a canjoe; he asked Chestnut how good a performer John really was. Chestnut, John said, told Snider, "He can play that thing as good as you can play that banjo." Snider agreed, but first he wanted to see John perform for himself. In three weeks he was going to be playing a show in Norris, Tennessee, and asked that John meet him there. When John arrived, the band was playing "Red Wing," an Indian love song that was first recorded in 1907. Snider acknowledged him as they played, and John jumped in, vamping the melody. After that, John said, Snider asked him, "CanJoe John, son, do you want to play the Opry?'"

Twelve years after assuring Sissy he was going to make it there, he was just a month away.

"I was so nervous the night before," John told me of his Opry debut. "My *fingers* were nervous." He kept asking himself, *How am I going to pull this off?*

That Saturday, hours before he went on, John went backstage, and he and Snider agreed they'd go with "Red Wing" for John's one-song performance. When it was finally his time, all his fear was suddenly gone. John walked out, and Snider announced to the crowd, "Hey, I got a guest right here standing beside me. This is his first time to play on the Grand Ole Opry." When he told them, "He's playing a can with a stick on it," that brought some tittering. "And it's got one string on it. And it's really a neat little instrument. He built it himself. And his name's CanJoe John — he's playing the canjoe here." The crowd laughed as if Snider had delivered a joke. "They ain't taking you serious, John, I can tell you already —" Off-mic, John said to him, "We're gonna have to show 'em." Snider said, "Yeahhh" and winked at him. Then Snider, who was playing mandolin on the song, proceeded to introduce the band and finished by saying — slowly, for comic emphasis — "And then on the can is John." Now the crowd was roaring. "We're going to let old John, CanJoe John kick us off on 'Red Wing' right here. Y'all listen close. You may"—and now Snider couldn't help but laugh himself—"you may have never heard nothing like this before."

Howls.

The Grand Ole Opry is, of course, a celebration of the traditional, so anything that flew in the face of that was ripe for ridicule. But when John launched the opening notes and the band joined in, the crowd understood this was no comedy act, but a high-end musician in the tradition of all the others who had come before him, and they cheered instantly. After John carried the first verse, the crowd lauded him again—perhaps as a mea culpa, but also for what he could pull off on this aberrant gizmo. The fiddler took the second break, sweeping through the melody like a windstorm. John came around again on the third, ricocheting off the highest notes, and the crowd whooped once more. At the end, the band stopped playing, save the guitarist, and John finished the song out with a final break. "Heeeeey!" Snider called out in delight.

It was all over in less than two minutes, and the crowd, John told me, leapt to their feet. He held the canjoe up in exultation—his as well as the instrument's—then turned and exited the stage.

Performing at the Opry was an inspiriting, thrilling event in John's life, but it didn't lead to bigger opportunities—there were no offers from Nashville labels, no coveted opening spots for established artists on tour, no reality-television pitches in which John moves to Hollywood and chases stardom with the canjoe. Still, he kept working his angles in promoting the canjoe however he could, and in 2012, he was ready for some company; he joined the long-established Notorious Nomadz Band as a full-time member. By the time I got to Tennessee, however, the Nomadz weren't wandering very often.

The band was still recovering from the loss of two members—drummer Travis Arend and guitarist Adam Graybeal, son of founding member Jim Graybeal. That left the Nomadz with three core members: Tony Malone, on guitar and vocals, had expertise in country, gospel, and rock; Jim, who split the lead vocals with Tony, mostly played electric bass and had a foundation in rock and blues; and John, who sang very little and played violin—only occasionally switching to the canjoe—favored bluegrass and Old Time. They amalgamated those disparate elements to form their unique variety of Americana.

Tony was in his early fifties, John in his sixties, and Jim in his early seventies, and they were past their days of playing bars. They preferred venues such as Moose lodges and veterans centers. "Most of our problem now is getting paid an appropriate rate," John explained. Some of the local clubs expected bands to play for up to four hours for a few hundred dollars, and that wasn't worthwhile for the Nomadz. The number of gigs, though, had dropped off significantly for the band. And the tough economy in Bristol didn't help matters.

When Jim, tall and lean, wearing a trim silver goatee and a boonie hat over shoulder-length hair, arrived, he wasn't carrying his electric bass but his dobro, which was a newer endeavor. Jim told me he had started the band when he was still in high school, in 1964. "We play the songs we like," he said. "We hope they like 'em, but if we don't have fun, we're not going to go back."

"So many out there that play have, quote, real jobs, so they don't care if they get paid," John said. "When we charge for a show, they say, 'Well, we can call somebody down the road and they'll come and do it for free.' So it's hard to compete with free."

When Tony, rounder than Jim and unshaven, arrived, they set up in John's living room. First they slid into "Red Wing," then some originals and other staples the band liked to fit in. They played the doleful "Faded Love," by Bob Wills, known as the King of Western Swing, then Bob Dylan's "You Ain't Going Nowhere."

There were a few canjoes lying on the table, and I asked Jim and Tony how the canjoe fit in with the band. "As far as I'm concerned, you need it every show," Tony said. "John has been picked on so much for that, like it's some kind of joke or something. I've seen it— you can just be with him and watch people look at it, and he'll start telling them about it, and they'll be like"—he made a snorting sound.

"That's why I like when he gets up and plays it because they find out it is a real instrument. It can be played on anything we play. That's when it blows their mind."

John remembered a time when maybe he blew too many minds. "I did the 'Star-Spangled Banner' at a festival in Bluff City, and I played what I called the 'Jimi Can-drix version,' with all the crunch, the grind, the sustain, and everything," he said. "Sounded a *lot* like Hendrix." That was his third appearance at the festival in a row, so Bluff City had clearly embraced the canjoe. But word got back to him that the town's mayor, who was in attendance and offended by John's rendition, told the director not to have him back.

Jim suggested they play a song sung by Tennessee Ernie Ford, who was from Bristol, but Tony ended up leading them through a relaxed take on Jimmie Rodgers's "Blue Yodel (T for Texas)" instead, with John's fiddle gliding smoothly over the twelve-bar blues structure like a man wiping the hood of a vintage car.

As rehearsal finished, they didn't know when they'd take the stage again, but they made loose plans to get together the following week. As musicians, as a band, all they could do was be ready when the call for a next gig came around.

Stephen Schoenecker, a recording engineer in Bristol, wouldn't be the first to record the canjoe, but the work he was about to do with John still put him in select company. For a while now Stephen had been thinking about 1927—and trying to draw inspiration from the man who single-handedly established Bristol as a musical haven. Ralph Peer, who was raised in Kansas City, started in the record business in 1909—originally for Columbia Phonograph Company, and later for the record label OKeh—and he would establish a career centered on what people wanted from music. Recorded music—and the business that served it—was still a fledging enterprise in the early part of the century, and labels were making new and important discoveries around the kinds of musical appetites consumers had. Peer had been particularly successful in finding audiences for music outside of the more established staples of the industry—"opera numbers," as a Victor catalog from 1925 referred to them, "sacred songs," and "dance" tunes—and tapping into those niche markets. Peer also became increasingly interested in "hillbilly" music. In 1927, no longer working for OKeh but contracted by Victor Records, Peer was looking for more southern sensations.

In July of that year, he and two fellow engineers created a make-shift studio in the Taylor-Christian Hat Company building—the company had recently closed—on the Tennessee side of Bristol. (The Tennessee-Virginia border cuts right down what had once been Bristol's Main Street.) Peer had communicated with numerous musical acts he'd been tipped off to before he arrived, and a couple of days in, he invited a reporter from the *Bristol News Bulletin* to witness the goings-on in the hope that an article would help get the word out. And it did. He recorded from July 25 to August 5, and over the course of those sessions he would document a broad range of music linked by the sound of the region but distinct in some key aspects: there were gospel songs, solo harmonica instrumentals, what could later be called country blues, traditional folk ballads, dance tunes, murder ballads. The nineteen acts—depending on how you quantify the lineups that had some of the same players—traveled to Bristol from other parts of Tennessee, Virginia, West Virginia, North Carolina, and Kentucky.

Two acts that recorded during those twelve days would shape not only the legacy of Bristol but country music itself. With his wife, Sara, and her cousin Maybelle, who was also Sara's sister-in-law, A. P. Carter drove up from Maces Spring, Virginia. They called themselves the Carter Family. They recorded on consecutive days, with Sara, who had just turned twenty-nine, playing the autoharp and singing lead; Maybelle, on guitar, was eighteen then and nearly twenty years younger than A.P., who was rather grim-faced and had ears as big as castanets. He could play a dandy fiddle, but he didn't use it for the sessions. What he did use was a trove of songs from Appalachia, secular and gospel, that he had rewritten or rearranged and that he and Sara had been performing for years—mostly at church events and local singing competitions.

In A.P.'s arrangements, Peer heard a regional music transcending place. Theirs were country voices about matters of country life—religious faith, love, and sorrow—but they were also outlining a blueprint for a new strain of popular music that would forever take its cues from these very recordings. The Carter Family's music would, in the coming decades, influence a range of artists, from Bill Monroe to Woody Guthrie to Johnny Cash and beyond.

If Peer had packed up and gone home when the Carters did, the Bristol sessions would still have been a pivotal event in music recording. But two days later another figure would show up whose impact would be no less seismic. Just shy of thirty, Jimmie Rodgers had spent a fair amount of his twenties earning money through railroad work, but he'd also been performing and chasing his dream of getting paid to sing songs for much of his life. What was distinctive about Rodgers, besides his emotive, forlorn voice, was his yodel. With Peer he recorded "The Soldier's Sweetheart" and "Sleep Baby Sleep"; in the lullaby, Rodgers's exquisite yodel rises above his guitar like smoke signals. Neither would prove to be a breakout song, though after Peer recorded him next, at the Victor studio in New Jersey, "Blue Yodel (T for Texas,") would make him a national star almost immediately. But his career was over just as abruptly when he died at 33 from complications of tuberculosis.

In 1928, Peer returned to Bristol for more sessions. He didn't make the extraordinary discoveries he had the previous year, but collectively the sessions would further shape the possibilities and the range of styles in country music and reveal the immense, broad-appeal musical talent in the deepest hollows of the South.

In his own career, Stephen Schoenecker had always been aware of that truth, and to commemorate the ninetieth anniversary of the fabled recordings, he'd decided to record area musicians for a kind of update. Once Stephen had the original vision for what could be, he contacted Jon McGlocklin of Virginia Ground, who, in addition to his performing and band-managing duties, ran a label called Middle Fork Records. McGlocklin agreed to put it out. "I love recording, and that's really where musical heritage is to me is in the recorded music," Stephen, in owlish glasses and a beard that spread to his chest, told me. He said the whole impetus was in wanting to know: what's the state of music ninety years later? "Does it have Appalachian influence? That's the core of it. It's also: What's local? What's going on?"

When McGlocklin and John were planning John's performance at the Celebrate Bristol! festival, McGlocklin told him about the project and encouraged him to be a part of it. John had a song he'd written a few years earlier that he thought could be right. He didn't think he was up to singing the lead, so he recorded a rough demo with another musician on vocals and sent it over. One Sunday evening, John showed up at Stephen's private studio to lay down the basic tracks.

For the session John brought his canjoe, a three-string instrument called the Strumstick, and an instrument called the chin cello—closer to the violin in appearance, but with the deeper range of the cello. John, who hadn't been in a studio in a couple of years, began unpacking his instruments in the airy, white-walled recording room. "When you wrote the song," Stephen asked him, "did you write it with the canjoe in your hand?"

"The canjoe is always in my hand," John said.

Stephen had a rhythm section lined up for the session, and after the introduction to Ric Burns on drums and Seth Jones on bass, John offered a quick preface to the canjoe, then ran through the song for them, singing the vocals. Ric got behind the drum kit and began to play a shuffling beat.

"Yeah, that's the beat I was going with," said Seth, and he began to work out an accompanying bass line. They went through the song with John on his Strumstick and also his chin cello.

"Hokie Karaoke: Are You Just Another Wannabe" takes the point of view of a bar patron observing someone giving a rocky karaoke performance.

> Was that you I heard last night trying to sing like Travis Tritt?
> If you coulda heard yourself you mighta been a hit
> But you were slurring all the words and singin' outta key
> Are you just another wannabe or another fool like me?

It featured a singsong melody and ended with an intentionally off-key clunker of a yodel, in keeping with the song's riff on thin talent, and perhaps a nod to Jimmie Rodgers. John's vocals were just north of croaky, but that didn't matter since another singer was due to record the true vocal. Stephen had John go in the booth to record a vocal guide, but he stumbled over the words in the first take. The second take was better, but he and Stephen agreed to try again. When John came in to listen to the third take, he couldn't help but show his pleasure in how he sounded. "I ain't no singer, but that's not intended to be perfect," he said.

Stephen recorded Ric's drums next, then Seth's bass, and now it was John's turn to record his instruments.

As John played, Seth told me that he started with piano at age five and later worked his way up through guitar and bass. Now he was the lead singer and bassist in a couple of bands. He was an ER nurse, and working twelve-hour shifts meant it was easier to arrange a gig or a session as they came up, since he had whole days free. Ric said he'd been playing drums since fifth grade. Like Seth, he played in a couple of local bands and did occasional session work, but his day job was director of the band at Castlewood High School in Castlewood, Virginia, where he'd just finished his sixteenth year.

When Stephen felt like he'd gotten what he needed from John, he brought him back in so that they could all listen to the track. Stephen had recorded the canjoe both in front of a mic and plugged in to the canjoe's pickup, then created a mix. "When you put the two together it's kind of pretty," he admitted.

As recording would go on over the next several months, Stephen would work with nearly forty artists for the project he was calling *1927 Jubilee: The New Bristol Sessions*, and he was pretty sure no one besides John had performed on an instrument that he or she had actually created. For Stephen, there was a satisfaction in that since it tapped into the same spirit of authenticity and originality of the first Bristol recordings. For John, there was the hope that once the song came out, it might, given the collection's ties to the landmark recordings and the attention it was likely to get, just possibly bring him back into the spotlight.

Every Friday night the Anderson Townhouse, a log cabin in Blountville built in the late 1700s, is the site of a jam session. Fiddler Ralph Blizzard established the weekly get-together here more than twenty years ago, and when you step inside, you have a choice to make: in one room you can hear bluegrass, the other Old Time and country. John showed up most every Friday, and he tended to head into the bluegrass room. On this night, he had brought his canjoe in addition to his fiddle, but here that was like bringing a peashooter to a gunfight.

Inside was a hardwood floor and a pale green wall with various newspaper clippings about some of the musicians who had walked through the door. There was a publicity picture of John, taken when his hair and beard were dark, holding his canjoe against a swirl of cans behind him.

On this evening, before the music got into high gear, the talk was over Rufus Thames's new guitar. "It's eighty years old," he told the group. "And I don't think I'll ever get one I'll like better. It's like the Holy Grail of guitars. It's never been refinished." Seated in a circle, the other bluegrass pickers—Clancy Mullins, on banjo, Ernie Shaffer on mandolin, Todd Markwalter on guitar—looked on admiringly. "It's got the original finish," he added.

Rufus told me that this wasn't the only place musicians got together to play. "There's jam sessions around here every night except for prayer meeting night—Wednesday—and Sunday night—church night. But Monday, Tuesday, Thursday, Friday, and Saturday somewhere in the Tri-Cities area there's jams going on."

And then they jumped into "Midnight on the Water," with John carrying the waltz's wistful melody before Ernie took a turn through it on mandolin, and then John delivering another break before the song ended. "The Girl I Left Behind Me," a centuries-old folk tune, came next, with violin, guitar, and mandolin jubilantly passing off the break to each other.

Justin Shaffer slipped into the circle—no relation to Ernie, except they both played the mandolin. And Doug Miller, on banjo, soon followed and found a seat in time for Rufus's singing of "Down the Road," with the assistance of a full-throated chorus. When that one ended, I could hear the musicians next door working through "Will the Circle Be Unbroken."

The group got bigger when Terri Thames, Rufus's wife, lugged in her standup bass before they commenced with "Three Men on a Mountain," with Terri's steady pulse giving the music new weight. John decided it was time to trot out the canjoe and said, "How about 'Red Wing' in G?" He stood up and picked off the opening notes he knew all too well, then the group fell in behind him. It was difficult for the canjoe to cut through the other instruments, though I'd never seen John strum harder. Ernie took a sunny break before Clancy kicked through it on banjo, then Doug had his say, mining the high notes at the bottom of the banjo neck. John took the last break and then comically flubbed the last note.

One of the musicians told John he'd once had a canjoe with a Spam can. It was hardly the first time John had heard that one. "I didn't make that," he said glumly. But before he put his canjoe away, he told them a story about one year at MerleFest, the North Carolina music festival celebrating "traditional plus" music and named for Doc Watson's son who died in a tractor accident. Earl Scruggs, the legendary bluegrass banjoist, told John of his canjoes, "Son, you're learning to play the banjo one string at a time!"

They jumped into an instrumental treatment of "Sally Ann" and followed that with "Blue Virginia Blues." Between songs, Rufus told me how the power of this music had originally seized him. He was raised in South Carolina and met a woman from Bristol who would be his first wife, and eventually moved up here. Before that, though, he was already on a path to Bristol. He had a friend who introduced him to artists such as bluegrass guitarist Tony Rice, Doc Watson, and the Carter Family. But for Rufus, who started playing guitar at nineteen, there was a bigger revelation to come. "I had a friend of mine give me a tape of the Stanley Brothers. I was driving down the highway—I popped it into the cassette—and I literally had to pull over to listen to their music. It struck me so—to listen to their harmonies and their singing and their guitar playing. They had a guy named George Shuffler doing all this cross-picking guitar playing, and I was on fire for it. That really sealed it. Then I came up here in the early 1990s, and I started going to the jam sessions in town." That first marriage ended, but he eventually met Terri here. They had their own collaboration.

Bill McCall, a local legend, walked in from the other room. Bill had been friends with the Carter Family and was a pallbearer at Sara Carter's funeral. Bill, his cheeks freshly shaven, wore a regal, white cowboy hat so wide it looked like it might flap away with him. His friend Tom Antenucci followed behind, clutching a case of Hohner harmonicas and a mandolin. Rufus insisted Bill play his new guitar, and they eased into "Dear Old Sunny South by the Sea," first recorded by Jimmie Rodgers. Bill offered a yodel, the high notes getting just enough liftoff (*yodeleee-hoo*) to pierce through the sea of strings around him. I could see why the other musicians had such affection for him: his yodeling let them glimpse, and briefly step into, a bygone era whose music they'd only listened to and read about.

For the second number, they played another Jimmie Rodgers tune, "Peach Pickin' Time in Georgia." Bill's voice and yodeling (*Di-odley e oh, oley e oh, oley*) were more potent this time. His yodels anchored the third selection, too—a song that everyone knew but no one could remember the title of. They played "The Wonderful City," originally recorded by Rodgers and Sara Carter, and when Bill yodeled, the notes suggested the plaintive wail of an old dog sure he'd been forgotten.

Tom selected a harmonica for a bluesy stomp through "Kansas City," which was certainly the only song of the night that had been recorded by Bill Haley and the Comets, Little Richard, the Beatles, James Brown, Peggy Lee, and Sammy Davis Jr., among countless others. Tom handled the lead vocals with a robust swagger, and he called out each musician by name to take a break, encouraging each of them to "take us to Kansas City!"

Before coming to Bristol, I'd never paid bluegrass much attention. Musically, I knew enough to separate it from country music, knew that Bill Monroe and Lester Flatts and Earl Scruggs were
spellbinders on their instruments in ways that had never been seen
since, but as I listened to the extraordinary level of improvisation
and musicianship—the interplay between guitar and banjo and fiddle and mandolin, followed all the unspoken communication that
darted back and forth, studied the musicians' ability to keep the
song barreling forward while staying out of each other's way, and
focused in on the economical but venturous storytelling in the playing, I felt gobsmacked. *This is prog!* I thought. Or maybe it was mountain prog. Ernie and Justin's dueling mandolins? That was like Yes's
Steve Howe and Rick Wakeman warring back and forth through
their intricate solos, like I'd seen them do so many times in concert.
Bill's angelic yodeling was as rarefied as Ian Anderson's flute solos.
Rufus wasn't stabbing his guitar with daggers like Keith Emerson,
of course, but when he stepped into his breaks, they were infused
with their own sense of melodic surprise and deep knowledge of the
song's harmonic fabric. Clancy's fingers hammering away on his
strings, John's bow sawing away on his fiddle. It was the show of instrument mastery I'd been drawn to my whole life, and I felt hum-
bled to be in a room of such master musicians as they dug into this
timeless, bracing music.

After "Kansas City," Bill and Tom were ready to call it a night,
and as they were leaving I followed them out onto the porch. Tom
had attended Harvard, and after law school he came down to these
parts to offer legal aid to those who worked in the coalfields. His wife
was a nurse practitioner and helped set up Lamaze classes for area
mothers-to-be. But, he said, "A lot of the reason we came down here
was because of the music."

Just a few months earlier, Bill, at age ninety-two, had married
for the second time—his bride, who was eighty-eight, was "an awful sweet little girl." He had been playing music all his life. "All them
fellas can play rings around me," he said, motioning back to the
bluegrass room, "but ain't none of them that likes it as much. When

I come along, everyone yodeled. I guess I was seven or eight years old — my uncle had one of those crank-it [phonograph players]. First time I ever heard Jimmie Rodgers made the hair on my arms stand up. He had so much feeling in his music. See, now I don't have the blues. He had the blues. Hank Williams — they had the blues."

I asked Bill, who had heard and been a part of so much traditional music from this region, if he had ever played with John and his canjoe. "Oh yeah," he said. "You know, it's just a tin can, but he gets music out of there." His preference, though, for the conventional sound embodied so much of what John and the canjoe were always up against: "his fiddle playing is what's always impressed me."

It was late, and Tom and Bill started toward Tom's car, but before they did Tom told me something to illustrate how deep the music went for them. "Bill and I will hop in our car, I'll pop in my iPod and kick in the Carter Family, and we'll sing harmonies all the way home. And you get home and you're lying in bed," and some nights, he said, the music *still* might not let you go.

It was the same for Bill. After a day of working on his farm and an evening of playing and singing, he could work his way into bed and know there was simply no room for sleep. "Sometimes an old song will go through my head all night," he said. It wasn't a complaint, and it was no kind of a curse. It was simply a way of living.

Because these days canjoe sales only added up to about 10 percent of John's income, and the gigs had never been harder to come by, he got by cobbling money from various sources: log cabin restoration; selling canned blackberries, venison jerky, logs, and recovered construction materials; canning friends' vegetables; carpentry work; restoring antique wood furniture; and doing fiddle repair. Also, every Saturday he hosted the six-hour Top Gun Mountain Matinee. He wasn't working as a traditional DJ, though he'd done that before. Instead, John brought in live music to fill the airwaves, usually securing three bands for two-hour slots each.

One activity that hadn't brought in any money, but reaped rewards of a different kind, was his fifteen years of playing hospitals and clinics. John and Sissy weren't able to have children, but as he embraced the name CanJoe John and the diverted life ahead of him, he began to focus on children anew, particularly those with cancer or other severe illnesses. After Sissy's death, he started to play regularly at various hospitals throughout Tennessee—for five years, he said, his appearances were nearly weekly. He'd walk through the halls carrying a bundle of instruments; he estimated he'd given away some fifteen hundred canjoes to sick children. When Niswonger Children's Hospital opened in nearby Johnson City, in 2009, John established relationships there, since the opportunity to travel shorter distances was a relief. But over time, as a new administration took over, he found its changing regulations and restrictions related to interactions with patients increasingly stifling. And as he began to struggle financially, giving away canjoes became too costly.

He'd gone a couple of years without playing in that setting, but he'd missed those experiences, so as a way to jump-start the routine, on a Friday morning he was back at the East Tennessee Children's Hospital, in Knoxville. He toured the pediatric hematology and oncology ward and played for children battling cancer or rare blood diseases, with one change this time: he was only going to make canjoes for those who expressed interest; then he'd have them shipped.

After John played for the last patient, we walked through the parking garage, and as we were about to get in my car he noticed, in the backseat of a minivan next to us, a boy and girl gawking at him. Immediately he took up "You Are My Sunshine"—at first, through the closed windows. "Awesome!" exclaimed the young mother, amused by this impromptu performance with the peculiar instrument. Then he played "Rocky Top," the unofficial fight song for the University of Tennessee. John told her and the children a little about the canjoe, mentioned his website. He asked if they were just visiting or here for an appointment, and the mother said the younger child was a patient. John then played "Over the Rainbow." Even as an instrumental it was hard, given the family's predicament, for me not to think about the song's wistful message of longing to be somewhere else (*Someday I'll wish upon a star / And wake up where the clouds are far behind me*). Earlier that morning he'd played it for a young teenager, the girl's head smooth and pale. It had been a frequent song for him at hospitals, since John focused on the affirming aspect of the lyrics: *And the dreams that you dare to dream / Really do come true.* He saw his life through that idea. Here in the parking lot, when he struck that last entrancing note, the mother clapped excitedly. He went on to tell them, "I'm the only canjoe picker in the world yet to make it to the Grand Old Opry."

For a while now I'd been turning over the fact that, despite the success of John's appearance at the Opry, they'd never invited him back. He didn't have an answer as to why that was, but he said part of the goal of getting on that stage, besides his promise to Sissy, had simply been to have that on his résumé so that it might open other doors. He told me he didn't care about not returning—he'd done it. But who wouldn't want to play the Grand Ole Opry again?

Maybe the venues in Bristol had seen the canjoe all they needed to, and maybe that's how the Grand Ole Opry folks considered it, too. Perhaps he was like a magician who had one great trick. But as the family in the van reminded me, so many people, here, everywhere, had never laid eyes on the canjoe, and they never failed to be fascinated by the very look of it and, more important, to be delighted by what he could do on it. With every scheduled show and off-the-cuff recital he was selling himself and the instrument, absolutely, but he was also selling something larger—the idea that you, anyone, could make music, too. The canjoe had proven to be John's salvation. There was no telling what it might be for others.

CHAPTER 8

Two for the Show

Sometimes I wonder if my friend Bob Funck's quest to make it as a musician would have turned out differently if his last name didn't have a *c* in it.

"Bob Funk Delivers on the Name with Latest Album"

"Singer-songwriter Brings the Funk on Tour"

Someone else, though, imagined his name another way when we were growing up and, at least once, spray-painted the *n* out on the Funcks' mailbox.

Bob's bedroom walls were covered with posters and album sleeves of Pink Floyd, Kansas, Rush, Black Sabbath, and Led Zeppelin, and his stereo was constantly on, so it wasn't lost on Bob's mother how much he loved music. None of the Funcks played an instrument, but when Bob was fifteen his mother gave him his first guitar, an acoustic, for Christmas. It was, he says, the most important gift he ever received. The following Christmas he got his first electric — a Memphis Les Paul copy. His progress as a player was swift. We knew a bass player named Sonny, and with me on drums and Bob on guitar, he decided we should be a band. He named us Ecuador. We had one rehearsal at my house, which Bob missed, that was most notable for how my mother looked on in horror as Sonny kept stepping out to our driveway to smoke.

The problem was, Bob had no natural singing voice. When you're just starting to play an instrument, you can make significant strides quickly. With singing you can learn better technique, develop better breathing skills, practice scales, but generally it's a much slower, more arduous process for someone whose voice is atonal. And despite all that work you still might be unable to sing with any pleasing effects. Bob was all throat. When he sang it sounded like a power tool. I was pretty sure that my sense of his voice and his were quite different. Bob knew it needed work, but only in the way you might be visibly disgusted by what a revolting mess your friend's apartment is, and your friend just mutters, "Yeah, I've been meaning to straighten up a little bit."

Still, by the time he entered college, Bob, who was two grades above me, was already writing his own songs and dreaming about a life in music — and how to find an audience. Most of his twenties, however, were about finding the Lord. At North Carolina State, Bob became a born-again Christian, and he quickly abandoned rock music. He gave all his albums away. When he picked up his guitar it was only to perform praise music at Bible study meetings. When I visited him once at his apartment, he sat on the couch and spoke in tongues.

Over time, an emptiness crept into his life of piety; without his music, Bob wasn't quite sure who he was anymore. He had gotten a graduate degree in recreation therapy, but he never worked in that field. Instead, he fanned through a myriad array of jobs. (He's been a carpenter, a social worker, a home-health inspector, a mediation counselor, a team-building coordinator for companies, a manager at a ropes course, a substitute teacher, a math tutor, and a bookkeeper

for an insecticide company. And that's just a partial list.) Around age
thirty he got back to his music. He didn't renounce God so much as
he cut the session short.

He formed a cover band, which lasted a few years, then a band
called Kernal Mustard, which played original material. After that it
was Bob Funck and the New World Heroes, World War Zero, then
several permutations of the Bob Funck Band. But in the competitive
musical environment of North Carolina's Triangle area — Raleigh,
Durham, and Chapel Hill — gigs were hard to come by, and Bob began concentrating on solo gigs to change up his strategy. Plus, his
focus was increasingly on his songwriting, and he believed the best
way for that to come through was to play for audiences by himself.
Most important, he undertook regular vocal training.

Throughout his forties Bob repeatedly tried to put out a CD, but
either the producer he had hooked up with could never get it finished
because of his day job, or musicians couldn't get away from their
families on weekends to finish up their parts. As hard as Bob was
working at his music career, nothing was panning out. He moved to
smaller and smaller apartments. He filed for bankruptcy. Bob never
married, despite the fact that he caught my wife's garter that I flung
into the crowd at our wedding, and there were few promising re-
ports from his dating life. He experienced severe depression.

To lower his expenses, he moved from Raleigh to Durham, eventually buying a camper that he parked on his friend Brian Hill's
property. He put out a crowd-sourcing plea for help to get dental
work done — he asked for $2,900; he got $400. Sometimes after we
talked by phone, I worried, given his bleak outlook, that there might
not be another conversation. Here was a man utterly committed to
making music in life, but it didn't seem as if life was going to allow
him to do that.

A few years ago, he had an inspiration. To showcase not only his
own talents but those of his musician friends, he came up with the
idea of NC Songsmiths. It would be a loose collective of individuals
who might be in bands or solo artists, but in a NC Songsmiths show

they'd be playing alone, songs presented as nakedly as possible to highlight the songwriting. The very name suggested that songwriters from North Carolina were their own precious commodity—like North Carolina pottery, North Carolina barbeque. For Bob, it meant new prospects.

As he closed in on fifty, he experienced his first stretch of real momentum. He and another guitarist and singer-songwriter in NC Songsmiths, Spencer Scholes, landed a gig in a Washington, DC, bar. Bob had almost never managed to play outside of North Carolina, and even the North Carolina gigs had become that much harder to come by. I'd gotten to see Bob perform only once before—with his cover band—but that night I was knocked out by his growth as a player, songwriter, and particularly as a singer. His voice had become notably stronger, more in control. More dynamic and textured. I mean, he hadn't turned into Van Morrison, but more than thirty years after he'd begun, he had transformed the voice he was given. "I'll never sing opera," he told me, "but I do have a voice that fits my music."

Onstage he exuded a fresh confidence, though almost none of the few people in the bar were paying attention. But I could see in Bob a renewed sense of joy, a promise I hadn't glimpsed before in his music—music that had become vital and honest and observant.

After landing some local gigs under the NC Songsmiths banner, Bob and fellow singer-songwriter (and landlord) Brian Hill put together a two-month, forty-gig tour across the country—in California, Nevada, Arizona, New Mexico, Texas, Florida, South Carolina. Their friend Kendra Warren joined them for many of the shows. These were house concerts, small clubs and pubs and cafes, mostly, a DIY tour that often consisted of pulling into town and trying to scare up a gig for that evening. They played for meals and tips, and there were frequent nights of musical synchronicity that ignited new connections. And there was the occasional gig, like the one in Plainview, Texas, that trapped seventy-five frustrated would-be dancers on the sidelines for two hours at a cowboy line-dancing club as Bob sang his song about governmental oversight.

I wanna know why elections are bought and sold
I wanna know and I wanna know now

For Bob that tour was a turning point. He barely made any money, but he was playing for new audiences nearly every night and often winning them over with a hard-earned perseverance. "Life is running out on me," he wrote me afterward. "If I want to leave any kind of meaningful impact on this world, it is going to be music."

When he got back home, he finally completed his first full CD — a collection of Americana-fueled songs he'd written called *Waitin' for the Rain*, by the Bob Funck Band, which he self-financed. The songs wrestled with familiar themes for Bob — love and longing, heartbreak and loneliness, hardship, but also new hints of perseverance. On the cover, he and the other three band members stood inside a large concrete pipe, four dudes with facial hair, a swirl of graffiti framing their somewhat stunned expressions. The low-fi image declared at least this much: if it did rain, the band would stay dry.

"I guess in a way, getting older started to become more of a motivator than a deterrent," Bob said. Now he had his music out there — if you knew to look for it, you could find it on iTunes, Spotify, bandcamp.com. But that was a big "if." No one outside the Triangle knew who Bob was. He was writing more songs than ever, and he had become a fluid, soulful guitarist who had no shortage of irresistible rock riffs and jazz-inflected fills, but that part of it almost didn't matter. He was trying to make it as a singer-songwriter, and no matter how strong the songs were or how adept his guitar work was, so much of it came down to his voice. The earliest instrument.

He decided the time had come for his first solo tour. Or "tour," depending on how you looked at it. He was fifty-one. And his whole life, as he saw it, had been building to this.

It began as a spreadsheet of possibilities — possible states, cities, clubs, or cafes; contacts, phone numbers, and e-mails. Since his latest job was working as a math tutor in the Durham public school system, his summer was free. At first, the skeletal information wasn't exactly auspicious. There were fields of empty spaces and cryptic notes about potential venues.

"left msg. for booking guy"

"No AC, not booking shows after July 15"

"Yes for party at store, I need to confirm exact date"

But in the weeks that followed, the spreadsheet began to bloom like a spring garden. From Washington to Maine. Under Bob's color coding system, green meant a gig was confirmed; yellow meant there was still a chance, orange a strong possibility but needing attention. Red meant no. Purple meant he had the day off. It all showed a new level of organization in Bob. Not everything was worked out by the time he drove to Washington for the first show, but there was still time to add gigs. He'd bought a 2001 Honda CRV with 169,000 miles to get him through. There was enough room in back for his tent, which he would rely on.

"Bob Funck's Sleep-out Tour!"

The Tree House Lounge showcased a variety of live music — jazz, folk, rock and roll, bluegrass. Colin Hoss, who did all the booking, was sitting on the steps watching the evening commuters pass by. Bob had sent him a few links to his songs from *Waitin' for the Rain*, and Colin agreed to give him a shot. Colin and his brother, Hammed, had owned the club for three and a half years; the nation's only university for the deaf — Gallaudet — was on the next block.

The brothers' family had fled Afghanistan during the Russian-Afghan war in 1982, and Colin and Hammed hadn't heard Western music until they moved to Washington, when they were fifteen and seventeen, respectively. One of the first bands the brothers heard was the Grateful Dead. They were hooked.

At fifty, Colin had booked forty thousand acts over his career, he estimated — or "one hundred and twenty bands per month for twenty-five years or whatever. You do the math." The math was close enough. He'd started at seventeen, and among those artists he'd worked with were Hootie and the Blowfish, Joan Osborne, and Dave Matthews as they were all starting out. ("I really never particularly liked his vocal," he said of Matthews, but "apparently it was the kind of voice that everybody wanted to hear because it doesn't sound like everybody else.")

Bob eventually joined us on the steps. The merciful temperature felt more like spring that evening, and as we watched people coming home from work, I pointed out to Colin that this was Bob's first night on his first solo tour—and that he had booked a string of shows up and down the East Coast.

"Road warrior, huh?" Colin said.

"Twenty-one days," Bob said, a slight smile divulging his pride in that.

Colin told Bob that he was splitting the night's show with another act, Twisted Tapestry, from Palm Beach Gardens, Florida. Twisted Tapestry arrived a few minutes later and, after introducing themselves—there was a keyboardist, singer, drummer, and, to our surprise, a harpist—began crossing back and forth between us to unload their gear.

One reason Colin had booked Bob, he said, was because he admired that Bob was pursuing his passion for playing despite his age. In their communications he had asked Bob if he had DC connections, by which he meant: *Do you have friends you can count on coming out?* Bob had replied that the number could be ten. (He'd get paid three dollars for each customer he brought in.) In this way, it was clear I had failed him, since neither my wife nor sons were willing to come. They had not fully recovered from hearing his four-song demo nearly ten years earlier.

Inside, a red velvet curtain hung behind the stage, with a modest bar situated at the back of the elliptical space. Hammed tended bar and worked the sound. As Twisted Tapestry set up, the keyboardist, Ali Sailer, played the opening piano intro to Styx's "Come Sail Away." There was no room for the harpist on the stage, and she positioned herself on the floor, which might have been problematic if there had been more than six people in the club.

"That keyboardist is cute," Bob said. He had lost thirty pounds in just a few months — he'd gone on a vigorous exercise routine, and his diet consisted mostly of salads now. The change had left him feeling more confident than he had in years.

Twisted Tapestry played a set of mostly covers while dishing out a bouncy brand of unselfconscious energy. The mix was a cultivated range of songs from four decades, including the Guns N' Roses staple "Sweet Child O' Mine," though as the harpist took on the anthemic guitar solo, the sensation was more like a band playing at a Renaissance festival. When their set was done, the band hustled to get its equipment off the stage. Ali and the singer stuck around for Bob's set. Ali told me the band was using its vacation days for this tour. She worked as a music therapist in a drug and alcohol addictions facility. The drummer, the only man in the group, worked at a skateboard park.

Bob set up a small suitcase to the side of the stage, and inside he had decorative lights and CDs of *Waitin' for the Rain* to sell. Not counting Bob, there were now just four of us in the club.

He started with "Bug," a playful, midtempo number whose a cappella chorus spoke to a one-sided love affair.

I was the boy with the hole in his heart
You were the girl who could tear it apart

His vocal was direct, amused. His eyes remained closed as he played, and he kept time by stomping his foot. As soon as Bob brought the song to a close, Hammed called out, "Fantastic! Very beautiful."

Bob launched into the raucous, country-tinged rocker "Lord Don't Leave Me Lonely." Sometimes solo guitarists carry the melody mostly through the vocal, and the guitar can be a dinky afterthought. But Bob is an aggressive strummer, and on this one the chord changes gushed under his blustering vocals. Next he played a song that wasn't on the album, an anti-establishment rant whose chief hallmark was not exactly subtlety: "Rise Up and Fight This Shit." His voice was grave, plaintive—the weight loss had clearly helped his range—but the verses *Come Muslim and orthodox Jew / Don't matter what you are / As long as you're not their sucker / Cuz it's gonna take all 99 percent of us to stop those motherfuckers* suddenly gave the room the feel of a Bernie Sanders rally.

He introduced a newer piece called "Three Black Buzzards" with an elaborate explanation about how breaking his collarbone in a bicycle accident had inspired the lyrics, but a minute into the story he was drowned out by a braying discourse among the remaining Twisted Tapestry members, so he began finger-picking the slight musical frame, and his voice dropped to a lower register. The words came through in a combination of singing and the style of stern talk one might use for a friend who has had one drink too many.

The set lasted forty-five minutes, and Bob had done an admirable job of shifting the dynamics within any given song—often letting the melody dissolve into a hush before pulling it back and having it roar back to life. The songs had sharp hooks, the choruses immediate and hummable. When I asked Hammed what he thought of Bob's performance, he said, "Fantastic. Really good, good material." He admired, too, that Bob had played all original tunes. Hammed had enjoyed Twisted Tapestry, but he wasn't impressed that they did so many cover tunes.

He had made almost nothing at the bar, but this didn't bother him. "We're here to do a show," Hammed said, and shrugged. He and Colin ran a business, yes, but what was most important to them was the music. "We came to America with no knowledge of English or the music, and to come here and create something like this?" he said. There was still a pronounced sense of wonder in his voice over how their lives had turned out. And he told Bob and me a story of how American music had woven itself into his and his brother's life so early.

"We ended up working at Andrews Air Force Base Officers Club. We were there for, like, two years. And plus, we were going to high school. That's how it started, actually: bartending and music. The main hall and all that stuff—that's where the music came from.

We used to work there every Friday and Saturday. And there was a guy — a colonel, right? He was a regular. And he used to always tell me: 'You need to put your heads up. Put your heads up, chins up.'" He did an impression of the colonel in a gruff, rough-throated voice, and even now it was clear the memory of the colonel hadn't lost its jolting effect on him.

It was time to close up for the night. Hammed owed Bob three dollars — but he paid him five and wished him well on his tour.

I hadn't eaten yet, so I had Bob drive behind me to a Burger King. As I was waiting for my food, I noticed that they were pumping in a bluesier style of music than you usually hear in a fast-food place — it wasn't the usual suspects such as Alanis Morissette, Aerosmith, or Bryan Adams. When we went downstairs, I was shocked to see it was coming from a live guitarist. A guy in a full gray beard and a grimy, crumpled baseball cap had a bundle of clothes with him in a crate on wheels, but he also had a small guitar amp and cradled an electric guitar as he sat in a booth. He was flicking out sparks of lead and coming back into a standard blues scale. He nodded toward us, and we nodded back.

When I asked Bob how he thought the show had gone, he pointed out that the remaining members of Twisted Tapestry had yakked throughout his set. "I've had that happen so often, it's just like, you roll with it," he said. "If I really am honest, deep down it's disappointing."

In the beginning years of playing solo gigs, he said, the crowd's indifference had been more common, but now, for every show like tonight and the competition against chatter, there were three or four more in which people were notably attentive. "There's also the gigs where nobody's there," he said. "It's just dead silence." He added that he played so much of his sets with his eyes closed that he didn't always know when people were getting up and leaving. Then, between songs, he'd open them again, and think, *Oh, OK.*

We talked about the weeks ahead, what he thought was at stake in this tour. "I know I'm older," he said. "And I wasted a lot of time when I was younger, when I could have really practiced and dug in more, like I'm doing now. But I didn't. If I had, what could have happened?"

We mulled that over as the homeless guitarist began to intone, though he didn't have a microphone, and his voice tucked itself in between the notes. And then it occurred to me that maybe we were just two more customers talking over his performance.

Bob's second gig was in the more bustling Georgetown area. The Vinyl Lounge was for those who wanted a drink before or after the show at the bigger room, Gypsy Sally's, which drew more nationally known acts.

"And if they like what they're hearing," David Ensor, who owned the place with his wife, explained to me, "maybe they buy a CD, maybe they start a conversation, maybe you make a fan for the next time you come through. So this is about pressing the flesh. You're right there"—he gestured toward the stage—"and people are right on top of you." He said the Vinyl Lounge tended to be Americana oriented. "That was the original idea for the *whole* place," he said, but he had come to see that "you can't make a living doing that." Thinking about how the original vision had evolved, he said, "I could turn this place into a dance club and make a freaking fortune overnight. So why do we do what we do? Because we're insane."

David, like the Hoss brothers, was a huge Deadhead, and in a long, rectangular section of the room he had framed portraits of the Grateful Dead members. David was a musician himself. He got his first guitar when he was fourteen, but he didn't devote himself to playing until he was twenty-five. Eventually he moved to Los Angeles in the hope of making it as an actor, but he found he had more fun hanging out with musicians. He formed his first band around 1988 and played the Sunset Strip and the Troubadour. When that band didn't work out, he formed another in 1989 under the name Silky Dave and played the same places. He had a friend at Capitol Records who passed around a demo David had made, but nothing ever developed, and he moved to New York in 1995. He kept writing but made a living through restaurant jobs until 2003, when, now in Washington, he started performing in Potbelly Sandwich Shops four to five days a week. Playing over the employees shouting "vanilla shake!" and "cup of broc!" was no ideal gig, but the constant playing sharpened his skills, and in 2008 he had saved enough to record his first full CD. He was in his late forties by then, and he gave it a prophetic title: *Building a Life.*

Soon after he met his wife, Karen, and they married in 2011. In 2013 they opened Gypsy Sally's. Because of the demands of family life and work, he had mostly put his own music on hold, aside from teaching a few lessons, which he said paid for his health insurance. But he was sure he would get back to his music one day. His experience as a struggling musician made one aspect of running a club "gratifying only half the time."

Sometimes your audiences "are morons," he said. "They're here for the party. They disrespect the bands and the performers, and I find it extremely frustrating." Recently at one of the Vinyl Lounge's open mic nights a performer let everyone know that he was live streaming his performance on his Facebook page. "I'm just like, can't it just be about the mic?" David said. "Does it have to be about how some dude in Outer Mongolia is going to see this on Facebook? Who gives a shit?" Just talking about these indignities got him worked up. "I defend that stage like a tiger. You will shut the fuck up or get the fuck out."

Unfortunately for Bob, David wasn't staying for tonight's show, and he was gone by the time Bob was getting oriented on stage—a platform with as much floor space as a service elevator. Behind him was a shelf of albums, which gave the spread a homey vibe; to one side of the stage was the original movie poster for the Bob Dylan documentary *Don't Look Back.*

He started off with "Nothing but Time for the Blues," a song that addresses despair more directly than any of his songs (*Well I've dragged around and I've hung my head / I've put myself down and I've wished myself dead*) and built around a vigorous verse and chorus, then a bridge that is almost a whisper. Tina, who was bartending mostly in the other room, stopped to watch. "He's got good energy," she said.

Just a handful of people were in the room, and Baptiste Bourgade, the bartender, listened thoughtfully. Baptiste, bearded and in a porkpie hat, was a percussionist from France; he'd toured in Germany and England in a band inspired by Led Zeppelin before moving here. He came to America for more touring opportunities. "I feel like people are more interested in music here," he told me. But he hadn't played many live gigs since arriving, and he was antsy to get back on the road.

With his eyes clinched tight, Bob shuffled and bobbed more energetically than he had the night before, and it was clear he was enjoying himself. After a couple songs, he said to the nearly empty room, "I'm cooking with gas. I don't know where everyone else is." Next was a bluesy, defiant romp called "Sell My Soul," with lyrics that speak to some of the situations Bob has known well—among them, life in a trailer. (*No job and no money / I'm reading into the future but maybe the writing's on the wall.*) He followed that with one of his most affecting songs, the tender ballad "Her Heart Is a Ruby Red," whose halting tempo is propelled by what feels like the musical distillation of heartbreak itself.

The eclectic mix and lively performances had made for a compelling set, but that began to be erased once he said, "This is for all our friends in DC. It's called 'Rise Up and Fight This Shit.'" It got no better with the tough-love harangue "Been a Long Night," when he sang:

> *So get your ass right*
> *You make your own luck*
> *You either gotta fight*
> *Or just don't give a fuck.*

Afterward he butchered a joke that Townes Van Zandt tells on *Live at the Old Quarter, Houston, Texas* about being too drunk to find his car. Behind the bar Baptiste's gentle smile was drooping.

The Vinyl Lounge was accumulating a few more callers, and a new group of four was carrying on an especially strident conversation directly in front of the stage. One man, his back turned to Bob and just a few feet away, was like a train agent announcing departure. Did he think Bob was a hologram?

Bob introduced the song "Big Smiles" by saying he hoped everyone had big smiles on their faces—a sentiment that felt painful, given the circumstances. The song follows a simpler chord pattern than most of his songs, but the vocal melody is carried by a staccato delivery that he sang in a rubbery, almost nasal pitch, which felt close to grating. But when it was over, the loud guy, who hadn't stopped blathering, turned quickly around and clapped gleefully, then stuffed a twenty-dollar bill in Bob's tip jar. Then another guy from the small group put a bill in as well.

Bob played "Three Black Buzzards," completing the story he'd abandoned the previous night. A younger woman broke away from her group to listen, then bought a CD—Bob's first sale of the tour. Her boyfriend put in twenty dollars, perhaps to show his alliance, and professed to like Bob's music very much.

When Bob finished the set and said good-bye to Baptiste, we stuck our heads in Gypsy Sally's on the way out, where the band Los Straitjackets had started up. Los Straitjackets, who had been around for more than twenty years, happen to wear Mexican wrestling masks—extravagant and sparkly—and in their navy blazers and tan turtlenecks they delivered a clean, if perfunctory style of modern surf rock. There were no vocals, and the mostly young crowd waggled and cheered each song, which seemed to me as distinct from one another as subway cars. It was clear the crowd was with them, though, and Bob and I admired the elegant tremolo of the lead guitarist, the loopy precision of the five musicians. But more than anything, we couldn't help but be fixated on their masks, which, under the lights, glistened like crushed diamonds.

Back at my house, where Bob was staying until his tour headed north, he said the night was at least a financial success—thirty dollars, plus a free meal and drinks. He felt that he'd been a little sloppy on some of the newer songs—and older songs that he hadn't played in a while, too. But he remained entirely encouraged. "By the end of the tour I'll be really tight."

A week later, we met up in Albany, New York, at the Ramada Inn. The sign out front read, on one side, "Best wishes Abraham & Elizabeth." On the other side, simply "sports team." In the days before, I called Bob to say I'd gotten hotel reservations for the next eight nights on the road, but based on online reviews of the places, some of these were low-rent stays where we might be jamming a chair in front of the door at night. But Bob was unfazed. "Dude, I've been sleeping in a tent for a week."

Once we'd checked in Bob said, "I know I'm pushing it, but I've got to hit the shower." He had not been able to shower, he said, since he had been at my house. In that time, he'd played five gigs. Nearby Schenectady had proven to be surprisingly fertile territory—tonight's gig was his second of three here. And he was looking at his longest show of the tour—more than two hours; he might have to throw in a few covers, play a couple of songs twice to make it through. When we got in his car, it smelled, predictably, like body odor.

We drove to Schenectady and pulled up at Stoney's Irish Grill, an Irish establishment. Inside, most everything was green—the carpet, the barstools, the tablecloths. There was an Irish flag—plaques of Irish sayings—but mostly I was struck that most of the people here having a quiet dinner appeared to be in their late fifties and older. I immediately wondered: is Bob going to sing that song about the motherfuckers?

There was also no obvious place where Bob, in shorts, a T-shirt, and sandals, was supposed to perform, but owner Mike Bennett, in a neatly trimmed beard and reading glasses around his neck, motioned right in front of him, across from the bar. Bob began to pull in his PA and equipment.

Mike said he tended to have live music a couple of times a week—traditional Irish music, jazz, singer-songwriter fare—and almost always it was a local act. But after Bob had gotten in touch and sent him some links, "It was different enough and unique enough that I thought, *What the heck?*" Mike told me. It was Saturday, but he said, "We're apt to have a pretty quiet night tonight. This is a slow time of year for me."

The regulars who came in and took a seat at the bar greeted Mike by name. *Hi, Cathy. Hi, Ken. Hi, Paul.* On TV the Yankees were playing the Giants; everyone was turned away from Bob. He strummed his guitar, and when he said he was ready to go, Mike said, "Not too loud in the beginning, OK? We have kind of a small crowd." In the opening notes of "Crushed into Smithereens," there were about ten people here, who responded to the early moments of live music with the quiet resignation of gas sufferers.

After a couple of numbers, Bob announced, "I'm on a twenty-one-day tour." And then he sprang into the roots rocker "Come On Down," which imagines the narrator surviving a flood by paddling to safety. He belted it with the cheer of someone glad to be singing and held the last note in a way he never could have ten years ago. Then he realized that he wasn't amplified yet. But in the small room no one was complaining.

He went on to play "California," a mellow ode to the good life out west. Overall he was singing with more restraint than he had shown at the Vinyl Lounge, which seemed to be a shrewd approach, given the crowd. "If you want to help a brother out," Bob said, and pointed out that he had CDs to sell. Then he played Johnny Cash's "Folsom Prison Blues." Mike occasionally whistled behind the bar to harmonize.

Bob eased into a tune called "1985," from the CD. "1985" benefits greatly from the three-part backing vocals that carry the song's infectious chorus, but as with all the songs from *Waitin' for the Rain*, he had to rethink the arrangements for playing solo. That year is right around the time Bob found religion, but the lyrics focus on a sixteen-year-old who has found his sense of purpose at the video arcade while trying to figure out where his life goes from there. Of all the songs written about the 1980s, it is surely the only one with a bridge that keeps repeating the line, *Asteroids, Missile Command,*

Space Invaders, and Pac-man. Cathy, at the end of the bar, elicited the most excitement yet when she won forty-two dollars from playing the lottery game Quick Draw.

In the second set he added a couple more covers — Paul Simon's "Me and Julio" and Tom Petty's "Last Dance with Mary Jane," flubbing the lyrics on the latter, but no one else seemed to notice. He had played his best songs in the first set, and now the second set was limping along. After he broke a string, a man named Bobby, in a tank top and jean shorts with his keys around his neck, took the occasion to make small talk with him. "I like your PA," Bobby said, giving it an inspection. "Yeah, you're all set." Bobby was a singer-songwriter himself and lived just around the corner. Bob seemed energized by the brief discussion, and when the set resumed, Bobby, sitting next to me, turned toward him and listened more carefully.

Bob uncorked the feisty "Sad," a song that might have too many words crammed into the main verse, but what makes it so charming is the juxtaposition of the sunny, swinging melody with the downbeat lyrics (*And that's when you poured your beer on my head / And that's when I told you I'd be better off dead*). Then came another new song called "Fuck It, Whatever," which struck me as a selection Mike and company might not appreciate since the chorus is a steady repeat of the title. Bob stretched the tone and pitch of his voice, and to me the song bordered on cheap novelty, a throwaway. But I could see that Bobby was into this one, too.

With time for just one more, Bob closed with the dramatic, rousing "Long Time," a meditation on life's difficulties, how the grind can wear you down. (*It's a game, it's a test, it's a dance / It's the end of the line, it's your one and only chance.*) It's in the key of D, and the chord progression goes D-A-G the first time, but the second time, Bob comes back to the root chord, which adds a nice a twist: D-A-D. The song doesn't have a bridge, but it manages to be hypnotic instead of repetitive. This was the third time I'd heard it, and already it seemed remarkable to me — the way it mounted to its blazing crescendo, Bob's voice pouring out as if he were on a sinking ship.

I wasn't alone in being swept up by the emotion in the performance. By this point, Bobby had turned around to face the bar again, but as the song ramped up, I saw that he was speaking to himself, or that's what I thought at first, but the more I watched him out of the corner of my eye, I saw that he was quietly singing along, harmonizing to a song he was hearing for the first time.

> *Been a long time, been a long time*
> *Chasing it down*

The chorus repeating, the words cascading over each other like waves. Bobby sang quietly but fervidly, as if it was a song he had loved his whole life.

Because we lived about a hundred yards apart, Bob and I never had actual sleepovers. But that night at the hotel, staying up late and tearing through snacks from the vending machine, we were like middle schoolers again, the way we laughed in our beds once we'd turned out the lights. Bob recounted the times he'd been caught sneaking out of his house, the lame excuses he offered his Dad when busted, and we reeled off the names of our fellow students we hadn't said out loud in decades. The teachers we had, the things they'd said that, for whatever reason, had etched themselves into our brains.

We remembered, too, the times we'd played music together, at his house, my house — a crude duet of guitar and drums. Two musicians trying to better understand their instruments and find syncopation, to create even a single moment that felt distinctive. To see what we could absorb and impart from each other, even as we were just in the earliest stages of learning.

We pieced together the time when we decided to walk to one of the X-rated drive-ins in town. Fayetteville is next to Fort Bragg, the second biggest military base in the country, which has always ushered in some decidedly tough elements to our city: strip clubs, prostitutes, not infrequent killings, all of which made for a darker backdrop to our childhood. As a young boy I'd opened the evening newspaper to the comics, and opposite "Beetle Bailey" and "B.C." were the ads for XXX fare playing at the drive-ins: "The Devil in Miss Jones," "Debbie Does Dallas," and "Insatiable." Black-and-white reproductions of movie posters featuring busty women with pouty mouths. After a while, I opened the paper only pretending to read the comics.

One Saturday night we'd let our parents know we'd be at each other's houses, then set off walking miles through residential neighborhoods, through a barren stretch of rock—a crater, really—named Kmart Canyon because it was behind a Kmart. We crossed hairy Bragg Boulevard as Trans Ams and bikers and vans with Vikings painted on the side charged across, then traipsed through a particularly unsavory warren of houses in disrepair, on to one particular house that someone, somehow had identified as having a backyard that, if you climbed over the fence, would give you access to the wooded area on one side of the enormous drive-in screen.

That night's movie was *The Seduction of Cindy*. What Bob and I remembered was that it was like watching giants having sex. We crouched in the woods and, despite our long and perilous pilgrimage, we stayed not much longer than ten minutes—we were more nervous than titillated—and began the long trek back home just as the skies opened up and rained on us like hammers driving nails. All these decades later, despite everything else that had happened—and hadn't happened—in our lives, those experiences we'd had together were no less meaningful to us now.

We finally drifted off to sleep. Then, at exactly three o'clock that morning, I was awakened to the most unmusical fanfare I would hear the entire tour: Bob was a vociferous snorer.

The next afternoon Bob called Gail Slavin to confirm his appearance at Geno's on the Avenue that evening. But Gail, who booked the music, said she thought Bob was coming by just to talk about the possibilities. Bob expressed his alarm, reminding her he had come up from North Carolina and that he was expecting the one hundred dollars they'd agreed to. Before they hung up they worked it out that he could play for tips, possibly dinner and drinks. And, Bob ventured, "Maybe depending on how it goes, you could take something out of the till?" That was left up in the air.

Inside the empty Geno's there was a foosball table, a jukebox, and a sign on the wall that said, "Time for a fuckin'." There was also a 3-D picture of a skeleton riding a motorcycle because, we soon understood, Geno's was a biker bar. After introductions, Bob and I ordered plates of barbecue as we watched a silent TV screen of women golfers lining up to putt. Outside, Gail smoked on the outside patio and regretted the confusion. "There was no advertising for it, nothing," she said. She had since reached one of the owners, who was putting a notice on Geno's Facebook page, but it was too late for that to make any difference.

With twenty minutes left until he was supposed to go on, Bob wondered if it was even worth it to set up. There were just six people at the bar, and it was hard to imagine the crowd would climb to even ten. When he asked Gail if he should go on, half hoping she would give him an out, she said, "I would, and if you play for an hour, hour and a half, and nothing happens, well . . ."

Bob got set up, and as soon as he commenced the two couples at the bar moved outside to the patio. Midway through the second song, one man got up to leave.

Afterward, Bob asked, "Is that too loud, Gayle?"

"It is a little loud," said Gayle, who had cranked up her own pealing amplitude once Bob had started. She resumed talking to Mark Ring, the lone customer.

Bob played "A Little Somethin' Somethin'," a tune about an aging boxer who's not yet done in the ring and whose main riff is so menacing a friend once said of it, "Dude, when you play that song I don't know if you're about to whip out a gun or your cock." Afterward, Bob asked, "Still too loud?"

"Yeah," said Gail.

When "Her Heart Is a Ruby Red" came and went, Bob and Gail had a further negotiation, and he turned it down even lower. Now I was the only one at the bar until one of the women came in from the patio to use the bathroom; on her way back she talked to Gail about the problem she was having both with her feet and her podiatrist.

"I'm going to sue this fucker," she said.

After a couple more songs, Mark Ring, who'd escaped to the patio for a while, reclaimed his stool as Bob played a majestic new song called "Chasm." It was built around a blues-country lick, followed by G, A major, and D chords before the lick came back around, with a quick, transitional riff that followed. After that, there was a walk down—a line that connects two chords whose roots are a third apart—which gave the song an almost lazy country turn. I'd heard it a few times now, and by this point I'd already found the song was constantly playing in my head. Lyrically, it's about life's leaps of faith (*You can put more gold in your wheelbarrow but you're probably gonna spill it / You can squash your dream 'til it splits the seams but you're never gonna kill it*), and when it finished Mark turned around toward Bob and called out, "Yeah! Nice song, nice song." Next he played the frisky "50 Bones," which is a takedown of an unnamed "you" who is guilty, seemingly, of corruption (*How many bribes have you taken? / How many debts have you paid to cover your ass today?*), and Mark chimed in again. "Yeah!" He turned to me and said, "He's awesome! I like his music."

As it turned out, Mark, bald-headed and sporting a walrus moustache, was trying to buy Geno's. He had a vision for how to bring in more people, and Bob was exactly the kind of performer he wanted. "I'd rather have him on, like, a Friday or Saturday—this place would be packed." He was changing the name of the place to "The Store." When a customer's wife called and said, "Where *are* you?" Mark explained, the customer could say, "Honey, I'm at the Store." That cleverness amused him. "I think it's a money maker."

He listened to Bob's "Sad," and said, "Yeah, this guy's awesome. I love his music."

Mark, who was a biker himself and drove a truck for the post office, was going to get the place all set up, then retire to Daytona Beach. He had two adult daughters who lived close by and could keep tabs on the place. And he'd let Gail run it. After another song, Mark turned to a man who had drifted in from the patio. "He plays good music, doesn't he?" The man, who hadn't paid Bob any attention, offered a masterful demonstration of the noncommittal nod.

There were no tips and no fee. All Bob had to show for the night was a plate of barbecue and beans and a few beers — and, depending on Mark's fortunes, an invitation to come back in the winter. So I was stunned when Bob said, on the drive home, that this had been the best show of the tour.

"I was in the zone," he said. "I think it's probably definitely one of the best shows, if not *the*. I definitely felt last night my guitar playing was off, and then tonight it was the exact opposite. I had control over everything I was doing, pretty much."

And the complete lack of attention, except from Mark Ring toward the end, didn't bother him? "Not at all. What happened tonight was almost more physical, and then that boosted my mental [energy], and then it was like some circular thing." He considered the strange spell of playing music, ultimately, for yourself. "It just gets better and better."

On the way to Portland, Maine, the next morning, we listened to some of the music that had so enthralled us in his bedroom when we were young: Yes, the jazz-fusion group Mahavishnu Orchestra, Santana. The sterling tone of Carlos Santana's guitar, his whistling sustain cutting through the percussive onslaught. We laughed over how deeply the sound of Santana's guitar captivated us, then and now.

Hearing all this music again with Bob, I could picture the sleeve of the live Kansas album *Two for the Show*, which Bob said was the first rock album to really have a big effect on him, taped on his wall. Steve Walsh, the singer, "looked like he was in gym class," I said. "He had his shirt off, he had the gym shorts, the sweat socks up to his knees."

"And he was ripped, too," Bob said.

He reviewed the LPs he had then — Jethro Tull's *Aqualung*, most of

Led Zeppelin's albums, the Who's *Meaty Beaty Big and Bouncy*, Rush's *All the World's a Stage*, Styx's *Paradise Theatre*, Blue Oyster Cult's *Some Enchanted Evening*, and Emerson, Lake and Palmer's *Welcome Back, My Friends, to the Show That Never Ends — Ladies and Gentlemen*. We remembered listening to "Stairway to Heaven" by rotating the album backward to hear the supposed Satanic messages the band had put in there — this was during the backward-masking hysteria of the early 1980s. Even Styx was supposedly a bunch of Satanists — in Greek mythology, Styx is both a deity and the river that separates earth and hell. (The news that the band behind "Babe" and "Lady" had been playing for the Prince of Darkness must have made for a confusing time for Christian warrior and Styx devotee Rick Santorum.)

Bob said that when he was a teenager he wanted to make it as a musician for the usual reasons — sex, drugs, money, fame. And then, when he became a born-again Christian, the dream "was pffft — gone." Now, he said, "I'm really doing it for the music. Just making music, good music, and hoping for the experience of having a real impact on people."

We stopped in Boston for the day, since he didn't have a gig that night. I showed him where I'd lived when I first moved here, then where Katherine and I had lived. We walked to Quincy Market, a tourist destination, but Bob had never been to Boston, and at one of the outdoor carts he bought a dark straw porkpie hat with a red band over the brim. He'd always wanted a hat like this, he said, but had never seen quite the right one. He put it on. Somehow the hat totally revamped him. Now he had the look of a musician on tour, hanging out on his day off.

As we circled through the Old Port neighborhood in Portland, in search of Andy's Old Port Pub, Bob was frustrated to not see any free parking. The public parking signs advertised ten dollars, which, as someone who works in Washington, struck me as a particularly good deal, but that was 20 percent of the fifty dollars he'd be making tonight, and he wasn't willing to spend that. After driving around for fifteen more minutes he found a space in a back alley. "Bam!" he said, decidedly pleased.

Out front, there was both a busker's sign announcing Bob's performance, just beneath the specials of the night, and a mini-poster of him on the front glass. In the picture, Bob is wearing sunglasses and a ski cap pulled over his brow. And frowning. Without his guitar in hand, it looked more like a Wanted poster from Crime Stoppers.

Inside Andy's the ceilings were high, with pictures of boats covering the walls, a sculpture of a mermaid above the bar. The performance space was in the front window, with stage lights overhead. Considering the general stir outside on Commercial Street, there was every reason to expect that Andy's would be a significant step up from the previous night. Gail Kent, one of the three waitresses, welcomed Bob warmly and took his order for dinner.

Andy's had live entertainment seven nights a week, Gail told me. After the show she or one of the other waitresses would record their impressions in a journal—how long the performance was, what the artist was like, how the crowd responded.

"How's everybody doing tonight?" Bob asked once he'd set up. The fact that there were seventeen diners and drinkers to even ask boded well. He was wearing his new hat and positioned himself on a stool. The first number was "Nothing but Time for the Blues," and his legs kicked out from underneath him. When he finished, he got more applause than he'd had the previous two nights combined. After a few songs, a man stuffed a bill in his tip bucket on the way out. "Thanks, man," Bob said, midsong. Another woman leaving gave him a thumbs-up and said, "Sounds good." By the time he got to "Ruby Red," though, the place was emptying out.

An hour in, Gail told me, "I always hate it when we have a talented musician and it's a dead night. This is a dead night."

Bob played "I Wanna Know," a fleet-strum workout that I'd remembered from his Washington gig because it was so different than anything he'd written—a societal rant on how badly we'd lost our way.

I wanna know why God is a Republican
I wanna know why we care about the Kardashians
I wanna know why we don't have universal health care
I wanna know and I wanna know now

That one got a few whoops. "That was a protest song, in case you didn't notice," he said. Then he turned to the plodding, overplayed Tom Petty hit "You Don't Know How It Feels," and a new frisson of excitement sparked through the room. Behind the bar Gail let out a hoot of approval and began to sway her head. Bart Gamache, sitting beside me in a Boston Bruins hat, began keeping time on the bar and singing along. To my ears, Bob had played a half-dozen songs that were more musically satisfying, but when the song came to an end he got the biggest hand of the night.

Since I'd noticed how Bart had perked up over the Tom Petty song, I asked him about his reaction. Bart said his favorite performers were singer-songwriters like James Taylor and Jim Croce. But "when I come to a place like this," he said, "I would prefer to hear more covers of things I know, rather than original music."

Do we really want new music at all? Are we just too gorged on the music we already know?

Most of us who've lived for some decades have a lifetime of music not only parked on our devices, but on CDs and albums and cassettes stacked away in the back of closets, and we have listened to it so often that our *mental* hard drives barely have room for any new music. I wasn't much of an exception to this. If you told me that I could never see another new movie, I'd be devastated, but if you told me I'd have to spend the rest of my days listening to the music I already know — and own — it would disappoint me, absolutely, but I could survive. I have so much music, and I love so much of it, and a lifetime of incessant listening has never dimmed my devotion to it. The list is endless: Wilson Pickett's "Hey Jude" with Duane Allman, Otis Redding's "Mr. Pitiful," the Bill Evans Trio's *Live at the Village Vanguard.* John Coltrane's "My Favorite Things." "Days" by the Kinks. "In a Silent Way" by Miles Davis. Yes's "Starship Trooper" and "My Funny Valentine" by Ben Webster. The music we know consoles us, even when other musicians are playing it, even playing it badly. But a new song from someone you've never heard of? It takes daring to really be open and listen to a new musician's offering. It requires generosity. We listen to musicians like Bob — if we listen at all — with skepticism. We think: *If I haven't ever heard of him, he can't be worth listening to.* Sometimes we simply resent new music.

Here we are now, entertain us

Not all the new music you could hear in bars or coffee shops on any given night anywhere in the world is worthwhile, of course. But every musician, every band you've ever loved started out, naturally, not being known. The Beatles playing clubs in Hamburg, Germany. Joni Mitchell playing her ukulele at a coffee house called the Depression in Alberta, Canada. Yes as one of the opening acts for Cream's final performance at Royal Albert Hall, before they'd recorded their first album. Those early performances were, for most everyone in those audiences, brand-new music, and maybe not all of it was electrifying. For those audiences, though, if they were truly attentive, they could see that there was something special happening, which demanded further, more careful listening.

Watching Bob perform that night, I couldn't help but think not that it was too late for him — I worried about that, yes, but that wasn't what I was thinking there at Andy's. Instead, I was thinking that maybe it was too late for the rest of us.

At least the waitresses were listening. "He's really talented," Gail said of Bob. "I just think he has a unique voice. I like a voice that's got a little bit of raw, scratchy kind of feel to it. And he's super into it, you know what I mean? Like when a guy closes his eyes, he's into it."

As Bob's set was winding down, more people started to come in, but they all worked their way to the back of the bar, and the conversations bubbled up loudly. He played a song called "Free (Waitin' for the Rain)," which is as manic and hard-charging as anything in his bag. The autobiographical observations speak to Bob's concessions about certain trying aspects of life—money troubles, for one—but they also address how you can cope with what drags you down.

> *Well it's all nice and pretty up in the big city*
> *And the bars are open into the next day*
> *But if you ain't got no money you're goin' home early anyway*
> *Well I gotta quit talkin' I gotta get walkin'*
> *My legs aren't as strong as they used to be*
> *And you don't need no money as long as your mind is free.*

Amber Allen, who had just started at Andy's, said Bob's music reminded her of Bob Dylan. "The best part about working here is you get to meet people, and then you get to say, 'Hey, I knew you when you were playing Andy's.'"

It was past 11 o'clock, and Bob was deep into the impassioned cry of "Long Time." Outside of Andy's, right next to the front door, there was a speaker to give passersby a sense of what they were missing, and now it carried Bob's last song of the night.

There was a steady breeze, and the music mixed in with the screech of the circling gulls. It drifted over Harbor Fish Market and the reeking crates at the end of the dock, drifting over Casco Bay and the twinkling lights across. From there, Casco connects to the Atlantic Ocean, and across the Atlantic Ocean Andreas Gerber, in Switzerland, who'd given me an afternoon of playing his hangs, had spent the day coleading a workshop called *The Music of Your Dreams* with musician David Gonzalez. There were thirty-five adults in the group, from conservatory-trained professionals to passionate amateurs, and they had broken out into three groups: songwriting, free improv, and groove-based improv. After dinner they gathered for a jam session that employed a wide variety of instruments and went well into the night.

Meanwhile, stateside, CanJoe John was in a jam session of his own with some musician friends in Tennessee. They wrote a song

called "Canjoe Can Blues" about a lonely can sitting on a shelf collecting dust and wishing it could become a canjoe.

Peter Frampton was nearing his performance of "Do You Feel
Like We Do" at the most unmusically named performance space in
the free world — Charlotte Metro Credit Union Amphitheatre. Yes
had just kicked off their summer tour in Lancaster, Pennsylvania,
the previous evening, but not at the baseball stadium where'd I'd
seen Frampton; on this tour they'd be playing exactly half of *Tales
from Topographic Oceans*. They were resting on this night and would
resume tomorrow at Ohio's State Fair, though by this point they
were without drummer Alan White as well, who was out of the
lineup as he recovered from back surgery. When they took the stage
the next night, only one member had played on all their great albums of the 1970s.

Bill Allen, in Maryland, had been resting at home for a couple
of hours after playing at his storage facility. Because of the day's
heat, he'd waited to go on in the late afternoon, and Spike, who had
since gotten a truck, had picked him up. The North Suburban Hammond Organ Society took the summers off, but Pig Destroyer's Blake
Harrison and J. R. Hayes were, improbably, at a Huey Lewis and the
News concert. It was a set that happened to feature five covers.

There are, of course, places where people go to hear new music. I'd
witnessed it in Baltimore, and in Portland that place wasn't far from
Andy's. Every Wednesday at the Dogfish Bar & Grille, downtown,
was open-mic night, and it was packed with people who wanted an
audience for their music and eager to support their fellow musicians — musicians still learning their strengths and limitations.

Bob was the featured artist on this Wednesday night, as was a
performer living in Utah whose real name was Columbia Jones but
who, inexplicably, went simply by Warren. The night's host was
Christine Rogers, and she introduced the first performer, Dan Knudsen; he wore a T-shirt that read, "Dogfish Open Mic Night Five Years
and Going Strong." Dan had the kind of quiet, restrained voice you
heard in *Sesame Street* sing-alongs, and his songs, too, were simple

musical parables. He performed a song called "Rain Falls Outside My Window," which was about just that.

When the rain falls
Quite often it brings me down
When the rain falls
Most of the time it brings me down
When the rain falls
It usually brings me down

Luckily for Dan, the skies had been clear all day.

"Here's another one from *Grass, Grain & Appleseeds*," he said afterward. In fact, Dan had recorded so many songs, you could purchase either *The Best of Dan Knudsen, 2000–2004* or, if you had that, *The Best of Dan Knudsen Volume II, 2005–2010*. His final song was "We All Make Mistakes," and when he was finished he told the crowd, "We all make mistakes. We don't die from them. Thank you, Dogfish. I'm going to be back here next Wednesday. See you then. Have an awesome week."

The next performer relayed an involved story about his wife being obsessed with Patrick Dempsey from *Grey's Anatomy*. And then he played a song about that.

Dogfish was smaller than Andy's, but the crowd was initially larger, and it was made up of as many friends of the performers as performers. The atmosphere was inspiring to Bob, but he got more animated when he heard the fourth act, Alex Millan, in dark-rimmed glasses and short dark hair. Before her first song, she announced that after ten years of playing open mics, she had, for the first time, booked studio time to produce her first full album. The crowd applauded approvingly. Then she played a song called "Free St." With its simple chord pattern and her disarmingly sincere voice, the effect was that the crowd quieted so that they could listen.

Every week I drink a little too much before I sing about my drinking
    problem,

And then I stumble back home to my private hell and say oh well
Is this the life I thought I would lead when I was fifteen?
Is this the life I always hoped I would lead?

She made the regret in those words both aching and pretty.

Her second song, which she had tentatively titled, "Drinking My Way through the Apocalypse," was similar in tempo and mood—and also in the intimacy and details of the lyrics—but no less commanding. When the applause subsided, Alex, who had a tattoo of an F-hole—the sound hole in some string instruments—said, "Any requests? Does anyone know anything about me?"

She had been writing songs since she was fourteen. When she was in fifth grade, Alex and her best friend, Heather, decided they should start a band. Heather would play guitar, with Alex on bass. Alex's parents were baffled when she told them she wanted an electric bass. How did she even know what an electric bass was, they wondered. Once she got it, the revelation was that she was naturally musical. Alex learned her parts on the songs she and Heather were covering—pop-punk songs, mostly, from bands such as Blink 182 and Green Day—so quickly that she would then show Heather the guitar parts. In addition to bass, Alex played saxophone in her school band.

Her band teacher in Hamden, Connecticut, Mr. Bottomley, also played bass, and he gave her lessons. He introduced her to the dexterous stylings of jazz fusion from the 1970s and 1980s, played her Jaco Pastorius, often referred to as the Jimi Hendrix of the electric bass. Pastorius's playing blew her mind. She read a biography of him when she was twelve; the book also focused on Pastorius's drug use and manic depression, but she was riveted. She studied other great bass players, too. Yes's Chris Squire was on her list.

She eventually got a guitar, and her parents began driving her to the open mics in town. Now 24, she'd landed in Portland just a year ago and soon found Dogfish. Though she'd always put most of her energies into the bass, in the last year she'd barely touched it, focusing more on her guitar and singing, her writing.

After a song called "Commercial St.," which followed the same verse-chorus-verse approach but was more melancholy and featured more complex chords (*It's not weird when you come home at two and I'm still up smoking by the windowsill*), Christine walked to the microphone, applauding. "Thank you, Alex," she said. "That was awesome. I love your songs because you've always got that one line that's so beautiful."

Alex, who was putting her guitar back in its case by the bar, called out, "One day it will be *all* the lines."

Next was Erin Fitzpatrick, who performed under the name Spinning Jennifer. With her tiny frame, hair in a ponytail, black T-shirt, baggie jean shorts, and tennis shoes, she looked like a girl who had snuck out from her parents' house. She announced that she was going to play songs she'd written in the past two weeks—and that she was still working them out. In her arms the guitar looked as big as a trunk, but she strummed vigorously. She played a song called "The Toothbrush," which told the story of a relationship gone bad—a toothbrush bought for a lover, eventually thrown away. Her voice ranged from a sedate whisper to a spritely yelp as she sang:

Who thought I'd find autonomy in a dentally hygienic device?
Who thought I'd sing about a toothbrush? It's really kind of nice.

She had a punkish, talk-singing approach to her songs, an *enfant terrible* who had a voice that would also fit right in on Broadway. Erin mentioned that she, too, was working on an album.

Like Alex, Erin was still new to Portland, having moved here in November. She grew up just outside New York City, and she missed being harassed as she walked the city streets.

She started first with the violin, around age seven. She asked for an electric guitar when she was nine and has been playing ever since. She got involved in musical theater, and she began recording herself playing her own songs when she was in middle school. During her time at Bowdoin College, she formed a band called the Navel Gazers with students who had no experience with musical instruments. She did her honors project on activism through feminist punk.

Erin liked her music to make people feel uncomfortable — in part because she felt as though some of her experiences, like being queer, didn't get enough attention in the more traditional open-mic situations, and she liked to see herself as disruptive. She didn't love the open-mic experience, exactly. She relied on a more shifting set of moods in her songs, and she knew that was different from most performers. She wanted to stand out. And every two or three weeks she made it to Dogfish to play the newest songs she'd written to test how they went over.

To Erin, also twenty-four, her onstage persona was an overemphasized version of herself. She thought she might return to school in a couple of years to study punk theory. If she didn't end up as a performer who recorded albums and toured the country, at least she saw her herself playing her songs for her students. For now, she was looking to pull a band together to record her first album. She'd talked to Alex about playing the bass.

Next up was Warren, who delivered an assured, thoughtful set while additionally playing a bass drum and sometimes a harmonica. His voice was as soothing as a warm drink, and his songs came the closest to the polished oeuvre of singer-songwriters that everyone in the room knew and had studied, yet the crowd paid less attention to him. Perhaps because he wasn't a regular. Bob, though, who listened to Warren's set intensely, standing just a few feet in front of him, came over to tell me, "This is the kind of vibe I like, dude."

When Bob's time came — he had the hat on and had taken it off only to sleep and shower — he put on his sunglasses, which had the ill-advised, affected look of someone playing putt-putt in a visor and golfing gloves. His performance of "Nothing but Time for the Blues" struck me as too forceful, his voice bending in extremes. By the end of the song he was practically shouting.

He performed "Chasm" over a network of table conversations, and the vocals on "Lord Don't Leave Me Lonely" got back to that edge of being unhinged, though the guitar work was dazzling. By now the crowd was starting to winnow; still, at the end of each song he was getting more applause than he had at most of the other shows. And then he played "Three Black Buzzards," which he introduced as a "flood ballad"; the song unspools the story of a calamitous flood, and it puts more emphasis on the narrative than the melody, but at Dogfish no one seemed to much want to hear a flood ballad, and it sapped his momentum.

He played "Long Time" earlier than usual, but by then the chatter had grown unruly, and the Portland musicians were tuning him out. The aggressive rhythm of "Somethin' Somethin'" perked some ears, but when he finished that, Christine, who had perched herself on a stool in front of the performers, let him know that it was 9:30 and his set was done.

A full band with three guitarists called 13 Scotland Rd. crammed the space. Delivering a rootsy, soul-flavored set and alternating between three singers, one of whom was blind, they mesmerized the room. "I may not even be the best one here," Bob said when they finished. He wasn't bitter, but as one of the two featured acts, he found the performers' range of talent sobering.

When the last act finished — with a seductive reading of "Killing Me Softly" — the staff started cleaning up. On the way home, Bob and I talked about how many notable songs we'd heard, how many formidable voices. "There's a lot of talent in every city, in every town," Bob said. "And it's good every week."

We considered all the singer-songwriters throughout the country, the world, that no one knew, and all the estimable songs that, ultimately, no one would ever hear. Some of them would get heard in open mics like Dogfish's, but so few would make it on the radio, or get recorded, or if they did get recorded, chances were you wouldn't come across them. On iTunes, Spotify, on all the other music-streaming services, it was a sea of songs whose depths nobody could ever fully reach. Who would even try?

Rock Harbor Pub and Brewery hosted live music a couple times a week, on average, and often the music consisted of cover tunes. On the outside of the U-shaped bar, in a dim spot under a TV tuned to ESPN, he began by saying, "My name's Bob Funck. I'm from North Carolina." It would be thirty minutes in before anyone thought to applaud.

But by that point Bob had already found a way to cope. "Thank you so much," he said a few songs in, when yet another last note hung over the din. At the bar drinkers carried on like a contentious session of British Parliament. Later, as the apathy continued, Bob told them, "Wow. You guys are tremendous."

Soon after, a guy got up from his stool and asked Bob if he knew any Waylon Jennings. Bob didn't, so the requester asked if he knew any James Taylor. The guy's friend joined them and wondered if Bob could play something by Neil Young. Bob, resigned to the night's fortunes, answered them both with the lesser-known "Traffic Jam" and "Vampire Blues," respectively. Neither of the two patrons seemed to understand that Bob had, in fact, honored their requests.

As the set went on, and despite the crowd's total impassiveness, it occurred to me that Bob had played his best show so far. His voice was unwavering and sure; he held notes for longer, pushing beyond his usual register, testing new harmonies. But by that point his transformation into apparition was complete. "You guys are too much," he said after another song avoided any notice. "I'm overwhelmed."

Even Tom Petty's "You Don't Know How It Feels" drew a blank. Afterward, Bob put his hands together, as if in prayer, bowed slightly, and offered this Indian greeting: "Namaste." *The divine light in me honors the divine light in you.*

When he played "Fuck It, Whatever" it was the first time it felt entirely right to me. He let loose on the rousing "Sad" as if it were an anthem of supreme joy, bobbing wildly as the three hours drained away. After that he announced, "This is the most miraculous evening I've ever had in my life."

Then he turned to "Long Time" and played it the best I'd heard. The outro fluttered for couple of minutes, Bob's passionate howl landing directly on the necks of the bar patrons ten feet in front

of him. When he struck the last chord, hitting it like a man chop-
ping a board, he took a long scan of the room, then looked at me and
pumped his arm in mock triumph. But maybe there was nothing
mock about it. He might have just played the best set of his life.

When he joined me at the bar, he couldn't suppress a roguish smile. "There was a switch that was flipped," he said. "Well, it
helped to go outside and smoke a little weed, I'll be honest." To my
surprise, this had been a habit, he told me, about every other show.
"The first set, I thought that I was good. But I wasn't really down
deep — I wasn't digging deep. I was letting myself be distracted by all
the people talking and all the backs turned, you know? Like, what a
horrible layout. Like, I should be there." He pointed to the midspot
of the bar. "No, I should be right here," he said and indicated behind
the bar, which everyone was facing. "People don't want music here,
or I suck. It's one or the other. So how do you test that? You don't
suck. You kick mother-fucking ass. And that's what happened."

He laughed — at what he had just endured and how he'd dealt
with it. And also at what he had accomplished musically. The whole
night, with all the feigned gratitude he'd expressed, the crowd's tuning him out completely, was "an experiment in social psychology."
He laughed some more. "Yeah, that was fun."

The next day we headed for Bangor, where Pete Hansen and his wife,
Annie Gamber, originally friends of Brian Hill's and now friends
of Bob's, were throwing a party, with Bob as the entertainment. He
looked forward to a different king of gig — more genial, more comfortable.

Pete had a little ministage on wheels he could roll anywhere in
his extensive yard, and when he got it in place he set up some LED
lighting in a potted plant in front. Pete knew all about lighting: he
had designed lighting systems for bands such as the Brian Setzer
Trio and Air Supply and had worked once for Radiohead, when they
performed at the Roseland Ballroom in New York. He had worked
various clubs and shows in Boston, too.

Pete, bearded and rangy in his early forties, explained that the lighting crew is the first in for a show and the last out. "So there's really not a lot of sleep going on," he said as he got the grill going. "So you make up for that by just constant partying." He emitted a machine-gun cackle.

He'd traveled all around the world in those years and had a lot of glorious memories. So why did he get out, I asked. I was sitting on one of the many chairs in the yard that Pete had made for the thrift store he and Annie owned. The back and cushion of the chairs were constructed entirely of old cassette tapes—Culture Club, Phil Collins, Pat Benatar. They were surprisingly comfortable.

Pete answered by telling me about a guy who did sound for the Brian Setzer Trio that everyone called Point Five. "He was Point Five because he was short," he said. "I was in my late twenties, early twenties, partying, traveling the world, having a great time, meeting women, this, that, and the other. Freshly separated." He said Point Five was fifty-five or sixty then, and he hung out with the much younger crew in all its shenanigans. For Pete, Point Five was the Ghost of Christmas Future, and Pete didn't want a similar fate. So he quit and got on with the next stage of his professional life: building helicopters.

Before Bob performed, Pete's father-in-law, Allen, took Bob's guitar for a half-dozen songs, belting out some classics from his era—including the Turtles' "So Happy Together" and "Gloria" by Van Morrison's Them. After Allen performed, Pete's mother-in-law, Terry Lynn, got up and performed an admirable rendition of the Janis Joplin a cappella gem "Mercedes Benz."

Bob was nursing a cold by the time he climbed onto the stage, and the effect on his voice was clear from the beginning. High notes were out of reach, and he bobbed and weaved his way through each song's vocal challenges like a man in an obstacle course. After each song he calculated what he could get by with and what he couldn't possibly attempt.

"Can you play any Eagles?" asked Danny, who lived across the street.

"No."

"Can you play 'Stairway to Heaven'?" Danny asked.

"I would never play that," Bob said, but realizing he'd been curt, he said, more softly, "Even if I knew it—I used to. It was the first song I ever learned, to be honest."

Danny looked forlorn. "You could play the guitar part," he said. "You don't have to sing it."

Now it was getting a little sticky. "How about Tom Petty?" Bob said. "You guys like Tom Petty?"

"I *like* Tom Petty," Danny said. "How about 'Won't Back Down?'"

"I don't play a lot of covers, but I could probably pull this one off." He then launched into "You Don't Know How It Feels" and made it look like spontaneous. When that finished, the small crowd responded with a willing cheer. Bob had struggled long enough, though, and announced he'd play just one more. "This is my newest song—it's called 'Long Time.'" What he couldn't deliver in voice, he made up with in new fanciful licks around the song's main verse. When the outro came, it was rougher, more agonized. In some ways, it sounded the way it might have ten years ago, but the musicality of his vocals wasn't entirely lost.

After the last chord hung in the night air, Danny broke the silence. "*Nice!*"

"That was fucking awesome," Pete said.

Bob joined the group, and Danny worked his way into the chair next to him to tell him, "I'm just a nobody, a carpenter from Maine, but I thought you were phenomenal."

Bob visited with Pete and Annie for a while longer, and they gave him sixty dollars for playing; in tips he'd made another forty. And he'd been able to catch up with a couple of friends and make a few new fans. Too, he'd had his anti-depression medicine, which wasn't ready when he left for the tour, shipped to Pete and Annie's. Back in the spring, even as he was planning the tour, Bob was having suicidal thoughts—he'd just told me this earlier that day. I wasn't entirely surprised because that had been a nagging concern I'd had about Bob for a long time now, but I felt particularly crestfallen to learn that he had been both planning his first tour and contemplating not actually being around for it. He had seen a therapist here and there over the years but nothing had much helped; when he saw a psychiatrist this time he got a prescription for Zoloft. And it had made a prominent difference.

At least, that's what he said.

The next morning, over breakfast at a Howard Johnson's in Bangor, where he was playing a place called Rock City Café later that evening, Bob and I talked about the literal costs of pursuing his dream. He was remembering when his good friend from high school, Scott, who lived in Atlanta, had invited him down about five years ago to help renovate a rental home he'd bought. Bob was on unemployment at the time, and Scott, who had enjoyed a successful career in global shipping, was paying him for his time. At some point Bob was talking about his music—and the hardships that went along with it.

"Dude, you've just got to let that go," Scott told him. That stung Bob, and it was clear the hurt of that had never really gone away. The lyrics for "Sell My Soul" were based on that conversation, he said.

> But some people are so funny
> They tell you which road you should travel on when they don't really
>   know you at all
> I'm livin' in a trailer on the outskirts of this dirty town
> When the roof decides to fail or when the walls proceed to come crumblin'
>   down
> Bury me with my guitar, let me cradle her down in the cold hard ground

He remembered, too, a similar comment from his mother, but this one had cut deeper. A few years before she died, she and Bob were talking about his trying to break through in the Durham music scene. He reminded her that she was the one who had put him on the path in the first place. "I told her, you know, 'You gave me my first guitar.' And she said, 'I kind of wish I hadn't done that.'"

But she had misunderstood the consequences of that gift—as a mother, she had concluded that she'd inadvertently put him on a kind of ruinous course for his life. Bob saw the gift in the opposite light. Despite all the immense struggles, the bad luck, the heartbreak, the countless hours of playing to so few or an indifferent crowd, that guitar she picked out for him had given him everything he had. Through his music he'd found ways to express himself, to share observations about life and love and what it meant to hang on. And he believed in his music in ways that let him play those songs fearlessly. He wasn't going to end up releasing a legendary live album or make it into the Rock and Roll Hall of Fame, or play a historic stage or be a main draw at a major festival. But that didn't take away from what that guitar had opened up for him — or the gratifying memories it had produced. He was a musician.

ON THE RECORD

Everything that anyone in this book is quoted as saying is what he or she said. However, there were some quotes that I shortened. At the *Washington Post*, where I work, we indicate when a quote has been abbreviated by using an ellipsis. And I started the book off that way, but I came to feel that those ellipses were a visual distraction to the reader and took them out. The words or phrases or sentences I cut in no way altered the meaning of the quote or took away any of the intended context.

LINER NOTES

Carlo Rotella and Lynn Medford were the George Martin and Phil Spector of this book. Three of these chapters have their origins in stories I originally wrote for Lynn at the *Washington Post Magazine*, and the rest of the book she advised me on like the sterling editor and dear friend that she is. It was Carlo who told me that I was writing a book in the first place, based on those stories — an idea I would have never hit on myself. When I came to see the possibilities, his generous and pitch-perfect counsel at every stage of the process was invaluable.

I thank my editor (and fellow drummer) at the University of Chicago Press, Doug Mitchell, for his commitment to this project, and also for his keen musical insights along the way. Also at the press I'm grateful to Leslie Keros, Susan Karani, and Kyle Adam Wagner for their great care of this book — and me.

Tom Shroder officially put me on the path to this book when he embraced my idea of going to Maryland Deathfest, in 2009, and exploring the world of death metal for the *Washington Post Magazine*. His excitement for and expert handling of that story began the opening notes of this long search.

For the writing of this book, I talked to and spent time with more musicians than I can name here, but I want to especially thank the following for sharing their stories so fully and openly with me: Peter Frampton, Aidan Mullen, Andreas Gerber, Hansruedi Reist, Walter Bachmann, Lorenz Mühlemann, Markus Plattner, Bill Allen, Mike Redmond, Eric Larson, Elizabeth Larson, Bill Lambert, Ginny Pratt, Miriam Linna, Jon Anderson, Chris Squire, Scott Hull, J. R. Hayes, Blake Harrison, Brian Harvey, John VanArsdall, Rufus Thames, Aaron Foster, Tim White, Alex Millan, Erin Fitzpatrick, David Ensor, and Bob Funck.

In addition, I want to thank Lisa Jenkins, Christian Billau, John Brabender, and Margaret Thresher for their kind assistance in making three of the chapters possible, and also David Morketter, Ben Ratliff, Bob Heil, Elaine Hayes, Jessica Dacey, Thomas Burkhalter, Theresa Beyer, Tom Günzburger, Alexa Horn, Lauren Onkey, Bill Reid, Ben Baker, Joe Cutshaw, Stephen Schoenecker, Mark Katz, Rene Rodgers, Pete Hansen, Marianne Merola, Caitlin Gibson, and Griffin Rowell for their charitable reflections.

I'm grateful to the Maryland State Arts Council for an Individual Artist Award, which helped with the cost of reporting expenses.

My parents, Glenn and Ann Rowell, bought me a drum set for my seventeenth birthday, which cemented a joyful pastime of playing music. In all the hours, days, and years I played in my bedroom, never once did they ever complain about the noise. That is love.

I'm deeply fortunate to have so many friends and family members who cheered me on throughout the work on *Wherever the Sound Takes You*. The cheering on of a writer sounds notably different than it does for a musician, but to the writer it's still an extraordinary sound.

SOUND CHECK

Faragher, Scott. *The Hammond Organ: An Introduction to the Instrument and the Players Who Made It Famous*. Montclair, NJ: Hal Leonard Books, 2011.

Mazor, Barry. *Ralph Peer and the Making of Popular Roots Music*. Chicago: Chicago Review Press, 2015.

Mudrian, Albert. *Choosing Death: The Improbable History of Death Metal and Grindcore*. Port Townsend, WA: Feral House, 2003.

Olson, Ted, and Tony Russell. *The Bristol Sessions, 1927–1928: The Big Bang of Country Music*. Bear Family Records, 2011.

Sharpe-Young, Garry. *Metal: The Definitive Guide*. London: Jawbone Press, 2007.

Welch, Chris. *Close to the Edge: The Story of Yes*. London: Omnibus Press, 2008.